Frontiers in Economic History

Economic historians have contributed to the development of economics in a variety of ways, combining theory with quantitative methods, constructing new databases, promoting interdisciplinary approaches to historical topics, and using history as a lens to examine the long-term development of the economy. Frontiers in Economic History publishes manuscripts that push the frontiers of research in economic history in order to better explain past economic experiences and to understand how, why and when economic change occurs. Books in this series will highlight the value of economic history in shedding light on the ways in which economic factors influence growth as well as social and political developments. This series aims to establish a new standard of quality in the field while offering a global discussion forum toward a unified approach in the social sciences.

Nils Herger

Switzerland and its Banks

A Short History

Springer

Nils Herger
Study Center Gerzensee
Gerzensee, Bern, Switzerland

ISSN 2662-9771 ISSN 2662-978X (electronic)
Frontiers in Economic History
ISBN 978-3-031-35903-3 ISBN 978-3-031-35904-0 (eBook)
https://doi.org/10.1007/978-3-031-35904-0

This Springer imprint is published by the registered company Springer Nature Switzerland AG
The registered company address is: Gewerbestrasse 11, 6330 Cham, Switzerland

To Meilin and Robin

Preface

> If you see a Swiss banker jump out of a window, jump after him. There is certainly money to be made. Voltaire (French philosopher, 1694–1778)[1]

Normally, banking neither appears in philosophical discussions, nor generates enough thrill to feature prominently in popular books or in blockbuster movies. However, as illustrated above by Voltaire's "bon mot", in the case of Switzerland, the situation seems to be different. To further illustrate this situation, Swiss bankers appear in several episodes of the film series about the legendary secret agent James Bond, conspiring with the forces of evil by laundering money through numbered accounts. Another famous example involves the cartoon figure Asterix on his visit to "Helvetia", where he and his companion Obelix hide from the pursuing legionaries in a bank safe crammed with stolen gold treasures in a town that was actually called "Geneva" by the Romans. These kinds of more or less humorous stories about a reckless financial underworld or gold depots hidden somewhere in the Alps have certainly contributed to the iconic status of Switzerland's banks. Of course, studying a country or a profession by watching James Bond movies or reading Asterix comic books is likely to create stereotypical images. Indeed, many widely held views about Swiss banking secrecy, numbered accounts, or the notorious gnomes in Zurich rest more on fiction than on fact. For example, there is scant awareness that most countries have some form of banking-secrecy laws. Numbered accounts neither were invented by nor are the exclusive domain of Swiss banks. Furthermore, such accounts obviously cannot guarantee complete anonymity, as at least some members of the bank management must be able to match the number with a personal identity. Is it truly believable that it is possible to store large amounts of gold in secretive Alpine vaults without anyone noticing? Despite countless claims to the contrary, tax evasion is not legal in Switzerland. In a similar vein, why should international fiscal fraud and money laundering be almost synonymous with offshore banking in

[1] Origin of quote unknown.

Zurich or Geneva, while other financial centres around the world would not lend themselves to these types of activity?

Among many other reasons, fact and fiction about Swiss banking have often diverged because there have hitherto been virtually no books to tell the corresponding history to an international readership. Of course, local as well as multinational Swiss banks have sometimes celebrated their fiftieth or one hundredth anniversary by publishing a company history. However, not even the most ancient Genevan private banks with roots going back to the eighteenth century have covered the entire development of Switzerland's banking sector. Moreover, a large number of articles and books have been dedicated to specific issues. In this regard, the role of banking secrecy looms particularly large. Then again, although the laws protecting financial privacy have gained a certain notoriety, they by no means represent the only chapter of Switzerland's banking history. Finally, this history has, unsurprisingly, been told by books written in the national languages of Switzerland, e.g., German, French, and Italian. However, these books are typically dedicated to a domestic readership and, therefore, take much background knowledge of the country's economy and political system for granted.

Against this background, this book endeavours to provide a broad and fact-based history of Swiss banking for an international readership. Following the discussion at the outset, one might wonder whether the resulting text will offer an entertaining read. In my opinion, there should be no reason to worry, as many actual developments, stories, and past events associated with Switzerland's banking sector are no less exciting than those told in movie scripts and fiction. Aside from the notorious banking secrecy and the corresponding scandals, the current book also discusses the intriguing early financial innovations by banks in Geneva to handle the sovereign risk on bonds issued in prerevolutionary France, the monetary chaos that led to the creation of the Swiss franc, the rather peculiar banknote competition and free-banking system in Switzerland during most of the nineteenth century, how the country and its currency became a financial safe haven after World War I, the golden age of Swiss banking when Zurich was briefly one of the largest financial centres in the world, and the extraordinary shocks during and after the recent Global Financial Crisis.

As specified by the title, this book presents a "short history". Within the present context, these words have a double meaning. First, they obviously refer to the goal of keeping the history concise. Second, they also refer to the fact that Switzerland's ascent in banking is quite a recent phenomenon. Unlike other iconic features of the country, such as the centuries-old political system with direct forms of democracy or the policy of neutrality in international affairs, the outstanding development of Switzerland as a banking centre began only around 1900. As mentioned above and discussed in more detail later, the banking history of Geneva is much older. Then again, it is not commonly known that this city did not become a full member of the Swiss confederation until 1815.

To turn to some practical issues, wherever possible, references will be made to books and articles written in English. Additionally, quotations from German and French publications are provided. Unfortunately, I did not include publications written in Italian for the simple reason that I am unable to read them. I grew up in the German-speaking part of Switzerland. Unlike French, Italian was an optional subject in our school curriculum and was scheduled on Saturday mornings between 10 am and noon. As a teenager, I obviously thought that I had better things to do on weekends than learning yet another national language. On another related issue, wherever it is sensible, Swiss banks will appear under their international (e.g., English) names. For example, Switzerland's central bank will be called the "Swiss National Bank" rather than the "Schweizerische Nationalbank", "Banque Nationale Suisse", or "Banca Nazionale Svizzera". However, to clarify which financial institute is meant, a table has been added to the appendix with the names of important Swiss banks in different languages.

I owe a great deal of gratitude to Ernst Baltensperger, Martin Brown, Oliver Buschan, Michel Habib, and Markus Staub, who took the time to read the manuscript. Their critical feedback has been very valuable for writing this book. It is almost needless to say, but any remaining errors or omissions are obviously my sole responsibility.

Gerzensee, Switzerland Nils Herger
April, 2023

Contents

1 **Introduction and Overview** ... 1
Reference ... 7

2 **Historical Background** ... 9
2.1 The History of an Unlikely Nation ... 9
2.2 Old Confederation Before 1848 ... 10
2.3 Modern Swiss Confederation After 1848 ... 17
References ... 26

3 **Banks in the Old Confederation and in Geneva (Before 1848)** ... 29
3.1 Early Swiss Banking in the European Context ... 29
3.2 Geneva ... 32
3.3 Banking Activities Within the Old Confederation ... 36
3.4 The Savings-Bank Movement ... 39
3.5 Overview of Swiss Banking Up to 1800 ... 41
References ... 43

4 **Free Banking and the Foundation of the Swiss National Bank (1826–1907)** ... 47
4.1 Banknotes During the Nineteenth Century ... 47
4.2 Unfettered Banknote Competition (1826–1881) ... 50
4.3 Regulated Free Banking (1881–1907) ... 52
4.4 The Role of the Cantonal Banks ... 55
4.5 Foundation of the Swiss National Bank ... 56
References ... 58

5 **Railway Boom, the Big Banks, and the Ascent of Zurich as Financial Centre (1848–1914)** ... 61
5.1 The Ascent of Zurich in Industry and Finance ... 61
5.2 Banking in Zurich before 1848 ... 62
5.3 Railways and the Big Banks ... 63
5.4 Big Banks Outside Zurich ... 68

5.5 Overview of Swiss Banking During the Nineteenth Century 71
References 72

6 A Safe Haven in an Unstable World (1914–1945) 75
6.1 The Safe-Haven Status and Its Origin 75
6.2 World War I and the Postwar Period 78
6.3 The Effects of the Great Depression 83
6.4 Federal Banking Act of 1934 92
6.5 Origins of Banking Secrecy—Myths and Reality 93
6.6 World War II: Gold Transactions and Dormant Accounts 97
References 101

7 The Golden Age (1946–1970s) 105
7.1 Washington Agreement as a Turning Point 105
7.2 Glorious Years and Growth Miracle in Swiss Banking 107
7.3 The Role of Banking Secrecy 113
References 117

8 Swiss Banking During Financial Globalisation (1970s–2008) 119
8.1 Causes and Consequences of Financial Globalisation 119
8.2 Paradigm Change in Governance 123
8.3 Real-Estate Crisis and Banking Merger Wave 126
8.4 More Setbacks During the 1990s: Swiss Economic Disease, European Integration, and US Lawsuits 130
8.5 Overview of Swiss Banking During the Twentieth Century 133
References 136

9 Global Financial Crisis, Too-Big-to-Fail Problem, and the End of Banking Secrecy (Since 2008) 139
9.1 Switzerland and the Global Financial Crisis 139
9.2 Too-Big-to-Fail Banks 142
9.3 Rescue of UBS and Too-Big-to-Fail Legislation 144
9.4 The End of International Banking Secrecy 147
9.5 Return of the Too-Big-to-Fail Problem: Downfall of Credit Suisse 151
9.6 Decline 152
References 155

10 Why Are There So Many Banks in Switzerland? A Tentative Answer 157

A Timeline 161

B Major Swiss Banks in Different Languages 163

C Data 165

D Glossary 175

Index 181

List of Figures

Fig. 1.1 Overview of Swiss banking across two centuries 3
Fig. 1.2 Further overview of the development of Swiss banking 6
Fig. 2.1 Evolutionary tree of the Swiss Confederation 12
Fig. 4.1 Swiss note-issuing banks (1826–1913) 49
Fig. 4.2 Banknote circulation in Switzerland (1826–1913) 50
Fig. 4.3 Exchange rate between the Swiss and French franc (1874–1913)... 54
Fig. 5.1 Overview of the early development of the Swiss railway network 65
Fig. 6.1 Inflation in Switzerland and in other European countries (1914–1939).. 80
Fig. 6.2 Industrial production during the Great Depression 84
Fig. 6.3 Balance sheet total of the Swiss banking sector during 1930s 88
Fig. 7.1 Development of Swiss banking during the golden age 108
Fig. 8.1 Globalisation in Swiss banking.. 121
Fig. 8.2 Effect of the public debt brake (1990–2020).......................... 131
Fig. 8.3 Main mergers and acquisitions of Switzerland's big banks during the nineteenth and twentieth centuries 134
Fig. 9.1 Size of the big banks in 1930, 2007, and 2018 142
Fig. 9.2 Capital ratio (unweighted) of Swiss banks (1906–2018)............ 143
Fig. 9.3 Amount of foreign assets collected and managed by Swiss banks 153

List of Tables

Table 6.1 Economic stability and instability (1918–2018) 77
Table 6.2 Restructuring of the big banks during the 1930s (in mio. Swiss francs) 90
Table 7.1 Five-year average growth rate of the balance sheet total by type of bank (1946–1980) 109
Table 7.2 Banking secrecy: an international comparison (as of 2020) 115
Table 8.1 Some banking scandals during the 1970s and 1980s 124
Table C.1 Number, and balance-sheet total of Swiss banks (1800–1943) 165
Table C.2 Number and balance-sheet total of Swiss banks (since 1944) 169

Chapter 1
Introduction and Overview

Why are there so many banks in Switzerland? The answer to this question is anything but obvious. Switzerland lacks many typical ingredients of an international banking centre. For example, unlike Amsterdam, London, New York, Tokyo, or Singapore, which are all seaside cities with busy ports, Swiss banks originated in landlocked cities, such as Geneva and Zurich. Naturally, they could not offer direct access to global trading routes, which have traditionally played a key role in the development and provision of trade finance, insurance, and cross-border payment services. Switzerland is also a relatively small and fragmented country. Hence, the capacity of the local economy to support a shining banking sector is limited.

Against this background, it is perhaps not surprising that the international success of Switzerland's banks has often been attributed to sinister business practices, such as tax evasion and the hoarding of illegally obtained money in secret numbered accounts. Although there are many examples of this type of misconduct, the role of Swiss banking secrecy should not be overrated because it was only codified during the 1930s, and its outstanding features have been dismantled by the international clampdown on tax evasion in the wake of the Global Financial Crisis of 2008. Another view suggests that the remarkable concentration of international wealth management in Zurich and Geneva reflects the quality and stability of the underlying political institutions and economic environment. Within this context, the exceptional stability of the national currency, the Swiss franc, is often mentioned. Then again, this view is not entirely consistent with historical facts. During the first part of the nineteenth century, Switzerland was rather known for its chaotic monetary system, and the franc was not seen as a particularly strong currency until World War I.

By providing a historical overview of the Swiss banking sector, this book endeavours to develop a more comprehensive and nuanced answer to the opening question. To begin with, the general historical background of Switzerland has obviously had a major influence on the local banking system. As summarised in Chap. 2, this history can be subdivided into two major periods. The years before 1848 cover the so-called Old Confederation, when Switzerland was not a state in the

N. Herger, *Switzerland and its Banks*, Frontiers in Economic History,
https://doi.org/10.1007/978-3-031-35904-0_1

modern sense, but merely represented a loose club of cantons (i.e., Swiss provinces) without a permanent federal government, a standing army, an internal market, or a common currency. The current political regime was adopted only with the Federal Constitution of 1848.

Owing to the landlocked location, which did not lend itself to long-distance trade via the sea, and the mountainous terrain in and around the Alps, which did not provide the land for a productive agricultural sector, Switzerland was not a financially advanced country in Europe during the preindustrial age. Concurrently, the banking sector did not play an outstanding role during this period. Unlike in the leading European financial centres, e.g., England and Holland, financial innovations, such as joint-stock companies, officially supported note-issuing banks, and an efficient government bond market, were more or less absent in Switzerland until well into the nineteenth century. However, as discussed in more detail in Chap. 3, this delay does not imply that ancient banking activities, such as changing coins or trade finance, were completely absent in Switzerland. Furthermore, the private banks in Geneva were an important financing source for the Bourbon kings before the French Revolution of 1789. Finally, as shown in Fig. 1.1a, the country's relatively early industrialisation around 1800 was associated with the establishment of literally hundreds of local savings banks, which mainly offered a safeguard against financial hardships for the emerging working class. However, the amounts of capital collected by these banks were modest and are, therefore, barely visible in the aggregate balance sheet of the Swiss banking sector depicted by Fig. 1.1b.

In contrast to the national unification that took place in the neighbouring countries of Germany and Italy during the nineteenth century, Switzerland's cultural diversity and fragmented history hampered a corresponding integration into a centralised state. Even after the foundation of the modern Swiss Confederation in 1848, the political system remained highly decentralised. As discussed in Chap. 4, in the area of money and banking, this decentralisation gave rise to a historically rather peculiar monetary system with a common currency, i.e., the Swiss franc; however, a large number of competing banks continued to issue private forms of paper money. This so-called free-banking" period ended with the relatively late introduction of a government banknote monopoly and the associated foundation of the Swiss National Bank (SNB) in 1907.

Industrialisation gave rise to far-reaching economic and social upheavals during the nineteenth century. For the banking sector, the new world of mass production required vast amounts of capital to build and maintain industrial mega projects: especially the railway network. Around the world, the resulting financial challenges paved the way for the establishment of large stock-traded financial firms that appeared under different names in different countries, including "crédit mobilier" in France and "investment banks" in the United States. In Switzerland, they are called "big banks", and early examples that appeared after the mid-nineteenth century were the nuclei of multinational financial firms, such as UBS. Furthermore, Switzerland's railway boom during this period was closely intertwined with the emergence of Zurich as a leading financial centre. Chapter 5 focuses on these developments.

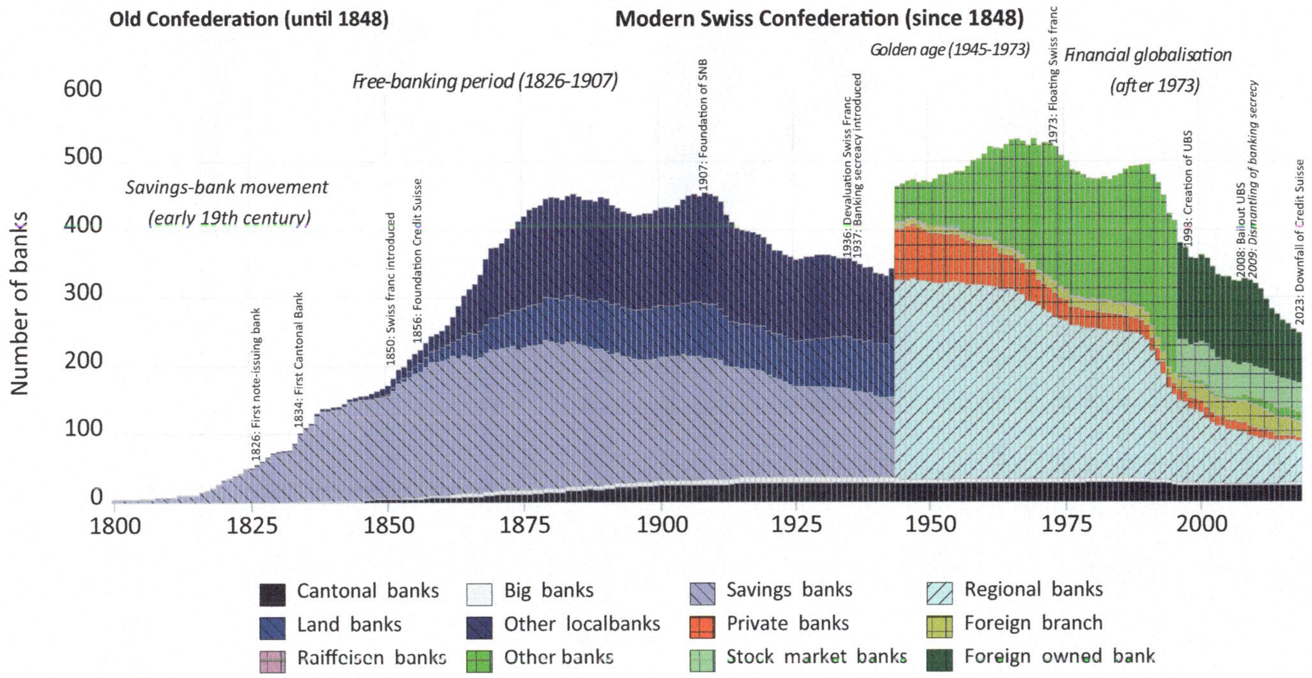

(a)

Fig. 1.1 Overview of Swiss banking across two centuries. (**a**) Number of banks in Switzerland since 1800. (**b**) Aggregate balance sheet of Swiss banking from 1800 to 1943. (**c**) Aggregate balance sheet of Swiss banking since 1944 (own figure. Data sources: Years between 1800 and 1943, Ritzmann, 1973, pp.263–266. During these years, private banks and stock-market banks are not recorded. Years between 1944 and 2018, Swiss National Bank (SNB), Historical time series, and banking statistics. During these years, regional and savings banks are merged into one group)

Chapter 6 is devoted to Switzerland's transformation into a safe-haven country between 1914 and 1945. On the eve of World War I (1914–1918), Switzerland had become an industrial economy with a modern financial system and capital market. In addition to the aforementioned big banks in Zurich, a large number of regional banks and state-supported cantonal banks had been founded to provide savings and transaction accounts as well as mortgages and loans to domestic households and firms (see Fig. 1.1a). However, Switzerland's foreign financial outreach remained very limited and was more or less confined to neighbouring countries. Ironically, the global ascent of Swiss banking began in earnest amid the turbulent political and economic world order between 1914 and 1945. During these years characterised by wars, political instability, financial disintegration, and economic depressions, Switzerland remained relatively stable and tranquil. The big banks benefited greatly

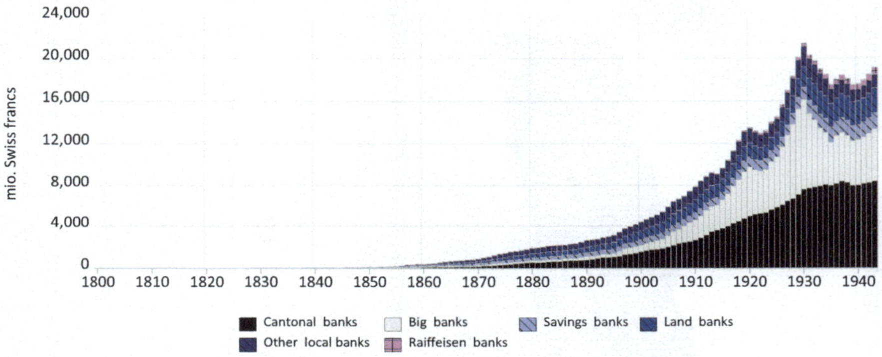

(b)

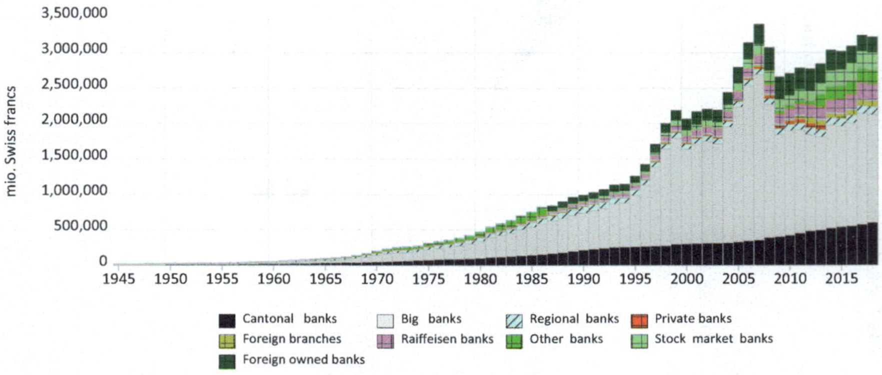

(c)

Fig. 1.1 (continued)

from this stability by attracting offshore capital in search of a safe haven. The result was a substantial expansion of their balance sheet (see Fig. 1.1b). However, the Great Depression of the 1930s and the contemporaneous destruction of the established monetary order through the rise of aggressive forms of nationalism and socialism were severe setbacks for Switzerland's journey towards becoming an important offshore financial centre. Another noticeable legacy of this period of pervasive instability was the codification of banking secrecy in 1934.

It was only during the decades following World War II (1939–1945) when Swiss banks became recognised global players. This period, which is often referred to as the "golden age", was characterised by several decades of exponential growth of the aggregate balance sheet of Swiss banking (see Fig. 1.1c). Notably, high levels of inflation around the 1970s explain only a small part of this spectacular nominal expansion. As shown by Fig. 1.2a, a conversion into real values portrays a similar picture, as do other indicators, such as the size of the balance sheet relative to GDP or the total employment in the banking sector within Switzerland (see Fig. 1.2b). The main drivers of this expansion were the big banks, especially their divisions dealing with international wealth management. It was these types of activities that transformed Zurich into one of the largest offshore banking centres in the world. Conversely, at the domestic level, the development was less dynamic because the main task of the various types of banks still encompassed the ordinary collection of savings and the provision of loans and mortgages. Indeed, according to Fig. 1.2c, the ratios between loans or mortgages and Swiss GDP remained at a comparatively low and stable level during the decades after 1945. Chapter 7 reviews this golden age and, in particular, assesses the importance of banking secrecy, currency convertibility, and other factors in explaining the extraordinary international expansion.

The collapse of the Bretton Woods System during the early 1970s paved the way for major financial liberalisations and inaugurated a renewed era of globalised cross-border trade and payments. Switzerland belonged to a pioneering group of countries with freely floating currencies. The era of globalisation was associated with profound restructuring, consolidations, and regulatory changes. In addition, for Switzerland's banks, the integrity of their international business was undermined by a series of scandals, which revealed the urgent need for tighter regulations to combat money laundering and tax evasion. At the domestic level, the number of small regional banks decreased as competition increased (see Fig. 1.2b). Many of these banks were taken over by larger rivals, especially by the big players with their increasingly universal approach to offering financial services. In a related vein, a series of mergers and acquisitions during the 1990s occurred among the big banks themselves, reducing their number from five to two, that is Credit Suisse and UBS. As discussed in Chap. 8, despite this consolidation, Switzerland managed to retain its position as a leading offshore centre for wealth management and head-office location for several multinational banks during this era characterised by a financial globalisation.

The Global Financial Crisis of 2008 created a degree of economic instability not seen since the 1930s. Liquidity shortages, correlated defaults on loans, collapsing

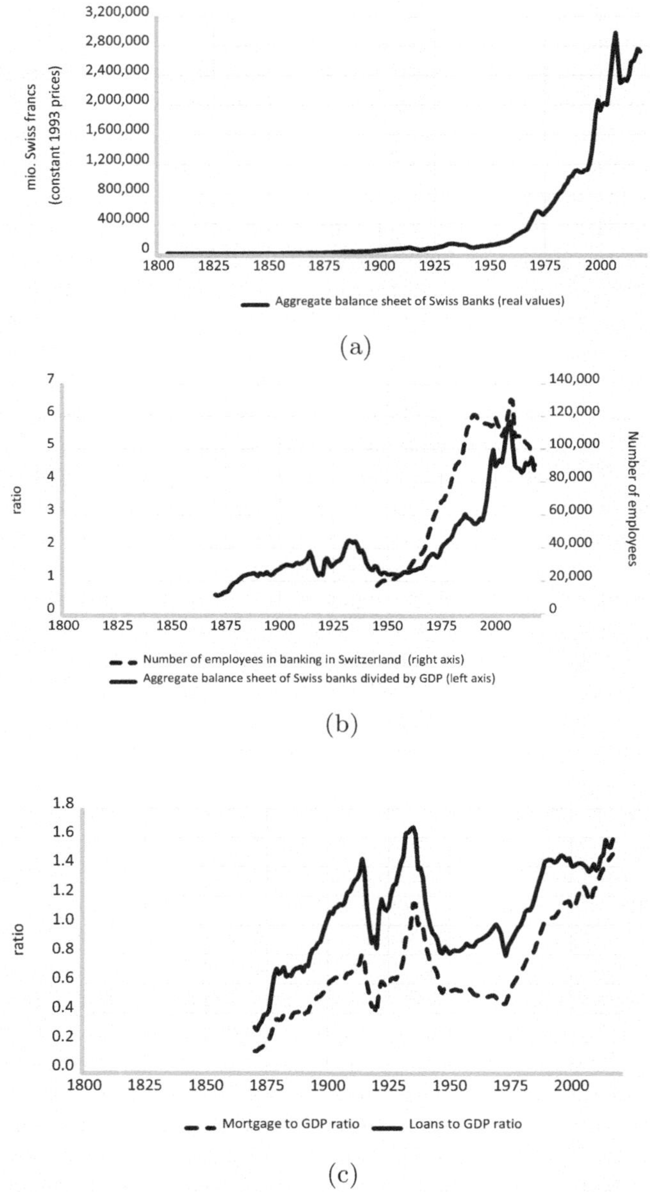

Fig. 1.2 Further overview of the development of Swiss banking. (**a**) Aggregate balance sheet of Swiss banking since 1800. (**b**) Employment and relative size of Swiss banking. (**c**) Bank loan and mortgage to GDP ratios (own figure. Data sources: The aggregate balance sheets are taken from Fig. 1.1b and c. These aggregates are divided by the consumer price index reported in the historical statistics of Switzerland (https://hsso.ch) and Swiss GDP taken from the Jordà–Schularick–Taylor macrohistory database (https://www.macrohistory.net/database). Data on the number of bank employees are published by the Swiss National Bank (SNB). Loans and mortgages to the non-financial private sector are taken from the Jordà–Schularick–Taylor macrohistory database)

asset prices, public bailouts, and in some cases outright failures shook the banking sector across the world. In addition, for Switzerland, the years after 2008 created the idiosyncratic challenge of how to deal with two banks that are too big to fail—and possibly even too big to be rescued. Furthermore, in many countries around the world, the bailouts of private financial firms by taxpayers and other forms of government support for struggling economies gave rise to a massive increase in public debt. Among other measures, an aggressive clampdown on tax evasion became an obvious political answer to the resulting fiscal problems. Given the status as a large offshore banking centre, Switzerland became a perfect target for international criticism of facilitating tax evasion. Regardless of whether these allegations were true, they resulted in the dismantling of banking secrecy for foreign customers during the decade after 2010. Moreover, this decade was characterised by further regulatory and political shocks that were associated with the declining importance of the banking sector in Switzerland. For example, in Fig. 1.2b, this decline is manifested in the reduction of the number of people employed in banking and the decrease of the aggregate bank balance sheet relative to GDP. The acquisition of the struggling Credit Suisse by UBS in 2023 represents the most recent event of the underlying consolidation process. Chapter 9 discusses these recent events.

Currently, there is not only a large number of Swiss banks but also a considerable variety, including the ancient private banks in Geneva, UBS as the main multinational player in Zurich, state-supported cantonal banks, institutes related to monetary policy, such as the Bank for International Settlements and the Swiss National Bank, and last but not least a whole range of ordinary commercial banks. As a summary and conclusion, the last chapter discusses how this variety came about and tries to answer the question of why Switzerland has managed to turn itself into an important banking centre.

Reference

Ritzmann, F. (1973). *Die Schweizer Banken. Geschichte - Theorie - Statistik*. Bern: Verlag Paul Haupt.

Chapter 2
Historical Background

2.1 The History of an Unlikely Nation

It is not unusual to tell the history of a country through the perspective of the nation, insofar as its political institutions and integrated economy are thought to be the outcome of a common language, shared ethnic background, or territorial integrity as in the case of an island nation. Although there is probably no perfect example of a one-nation state, Switzerland does not at all lend itself to this type of national history because there is no common language, shared ethnic background, or naturally delimited territory to begin with. In particular, reflecting long-standing influences from neighbouring cultures, German is predominantly spoken in the northern and eastern parts of the country, whereas French and Italian are the lingua franca of the west and the south, respectively.[1] These language regions have barely changed across centuries and still show the carving out of territories where Germanic tribes replaced the Latin-based culture, when the Roman empire collapsed more than 1,500 years ago. Regarding territorial integrity, although Switzerland is famously mountainous, it covers only a part of the Alpine range, which represents a major natural barrier between northern and southern Europe. Moreover, the most densely populated areas, including the cities of Geneva and Zurich, are actually located on a plateau at the foot of the Alps. Finally, there is hardly a common Swiss culture. For example, in addition to its linguistic fragmentation, Switzerland was once a hotbed of the Reformation, which was preached by Huldrych Zwingli (1484–1531) in Zurich and, more famously, by Jean Calvin (1508–1564) in Geneva, among others. Nevertheless, Catholicism has remained the dominant faith in the Alpine heartland, from which the papal Swiss Guard in Rome is still recruited today (Thürer, 1970, pp.53ff.; Reinhardt, 2013, pp.169ff.). Across centuries, these

[1] In southeastern Switzerland, a small minority speaks "Romansch", which is a Latin-based language similar to French and Italian.

N. Herger, *Switzerland and its Banks*, Frontiers in Economic History,
https://doi.org/10.1007/978-3-031-35904-0_2

different interpretations of Christian belief represented an insurmountable obstacle to national unification and were even the source of severe conflicts that culminated in several civil wars in 1531, 1656, 1712, and 1847.

Nevertheless, with an ordinary government, an own legal system, a common currency (the Swiss franc), internationally recognised borders, and a police force and army, Switzerland today has every feature of a sovereign state. However, it is often said that the country has kept the character of a "club" of cantons (i.e., Swiss provinces) rather than a nation. According to this analogy, club membership is not only a matter of pride and tradition but also the result of a crude analysis of the corresponding political and economic costs and benefits. As with other clubs, some cantons were the founding members. Others joined later, sometimes after a long period with some form of collaboration or alliance with the existing members.

To appreciate the development of the Swiss banking sector, the corresponding historical context matters, as it has left a peculiar institutional and political legacy in terms of a highly decentralised form of government, elements of direct democracy, and a long tradition of neutrality in international conflicts. Following the seminal work of North (1990), such institutions—that is, the formal rules and informal norms underpinning a political and social system—can impact upon economic outcomes. In this regard, the role of institutions has also been highlighted in the development of the financial and banking system, which can arguably flourish only within an environment that safeguards property rights (see, e.g., Herger et al., 2008). Hence, to prepare the ground, this chapter provides a synoptic overview of those events of Switzerland's history that matter, directly or indirectly, to the development of the banking sector.[2] In doing so, the storyline begins with the Old Confederation before 1848 and subsequently moves to the political and economic events during the period of the modern Swiss Confederation. The discussion will give more weight to the years after 1848 because only since then has Swiss banking emerged as a genuinely important force, both domestically and internationally.

2.2 Old Confederation Before 1848

The origins of Switzerland can be traced back to the thirteenth century, when several cantons in the mountainous region around Lake Lucerne began to form an alliance. The various pacts and treaties underpinning this so-called Eidgenossenschaft—i.e., a confederation bound together by oath—were concluded primarily to defend regional autonomy by joining military forces (Thürer, 1970, pp.23ff.; Reinhardt, 2013, pp.31ff.). Although this "Old Confederation" grew steadily into a larger and more integrated club of cantons, recurring internal and external conflicts also

[2] In English, a concise, but increasingly outdated, Swiss history can be found in Thürer (1970), which is based on an earlier German edition first published shortly after World War II. In German, Reinhardt (2013) provides an up-to-date account of the history of Switzerland.

hampered this development.[3] Nevertheless, across the following centuries, the existing alliances were regularly renewed to promise mutual military support in case of an external attack, to recognise regional autonomy, or to arrange relationships with neighbouring powers, especially the Holy Roman Empire of the German Nation and the Kingdom of France. As indicated by these relationships, the history of the Old Confederation is intertwined with the major events on the European continent, including the emergence of the House of Habsburg as the dominant dynasty within the Holy Roman Empire of the German Nation, the development of France into a centralised state and hegemonic power, the economic and financial success of Italian city states (in particular nearby Milan), the Reformation, and the rise of absolutist forms of government and their subsequent downfall after the French Revolution (Thürer, 1970, ch.3–6).

By the sixteenth century, the Old Confederation had developed into an alliance among thirteen cantons, including the founding members, as well as the city states of Bern, Basel, Fribourg, Lucerne, Schaffhausen, Solothurn, Zug, and Zurich. However, the structure within this alliance was extremely complicated, as the influence and status of the various cantons differed markedly. Of note, most of the current French- and Italian-speaking cantons of Switzerland were not members of the Old Confederation but were either loosely aligned, or had the even lower status of a protectorate. As illustrated by the evolutionary tree shown in Fig. 2.1, several cantons, including Geneva, fully joined the Swiss confederation only during the nineteenth century.

Some of the iconic features of the Swiss political system can be traced back to the premodern age. In particular, in contrast to neighbouring France—and farther away in, e.g., Prussia, Russia, or Spain—the Old Confederation did not turn into an absolute monarchy and, hence, did not make the transition towards a centralised form of government during the seventeenth and eighteenth centuries. The cantons simply lacked the aspiration to establish a strong and permanent centre of political power, a standing army, a professional bureaucracy, a national tax system, or a common currency (Thürer, 1970, p.69). Despite the absence of an absolutist monarchy, the Old Confederation was not a democracy in the modern sense. At the federal level, there was no representative government or parliament, but merely a diet (called the "Tagsatzung"), which summoned delegates, who voted

[3] The official foundation day of the Old Confederation on the 1st of August 1291, which is celebrated each year on the occasion of Switzerland's national day, is probably mythology (Reinhardt, 2013, pp.33ff.). In a similar vein, the interrelated story of Willhelm Tell as a freedom fighter against foreign tyranny is scantly documented by historical evidence (Marchi, 1971). Nevertheless, Willhelm Tell has become a famous figure thanks to his appearance in a stage play written in 1804 by the German author Friedrich Schiller, and in an opera completed in 1829 by the Italian composer Gioachino Rossini. Furthermore, the national mythology of Switzerland's foundation contains a grain of truth in the sense that historical documents indeed suggest that a medieval alliance emerged between cantons within the Alpine heartland and that the resulting confederation was quite successful in maintaining its freedom and independence from foreign influence.

Fig. 2.1 Evolutionary tree of the Swiss Confederation (Lithography produced around 1909. Picture reprinted with the permission of the Swiss National Library (NL), Graphische Sammlung: Sammlung Druckgrafik Heraldik. In 1909, the Swiss Confederation encompassed 22 cantons. A 23rd canton called "Jura" was founded in 1979)

on the instruction of their cantons (Thürer, 1970, p.69). Furthermore, although some rural cantons retained their ancient representative assemblies, the so-called Landsgemeinden, where citizens regularly gathered to make political decisions, only a small elite could afford to stand as candidates for (unpaid) government positions (Thürer, 1970, p.70). Moreover, only native and sufficiently wealthy men had the right to vote (see Möckli, 1987, pp.12ff.). City cantons, such as Bern or Zurich, were even directly ruled by an oligarchy encompassing the aristocracy or the leading members of the craft guilds.

From the mid-sixteenth century onwards, the concept of neutrality began to take shape as the Swiss elites began to realise that they could not keep up with their increasingly powerful neighbours (Bonjour, 1946, pp.11ff.). Amid the emergence of potent absolutist monarchies in, e.g., France, abstaining from foreign warfare seemed the most promising way to remain autonomous (see, e.g., Somm, 2015). In general, the Old Confederation had been remarkably successful in achieving this goal. Although the thirteen cantons initially belonged to the Holy Roman Empire, which subjected the German-speaking nation to an emperor recognised by the papacy, they managed to limit the influence from the corresponding rulers of Austria and other powerful German kingdoms and principalities. In this way, neutrality was upheld during the Thirty Years War (1618–1648), which devastated large parts of central Europe (Thürer, 1970, pp.64ff.). In the Peace Treaty of Westphalia, which ended this war in 1648, the major European powers even agreed to officially recognise the full sovereignty of the Old Confederation and granted it a complete independence from the Holy Roman Empire of the German Nation (Reinhardt, 2013, pp.223–225).

Why were the leading monarchies on the European continent ready to accept the sovereignty and independence of the Old Confederation? After all, various parts of Switzerland share the culture of their powerful neighbours and would, in principle, have lent themselves to becoming mere provinces of the French, German, and Italian nation states. To explain this development, it is perhaps important to realise that before the industrial age, the Alps were a peripheral, and economically rather underdeveloped, European region. Aside from controlling some Alpine passes, conquering this inhospitable territory was perhaps not worthwhile. Furthermore, some early attempts to do so had failed remarkably. Possibly the most famous example of such a failure occurred during the Burgundian War. By controlling economically advanced territories across Flanders and what is today eastern France, Burgundy became a potent duchy during the fifteenth century. Nevertheless, the last duke of Burgundy, Charles the Bold (1433–1477), failed to expand his territory southwards towards Switzerland, as he lost a series of battles against the Old Confederation (Thürer, 1970, pp.42–44). Among other episodes, it were these stunning military victories that enhanced the reputation of the Swiss as skilful soldiers. Foreign powers began to draw on these military skills by recruiting Swiss mercenaries. This arrangement was mutually beneficial, because the papacy or French monarchs managed to enhance their military power and employed Swiss soldiers as personal guards who were unlikely to fraternise with the local population in case of a revolt. Meanwhile, the Swiss cantons had found a way to deal with the chronic population surplus on a terrain offering little room for increasing agricultural production. Moreover, for the Swiss elites, mercenary work became a lucrative business in terms of opening positions for officers in the corresponding foreign regiments and generating substantial revenues in the form of the so-called pensions in exchange for recruiting an agreed-upon number of troops (Bauer & Blackman, 1998, p.52). Throughout the seventeenth and eighteenth centuries, France was the dominant power on the European continent and therefore became the main destination for Swiss soldiers (Thürer, 1970, pp.71–72, 79–80; Mottet, 1987, pp.18ff.). They served the Bourbon kings as personal guards, but also fought as regular forces in Napoleon's military campaigns (Reinhardt, 2013, pp.266ff.).

The mercenary business yielded considerable amounts of foreign income. For example, the treaties concluded with France around 1520 alone led to the payment of 400,000 livres in annual pensions (Ritzmann, 1973, p.17).[4] The lucrative export of goods to the belligerents during the Thirty Years War (1618–1648), or during the Spanish War of Succession (1701–1714), added to this capital inflow. The influx of wealthy refugees, especially the Huguenots—i.e., French Protestants—fleeing from war and oppression had a similar effect. As there was no need to maintain a standing army, because the cantons managed to avoid external conflicts[5] between the middle of the sixteenth century and the end of the eighteenth century, or to maintain a lavish royal court, these foreign inflows resulted in an entrenched capital surplus within the Old Confederation (Bauer & Blackman, 1998, pp.59–60; 81–82; Ritzmann, 1973, p.16).

In Switzerland, the period until the end of the eighteenth century also offered fertile ground for progressive ideas (Thürer, 1970, pp.73–77). Especially in science, remarkable contributions to anatomy were made by Albrecht von Haller (1708–1777) in Bern, to mathematics by Leonhard Euler (1707–1783) and Daniel Bernoulli (1700–1782) in Basel, and to political science by Jean-Jacques Rousseau (1712–1778) and to geology by Horace-Bénédict de Saussure (1740–1799) in Geneva. Conversely, there was virtually no political reform, as the estate-based society, the political privileges of the ancient elites, and the separation between autonomous cantons and their protectorates remained largely untouched (Thürer, 1970, pp.69–72). In France, a similar, but probably more extreme, contrast between economic as well as scientific progress and social as well as political stagnation eventually sparked the revolution of 1789. The era of turmoil following the French Revolution had far-reaching repercussions, especially for a neighbouring country, such as Switzerland. Owing to geographical and cultural proximity, and given the discriminatory status of citizens within and between the cantons, large parts of the Swiss population welcomed the enlightened ideas of equality before the law, and of all

---

[4] One "livre tournois" was at the time equivalent to 80.88 grams of fine silver. Hence, 400,000 livres were approximately equivalent to 32 tons of silver.

[5] As mentioned above, between the sixteenth and eighteenth centuries, several brief civil wars were fought between the Protestant and Catholic cantons.

human beings being endowed with unalienable rights. The revolutionary call for "liberté, égalité et fraternité" irrevocably undermined the authority of the aristocracy and the guilds in city cantons and, to a lesser extent, the local elites in the rural cantons. It is therefore not surprising that the Old Confederation was unable to put up much resistance when several French armies invaded Switzerland in 1798 (Thürer, 1970, pp.80–84). This invasion was even welcomed as a liberation in areas that for centuries had been mere protectorates of the Old Confederation, such as the French-speaking region around Lausanne, or the Italian-speaking Ticino. Based on the blueprint of the French Republic, Napoleon tried to rearrange Switzerland into a "Helvetic Republic" with a potent central government. Among other political changes, the ancient protectorates were dismantled and converted into several new cantons. However, the desire for centralised government quickly collapsed with the French hegemony over continental Europe when Napoleon was finally defeated during the Battle of Waterloo in 1815. The Congress of Vienna, which was held during that year to negotiate peace across Europe, essentially restored the international status of the Swiss Confederation. In particular, the major European powers reaffirmed its sovereignty and independence and enshrined Switzerland's neutrality in international law (Bonjour, 1946, pp.54ff.). Conversely, the recently established cantons outside the German-speaking heartland were preserved and formally joined a confederation that now counted 22 equal members (Thürer, 1970, pp.97ff.).[6] Although the central government was reduced to a bare minimum, the decades until 1848 were characterised by fierce debates over whether it was necessary to establish a permanent federal government, expand democracy, abolish all forms of press censorship, and guarantee freedom of speech, association, and settlement (Thürer, 1970, pp.100ff.). These progressive political ideas fell on particularly fertile ground in the newly founded cantons as well as in the former subject territories surrounding the major cities. For example, in Zurich, a rural uprising in 1830 paved the way for adopting a revised, and quite "liberal", constitution in 1831. Conversely, a group of the so-called conservative cantons in the Alpine heartland remained strongly opposed to the foundation of a modern state. Unfortunately, the liberal and conservative cantons were, by and large, also divided along Protestant, and Catholic beliefs, which further aggravated the tensions. To secure its position, the conservative camp eventually formed an inconspicuous alliance, the so-called Sonderbund, and resorted to secret diplomacy to secure the backing of France and Austria-Hungary in the event of a civil war (Thürer, 1970, pp.106ff.). When the existence of the "Sonderbund" became known in 1847, an armed conflict between the liberal and conservative cantons was unavoidable. During this Civil War of 1847, the conservative cantons, most of which were small and sparsely populated, were quickly defeated.

[6] The 23rd canton was founded only in 1979, when the French-speaking and overwhelmingly Catholic "Jura" broke away from the Protestant and mainly German-speaking Canton of Bern (Reinhardt, 2013, pp.458–461).

The turbulent decades that followed the French Revolution gave rise to severe financial and economic problems. For example, massive losses hit Geneva when France defaulted on the loans granted to the Bourbon kings before 1789, and when state treasures, such as that of Bern, were confiscated during the French occupation. Furthermore, the mercenary business began to fall apart as the "ancien régime" collapsed and, with the exception of the papal Swiss Guard in Rome, was finally outlawed in 1859 (Thürer, 1970, pp.138–139). The loss of the corresponding sources of foreign income posed a problem because the contemporaneous dawn of the industrial age was associated with an increasing domestic demand for capital. In particular, within the primitive silk and cotton manufacturing clusters that had sprung up in and around cities, such as Zurich and St.Gallen, since the sixteenth century, the first textile machines appeared around 1800. Hence, the transition from manual to mechanical production occurred a couple of decades later than in Great Britain, but substantially earlier than elsewhere on the European continent (Thürer, 1970, p.129; Bergier, 1983, pp.188ff.). After importing industrial technology and equipment, domestic manufacturers soon began to replicate and subsequently to produce and export the novel textile machinery around the world. Watches, foodstuffs, such as chocolate, and chemical and pharmaceutical products that are famously "made in Switzerland" soon followed. Potential reasons why the industrial era began relatively early on Swiss territory are the lack of agricultural employment opportunities due to the inhospitable terrain, a relatively large degree of economic freedom, as well as the technical know-how and entrepreneurial spirit of the Protestant refugees, who arrived in large numbers during the seventeenth and eighteenth centuries.[7] Furthermore, the Continental Blockade imposed by Napoleon was not only a burden for Swiss entrepreneurs, who found themselves temporarily cut-off from the world market, but also incidentally protected an infant industry from superior competitors from across the English channel. However, in several regards, the Alpine version of industrial development differed markedly from what happened elsewhere. First, Switzerland lacks a large domestic market and, as a landlocked country, direct access to overseas territories. Before 1848, this situation was exacerbated by economic fragmentation across and within the cantons, which used different currencies and obstructed internal trade by collecting customs, bridge tolls, and other fees in literally hundreds of places (Thürer, 1970, p.100). Owing to the scant domestic demand, as well as the lack of privileged access to a colonial empire, Swiss entrepreneurs could only succeed, when they were able to specialise in niche products and hence secure a leading position in the global

[7] The development of the watchmaking industry in the rolling hills between Geneva and Basel is a case in point. Huguenot refugees settled in this region after the Edict of Fontainebleau of 1685 ended approximately one hundred years of religious tolerance towards Protestants in France. Among other things, the Huguenots brought with them the know-how to produce clocks and watches and, hence, laid the foundation of an industry that characterises the region to this day (see Donzé, 2015; Thürer, 1970, p.128). In a similar vein, the establishment of a silk manufacturing sector in Zurich was largely caused by an influx of Protestant refugees during the sixteenth century (Somm, 2022, pp.43ff.).

market. Second, in and around the Alps, there are no major coal deposits, and as a consequence, the potential to rely on steam power was severely limited before the railways offered a cheap means to transport bulk commodities. Instead, early Swiss factories turned to water power as a source of energy (Thürer, 1970, pp.127–128; Bergier, 1983, pp.200–201). Exploiting the currents of the Alpine rivers implied, in turn, that Switzerland's industrialisation began in the hinterland and occurred in a dispersed manner across large rural areas, rather than being concentrated in rapidly growing industrial cities (Thürer, 1970, p.128). Especially in machinery and watchmaking, a decentralised industrial structure characterised by small- and medium-sized companies has survived to the present day. However, the lack of large factories and mass production also implied that this type of early industrial development was largely self-funded and could long cope without the support of a sophisticated commercial banking sector (Mottet, 1987, p.29; Ritzmann, 1973, p.16.).

2.3 Modern Swiss Confederation After 1848

During 1848, a wave of popular uprisings swept across Europe with demands for far-reaching reforms, such as national unifications, the abolishment of press censorship, and the expansion of the right to vote. Unlike in neighbouring Austria–Hungary, Italy, and Germany, where these uprisings were crushed by the authorities, a new era began for Switzerland. In particular, the brief civil war at the end of 1847 paved the way for the rather fundamental reforms enshrined in the Federal Constitution of 1848. For the first time in history, the cantons had reached an agreement to install potent political institutions at the federal level, including an elected parliament, a national government supported by a professional administration, and a supreme court called the "Federal Tribunal" (Thürer, 1970, pp.113ff.). Furthermore, Bern became the permanent capital city. The conservative cantons, which were defeated in 1847, eventually learned to live with this new type of government that they had long opposed because the Constitution of 1848 managed to strike an enduring compromise, which honoured the widespread desire to preserve a large degree of local autonomy. Key elements of this compromise included a bicameral parliament designed after the US Congress, with chambers equipped with equal powers called the "Council of States" (Ständerat, Conseil d'états, Consiglio degli stati) with two delegates per canton, and a "National Council" (Nationalrat, Conseil national, Consiglio nazionale), in which cantonal representation is weighted according to population size.[8] Moreover, federal authority was heavily restricted and encompassed, initially, mainly foreign policy and national defence. In important areas, including policing and jurisprudence, basic and higher education, public

[8] For historical reasons, three cantons (Appenzell, Basel, and Unterwalden) are split into two "half-cantons", which can send only one delegate to the Council of States.

infrastructure, and health care, the cantons were, and still are, quite autonomous. Furthermore, they have remained sovereign states in terms of having their own constitutions with proper powers to collect and spend various kinds of taxes and to determine the electoral system (Thürer, 1970, pp.116ff.). Finally, Switzerland is governed not by a single president, but by a so-called Federal Council (Bundesrat, Conseil fédéral, Consiglio federale), which is elected for a renewable term of four years by both chambers of parliament. This Federal Council involves a cabinet of seven ministers drawn from different cantons and typically representing the main languages and political parties of the country.[9] Picking the representatives of government from various backgrounds reflects a desire to rule by consensus. Initially, the liberal and conservative parties had to find an acceptable balance of power. However, with the emergence of other political ideologies, the constant search for consensus has been extended to other parties, such as the social democrats (or labour party). Taken together, across the political and economic changes since the mid-nineteenth century, the Federal Constitution of 1848 has been very successful. Its main elements have survived to the present day.

In addition to installing a federal system of government and enshrining human rights, such as the freedom of speech and assembly, the Constitution of 1848 led to a deeper integration of the Swiss economy by, among other things, guaranteeing the freedom of settlement across the cantons, abolishing internal customs and tariffs, and nationalising postal and telegraphic services (Thürer, 1970, p.117). In the area of banking and finance, an important innovation was the introduction of a common currency, called the "Swiss franc" (Baltensperger & Kugler, 2017, pp.26ff.). However, the right to issue the corresponding banknotes remained under the jurisdiction of the cantons, which typically gave commercial banks a large degree of freedom to print their own forms of paper money. Competition in the market for paper money ended only in 1907 with the foundation of the Swiss National Bank (SNB) (Baltensperger & Kugler, 2017, pp.45ff.).

The new political system and integrated internal market laid the foundations for several decades of vigorous industrial growth (Thürer, 1970, pp.127ff.; Bergier, 1983, pp.228ff.). This economic progress was heavily driven by the railway industry, the development of which had long been hampered by the cantonal fragmentation before the era of the modern Swiss Confederation. In the area of banking, the railway boom warranted a new type of financial institute to mobilise large amounts of capital (Kindleberger, 1984, pp.199ff.; Cassis, 2010, pp.54–60). To meet this challenge at the time, the big Swiss banks, which later developed into multinational firms, were founded. The emergence of these big players was also closely associated with the replacement of Basel and Geneva by Zurich as the leading Swiss financial centre (Cassis, 2010, p.127).

[9] One member of the Federal Council acts as its president. However, this presidency typically rotates between the seven members on an annual basis and is not associated with an increase in political power. Moreover, the highest representative of the Swiss Confederation is, actually, the president of the Federal Parliament.

At the social level, the railway boom gave rise to a disturbing concentration of political, financial, and economic power in the hands of an industrial elite. Although a multitude of private railway companies existed in Switzerland, they were controlled by "railway tycoons", such as Alfred Escher (1819–1882), who had managed to accumulate key positions in business and politics (Jung, 2015). Business tycoons were of course not unique to Switzerland, as Escher had more famous American contemporaries including Andrew Carnegie, Cornelius Vanderbilt, and John D. Rockefeller. On both sides of the Atlantic, their corporatism was met by a mixture of concern and envy and eventually unleashed a political counter-reaction. Unlike in the United States, where legislation was enacted to break up the large trust companies, Switzerland embarked on a so-called democratic movement to address the concentration of political and economic power. This process, which began in the cantons, eventually gave rise to a remarkable expansion of direct-democratic rights (Thürer, 1970, pp.118ff.). For example, during the 1860s, Basel-Country and Zurich introduced a "legislative referendum" that offers the right to repeal any piece of legislation passed by local parliament through a popular vote (Thürer, 1970, pp.120–122). Conversely, at the federal level, the Constitution of 1848 enshrined only the "compulsory referendum", according to which constitutional amendments, but not laws, require the approval of the people. However, under the impression of national unification in neighbouring Germany, which had demonstrated its military might with a rapid victory during the Franco-Prussian War (1870–1871), the Swiss constitution was substantially revised in 1874, in order to strengthen the army (Thürer, 1970, pp.122ff.). Although the centralisation of national defence was widely seen as necessary, the corresponding constitutional change was controversial and required a political bargain, which introduced the legislative referendum at the national level to counterbalance the enhanced federal authority (Reinhardt, 2013, p.384). Since 1874, any law adopted by the Federal Parliament can be put to the ballot, when a given number of citizens sign a corresponding petition within a certain period (currently, 50,000 signatures within three months). In a subsequent vote, the law requires a simple majority for approval. At the federal level, the instruments of direct democracy were supplemented in 1891 with the so-called popular initiative, which offers citizens the right to call for a partial amendment of the constitution, when they manage to collect 100,000 signatures endorsing the proposed clause within 18 months. To be approved, an initiative requires a double majority: the support of more than half of the voters and the majority of the cantons. A final breakthrough of the democratic movement occurred with the transition, in 1919, to the proportional electoral system for the "National Council", i.e., the chamber of Federal Parliament representing the population (Thürer, 1970, p.124). During the nineteenth century, the majoritarian electoral system had strongly favoured the dominant parties at the time, i.e., the liberals and the conservatives. Conversely, the social democrats, whose party was founded in Switzerland in 1870, had long been disadvantaged by the electoral system, but quickly managed to become the largest faction in parliament after the introduction of the proportional electoral system (Thürer, 1970, p.123; pp.147–148).

The instruments of direct democracy can be, and frequently have been, used to promote vested interests and, in this way, to infringe on economic freedom (Thürer, 1970, p.120). Although many proposals catering to narrowly defined privileges fail to win a majority at the ballot box, the democratic movement opened the door to expanding the role of government to deal with economic activities that represent a so-called public service. An early manifestation of this development was the nationalisation of the railways, which was approved at the ballot box in 1898 (Thürer, 1970, p.131). In the financial industry, the foundation of several cantonal banks to support the local economy and the aforementioned Swiss National Bank as a central monetary authority are additional examples of the growing government influence during the democratic movement.

Owing to international stability during the era of the classical gold standard, and technological innovations in transportation (e.g., railways and steamships) and communication (e.g., telegraph and telephone), cross-border trade in goods, services, and assets surged during the decades before 1914 (Obstfeld & Taylor, 2004, pp.24ff., 126ff.). As a small open economy, Switzerland participated in this economic globalisation, not least by becoming a major destination for foreign tourists (Thürer, 1970, p.133). However, the happy years of tranquillity and prosperity ended abruptly when World War I (1914–1918) broke out, marking the beginning of three decades of more or less uninterrupted political and economic turmoil around the world. Following the traditional foreign policy in times of conflict, Switzerland remained neutral and, therefore, had to comply with the rules that had been enshrined in the "Conventions Relative to the Rights and Duties of Neutral Powers" at the Hague in 1912. This piece of international law obliges a neutral country to prevent the passage of foreign troops and military supplies through its territory, but allows the export of arms on equal terms to belligerent countries, and permits the passage of wounded soldiers (Thürer, 1970, p.144; Bonjour, 1946).[10] In any case, when Germany invaded neutral Belgium at the outset of World War I, it became clear that international laws provide no protection against an invasion. Confronted with the threat that France or Germany could launch a similar outflanking manoeuvre through Swiss territory, the army was mobilised in 1914 to guard the western and northern borders. However, Switzerland was ill-

[10] These obligations are not restricted to a specific group of countries. In principle, every country around the world can declare, on a case-by-case basis, its neutrality in an international armed conflict. During both world wars, e.g., Belgium and the Netherlands were neutral. However, Switzerland pursues a policy of a so-called perpetual neutrality, which rules out all forms of military alliances, and alignments with belligerents in any future conflict between foreign countries (see Bonjour, 1946). Furthermore, there is a crucial distinction between the legal obligations, as stipulated in The Hague in 1912, and the broad policy with regard to neutrality. In Switzerland, the policy of neutrality has regularly been adapted to the prevailing world order. For example, during the "ancien régime", the supply of mercenaries to foreign armies was deemed compatible with neutrality. Nowadays, this would be seen as a clear violation. In a similar vein, Switzerland participated in the League of Nations and took part in its economic sanctions but did not join the United Nations during the decades after World War II. During this period of the Cold War, a relatively strict policy of neutrality was pursued.

prepared for four years of international conflict. In addition to several skirmishes at the border, it became quite challenging to replace the income of soldiers away from their peacetime jobs, secure food and other vital economic supplies in a landlocked country surrounded by war, and uphold morale after it was revealed that senior officers had breached neutrality by regularly leaking confidential information to the German and Austrian–Hungarian military attachés (Thürer, 1970, pp.145ff.). That the German- and French-speaking populations of Switzerland held, by and large, opposite views about the neighbouring countries further aggravated the situation (Reinhardt, 2013, pp.417ff.). The corresponding tensions became quite serious towards the end of the war. Amid the sufferings caused by the Spanish influenza pandemic, in early November 1918, Switzerland was virtually paralysed for a couple of days by a massive industrial strike. That this so-called General Strike erupted almost exactly one year after the Russian Revolution was, perhaps, no coincidence, because leading Swiss socialists had been able to establish close contact with prominent Russian revolutionaries including Lenin (1870–1924), who had lived as a political refugee in Bern and Zurich between 1914 and 1917. During this period, clandestine conferences attended by leading socialists were also held in the Bernese villages of Zimmerwald, and Kiental (Thürer, 1970, p.147). Nevertheless, the General Strike quickly collapsed due to the scant support in the French-speaking part of Switzerland, and the deployment of the army to restore order.[11] Additionally, parliament reached out to the labour movement to meet some of its key demands, including the introduction of the eight-hour workday, which further eased the tensions. Furthermore, the socialist movement was divided between a democratically oriented and a communist faction seeking reform through constitutional means and a coup d'état, respectively (Thürer, 1970, pp.147–148). The aforementioned transformation to a proportional electoral system in 1919 mainly strengthened the social democrats, who managed to greatly expand their political influence during the 1920s, while the communist faction became marginalised. Approximately two decades later, this development culminated with the election of a social democrat to the Federal Council (i.e., the Swiss government) in 1943. In a similar vein, during the 1920s and 1930s, many trade unions moved to a consensus-oriented policy. In particular, in 1937, they struck a landmark agreement to settle labour disputes in the metal and watchmaking industry through negotiations, rather than industrial action. As these types of negotiations between employers and employees have become standard practice across all economic sectors, strikes have become very rare in Switzerland.

Compared with the massive number of casualties in the belligerent countries, as well as the severe turmoil after the collapse of the Austria-Hungarian and German empires, the skirmishes at the Swiss border during World War I and the violence

[11] Schaltegger and Schmid (2021) provide a detailed analysis of Swiss government bond prices between 1914 and 1918. According to this analysis, bond yields increased significantly towards the end of 1918 suggesting that, in the opinion of investors, the instability of Switzerland during World War I peaked around the General Strike.

during the General Strike were relatively harmless. The same can be said of the wartime inflation that resulted from the suspension of the gold convertibility of the franc (see Baltensperger & Kugler, 2017, pp.59–62). Similar to the economy of Britain, the Swiss economy underwent a postwar deflation and recession, because the wartime monetary expansion was reversed around 1920 to prepare the ground for returning to the gold standard at the prewar mint-par in 1925 (Baltensperger & Kugler, 2017, pp.62–67). Then again, the economic problems associated with these episodes of price instability bear little resemblance to the chaos during the hyperinflation period in neighbouring Germany around 1923. In terms of political stability, the General Strike was obviously a manifestation of entrenched labour conflicts. However, these conflicts never undermined democracy as a broadly accepted form of government. Therefore, they had little in common with the rise of Benito Mussolini's fascism in Italy, or the deep aversion of the national socialists to the Weimar Republic in Germany. Taken together, the resilience of the Swiss political and economic system during the early twentieth century helped to brand the country as a safe haven with a relatively strong currency, low interest rates, and foreign capital inflows in times of crisis (Baltensperger & Kugler, 2016). Owing to this stability, Swiss banks eventually gained a leading position in international wealth management.

Although Switzerland did not participate in the Versailles Peace Conference, which was held in 1919 to renegotiate the world order after the Great War, the corresponding treaty left a far-reaching legacy for Geneva as a centre for international organisations. Neutral Switzerland had already become the domicile for several international organisations during the nineteenth century. Above all, the Genevan businessman Henry Dunant (1828–1910) had launched the Red Cross as a humanitarian organisation in his hometown in the 1860s (Thürer, 1970, pp.140–141). However, the decision made in Versailles to establish the League of Nations—e.g., the forerunner of the United Nations (UN)—in Geneva, put the city of Calvin and Rousseau definitively on the map of international affairs. Despite concerns on whether economic sanctions imposed by an international organisation are compatible with the concept of neutrality, Switzerland joined the League (Thürer, 1970, pp.149–153). Moreover, Basel was chosen as the head-office location for the Bank for International Settlements (BIS) in 1931. Although the BIS was originally designed to facilitate the transfer of German war reparations, it later converted itself into an international organisation for central banks around the world (see Cassis, 2010, pp.177–178).

On both sides of the Atlantic, a short period of optimism, economic prosperity, and political stability during the roaring twenties was cut short by the Great Depression. In Switzerland, the corresponding economic downturn affected primarily export-oriented firms. Between 1929 and 1932, total exports declined by approximately two-thirds in nominal terms, and by one-half in terms of volume, while wholesale prices contracted by almost 40 per cent until 1935 (Zurlinden, 2003, p.96). Although domestic demand remained remarkably stable, and the Swiss banking sector did not suffer from the catastrophic failures that had crippled the financial systems of the United States and Germany, economic recovery occurred a couple of years later than elsewhere (Baltensperger & Kugler, 2017, pp.73–82). The main culprit for this sluggish return to full employment was arguably that the Swiss franc was devalued only in 1936, which was well after sterling or the US dollar (Bernanke & James, 1990; Baltensperger & Kugler, 2017, pp.82–87). This hesitation to abandon the principles of the gold standard, such as preserving a fixed mint-par and free capital movements in times of peace, reinforced the status of the Swiss franc as a safe-haven currency. This status acted, in turn, as a magnet for foreign money, assets, and gold during the first half of the 1930s (Baltensperger & Kugler, 2017, p.73).

In addition to the economic havoc caused by the Great Depression, Europe was destabilised politically by the transformation of Germany into a Nazi dictatorship after 1933. Encouraged by this transformation, members and sympathisers of the far-right movement in Switzerland also began to openly support authoritarian forms of government. However, the majority of the Swiss electorate fortunately withstood this temptation (Thürer, 1970, p.153). For example, when the liberal party formed an alliance with the emerging right-wing "National Front" during local elections in Zurich in 1933, this decision did not fall on fertile ground with the electorate, but rather met with the victory of the social democrats, who had refused to join forces with the communists (Reinhardt, 2013, p.429). Furthermore, during the national elections of 1935, the "National Front" managed to win no more than two seats in the Federal Parliament. During the same year, the "Fronten Initiative", which proposed transforming the Swiss Confederation into a centralised state run by a powerful leader, was rejected by more than 70 per cent of the voters (Reinhardt, 2013, p.429). From today's perspective, it may seem strange that this initiative was not rejected by an even greater margin. However, this result reflected a relatively widespread feeling at the time that the future belonged to centralised and powerful forms of government, which were supposedly more effective at resolving economic problems than the tedious procedures of democratic rule.[12]

During the late 1930s, most members of Swiss society began to realise that the aggressive combination of nationalism and socialism in neighbouring Germany posed a direct threat to the very survival of their country (Thürer, 1970, p.153). Hence, before World War II (1939–1945) broke out, hasty preparations were being made by passing bills, supported by all major political parties, to strengthen the Swiss army, which was mobilised as soon as hostilities broke out in Europe in September 1939 (Thürer, 1970, p.155). The country had learned its lessons from World War I; soldiers were paid through a dedicated compensation scheme, and wartime expenditures were funded mainly through the capital market and tax increases rather than ad hoc monetary expansion, with inflation as a result. Furthermore, economic plans were implemented to increase domestic food production and to manage the supply of other vital goods (Baltensperger & Kugler, 2017,

[12] Within this context, it is worth mentioning that the national socialists were openly hostile to Switzerland's democracy. For example, Adolf Hitler referred to the Swiss as the "mortal enemies of the new Germany" and "the most despicable and wretched people of our nation".

p.88; Thürer, 1970, p.1571). Finally, tensions between the German- and French-speaking parts of the country were, by and large, absent during World War II (Reinhardt, 2013, pp.436–438). Despite the internal cohesion, the encirclement by Hitler's "Third Reich" and Mussolini's "Impero Italiano" after the surprisingly quick defeat of France in 1940 created a perilous situation during the subsequent years.[13] Although Germany had developed concrete plans to annex Switzerland, an attack never happened and, hence, one can only speculate about how long the resistance would have lasted (Urner, 2001; Reinhardt, 2013, p.439). Why did Switzerland remain an island of peace in the centre of a European continent torn apart by war? That the Swiss army was reasonably well equipped and could mobilise up to half a million men certainly mattered (Thürer, 1970, p.157). However, a role was also played by nonmilitary factors, such as allowing the passage of German and Italian transports on the transalpine railway lines, the conclusion of trade and financial agreements with Hitler's regime, and plain strategic luck that no major battles erupted within the vicinity of the Swiss border (Reinhardt, 2013, pp.442–447; Thürer, 1970, p.158). For the Swiss banking sector, it was mainly the gold transactions with the German Reichsbank as well as the way in which commercial banks dealt with the assets of Jews murdered during the Holocaust that would give rise to delicate questions after the end of World War II in 1945.

Except for several mistaken air raids by Allied bombers on towns located close to the German border, Switzerland emerged from World War II almost unscathed. After 1945, the intact political system and infrastructure provided the basis for a rapid economic recovery and expansion (Bergier, 1983, pp.274ff.). During the second part of the twentieth century, Switzerland became one of the wealthiest countries in the world and began to attract large numbers of immigrants, especially from Southern Europe, and later from other parts of the World as well (Thürer, 1970, pp.170ff.; Reinhardt, 2013, pp.451ff.). This development stands in sharp contrast to previous centuries, when large parts of the Swiss population saw no future other than to emigrate by, e.g., enlisting as mercenaries in foreign armies (see Chap. 2.2). Economic growth also provided the foundation for expanding the welfare state, including the introduction of a state-pension scheme in 1948. Nevertheless, compared with other countries, state benefits remained relatively modest until the end of the twentieth century. For example, a national health-insurance scheme was introduced only in 1995. During the decades following World War II, the banking sector extended its reach across the globe and benefitted from large inflows of offshore capital and assets (Cassis, 2010, pp.232–235).

In contrast to the globalisation of the economy, Switzerland maintained a quite low international political profile throughout the twentieth century. Because

[13] Until 1940, the Swiss military strategy against an attack by large German forces rested on holding the line along the major rivers until the French army would come to the rescue (see, e.g., Ribi, 2010; Somm, 2010). The French defeat left this strategy in tatters. As an emergency solution, it was decided that the army should retreat to strongholds in the Alps, the so-called Réduit Nationale (or national fortress). This réduit strategy after 1940 left substantial parts of the country, and population almost completely exposed to a German attack.

neutrality had served the country well during both world wars, joining a military alliance, such as NATO, was not seen as desirable (Thürer, 1970, p.164). During the decades after 1945, the policy of keeping out of international affairs went even so far as to prevent a membership in the United Nations (UN), despite the location of the European headquarters of this international organisation in Geneva. Furthermore, by lacking the motive of seeking reconciliation with a former enemy through economic co-cooperation, Switzerland did not join the European Community, which later became the European Union (EU). Finally, although the Swiss franc was closely aligned with the dollar between 1945 and 1973, widespread mistrust of government-controlled capital movements long prevented a formal membership in the Bretton Woods Institutions, i.e., the International Monetary Fund (IMF), and the Worldbank (Baltensperger & Kugler, 2017, pp.94, 104). When it turned out that the international gold-dollar standard was no longer compatible with domestic price stability, the Swiss franc also became part of a pioneering group of freely floating currencies in 1973 (Baltensperger & Kugler, 2017, pp.106ff.). The comparatively large degree of monetary independence has continued to the present day. Above all, unlike neighbouring countries, Switzerland has not replaced its national currency with the euro (Baltensperger & Kugler, 2017, pp.122ff.).

The collapse of the Soviet Union in 1991 marked the last historical turning point during the twentieth century. For Switzerland, the economic liberalisation and democratisation of Eastern Europe implied that for the first time in decades, there was no imminent military threat. This development, which was in itself benign, also gave rise to questions regarding whether neutrality had become outdated, and created a momentum to expand the political cooperation with Europe and the rest of the world. In particular, Switzerland finally became a full member of the IMF as well as the Worldbank in 1992 and formally joined the United Nations, as one of the last countries in the world, in 2002. Conversely, the widely shared aspiration of the political, intellectual, and economic elites for a closer European integration suffered a severe setback, when an agreement to enter the single market was rejected in a referendum in 1992.[14] After several new members had joined the European Union around 2000, the Swiss economy became an enclave within the single market and the euro area. To reduce this isolation, the relationship with the European Union has been organised, on a selective basis, through the conclusion of numerous bilateral agreements. Above all, since 2008, Switzerland has been a part of the Schengen area and has granted the free movement of labour to most European countries. However, the corresponding policies have remained controversial, especially when the level of European immigration increased dramatically after 2008. Reflecting this controversy, an initiative calling for a reduction of "mass migration" was adopted in 2014.

[14] In particular, the referendum referred to joining the so-called European Economic Area (EEA), which is an international agreement enabling the participation of non-EU countries, such as Norway and Iceland, in the European single market. The result of the referendum was narrow in terms of vote shares (50.3 per cent voted against joining the EEA) but fell clearly short of the cantonal quorum that was also required (16 cantons "no" versus 7 cantons "yes").

Regardless of these political events, and similar to the developments taking place approximately one hundred years earlier, Swiss companies have been keen participants in the globalisation of economic and financial activities since the 1990s. Together with some highly specialised medium-sized enterprises, which export their sophisticated products to countries around the world, multinational firms have been at the forefront of this globalisation. Today, an astonishing number of firms with complex international chains of production and distribution are headquartered in Switzerland, including financial firms, such as UBS, and Swiss Re, but also Novartis and Roche in the pharmaceutical industry and Nestlé in the food industry. Thanks to developing innovative technologies and offering well-paid jobs, these firms are important sources of Switzerland's current prosperity (Walser & Bischofberger, 2013). Of course, this openness and international integration expose the country also to external shocks. For example, after the Global Financial Crisis of 2008, UBS had to be supported by a government bailout. Moreover, the instability of the euro during the European debt crisis led to a substantial appreciation of the Swiss franc, which was only briefly interrupted, when the Swiss National Bank imposed an exchange-rate floor between 2011 and 2015. The recent effects of the Covid-19 pandemic, the war in Ukraine, and the financial instability that led to the downfall of Credit Suisse only provide the latest examples for these types of external economic shocks.

References

Baltensperger, E., & Kugler, P. (2016). The historical origin of the safe haven status of the Swiss Franc. *Aussenwirtschaft, 67,* 1–30.

Baltensperger, E., & Kugler, P. (2017). *Swiss monetary history since the early 19th century*. Cambridge: Cambridge University Press.

Bauer, H., & Blackman, W. J. (1998). *Swiss banking–An analytical history*. Basingstoke and London: Macmillan Press.

Bergier, J. F. (1983). *Die Wirtschaftsgeschichte der Schweiz: Von den Anfängen bis zur Gegenwart*. Zürich und Köln: Benzinger Verlag.

Bernanke, B., & James, H. (1990). The gold standard, deflation, and financial crisis in the Great Depression: An international comparison. In G. Hubbard (Ed.), *Financial markets and financial crises*. Chicago: University of Chicago Press.

Bonjour, E. (1946). *Swiss neutrality, its history and meaning*. London: George Allen and Unwin.

Cassis, Y. (2010). *Capital of capital. The rise and fall of international financial centres 1780–2009*. Cambridge: Cambridge University Press.

Donzé, P. Y. (2015). *History of the Swiss watch industry* (3rd ed.). Bern: Peter Lang.

Herger, N., Hodler, R., & Lobsiger, M. (2008). What determines financial development? Culture, institutions, or trade. *Review of World Economics, 144,* 558–587.

Jung, J. (2015). *Switzerland's success story: The life and work of Alfred Escher (1819–1882)*. Zurich: NZZ Libro.

Kindleberger, C. P. (1984). *A financial history of Western Europe*. London, New York: Routledge.

Marchi, O. (1971). *Schweizer Geschichte für Ketzer oder die wundersame Entstehung der Eidgenossenschaft*. Zurich: Praeger.

Möckli, S. (1987). *Die schweizerischen Landsgemeinde-Demokratien*. Bern: Verlag Paul Haupt.

Mottet, L. H. (1987). Die Schweiz und ihre Banken. In L. H. Mottet (Ed.), *Geschichte der Schweizer Banken*. Zurich: Verlag Neue Zürcher Zeitung.

North, D. (1990). *Institutions, institutional change and economic performance*. Cambridge: Cambridge University Press.
Obstfeld, M., & Taylor, A. (2004). *Global capital markets integration, crisis, and growth*. Cambridge: Cambridge University Press.
Reinhardt, V. (2013). *Die Geschichte der Schweiz* (2nd ed.). Munich: C.H. Beck.
Ribi, R. (2010). General Henri Guisan. Heart of the resistance, saviour of the nation. *Swiss Review, 3,* 8–11.
Ritzmann, F. (1973). *Die Schweizer Banken. Geschichte - Theorie - Statistik*. Bern: Verlag Paul Haupt.
Schaltegger, C. A., & Schmid, L. A. (2021). Public perceptions and bond markets during the Great War: The case of a neutral country. *Public Choice, 186,* 537–561.
Somm, M. (2010). *General Guisan. Widerstand nach Schweizerart*. Bern: Stämpli Verlag.
Somm, M. (2015). *Marignano. Warum die Schweiz keine Grossmacht wurde*. Bern: Stämpli Verlag.
Somm, M. (2022). *Warum die Schweiz reich geworden ist - Mythen und Fakten eines Wirtschaftswunders*. Bern: Stämpli Verlag.
Thürer, G. (1970). *Free and Swiss-the story of Switzerland*. London: Oswald Wolff.
Urner, K. (2001). *Let's swallow Switzerland - Hitler's plans against the Swiss confederation*. Lanham: Lexington Books.
Walser, R., & Bischofberger, A. (2013). *Multinational companies: Fact and fiction the wide ranging contribution of multinationals to Swiss prosperity*. Zurich: Avenir Suisse.
Zurlinden, M. (2003). *Gold standard, deflation and depression: The Swiss economy during the Great Depression*. Zurich: SNB Quarterly Bulletin 2/2003.

Chapter 3
Banks in the Old Confederation and in Geneva (Before 1848)

3.1 Early Swiss Banking in the European Context

This chapter contemplates the years before 1848, which cover the period of the so-called Old Confederation, when Switzerland was no more than a loose club of cantons without a permanent central government, common internal market, or uniform currency (see Sect. 2.2). Owing to this economic and political fragmentation, and for other reasons, the development of Swiss banking before the nineteenth century was relatively slow and lagged behind the progress made in the leading European financial centres at the time.

In medieval Europe, the need for banking services often emerged in connection with the financial challenges of long-distance trade, including covering delays between selling merchandise and receiving payment, and absorbing the risks of transporting goods over land or by sea (Kindleberger, 1984, pp.35ff.). In a similar vein, when shipping goods to other cities, merchants regularly required the financial service of exchanging various kinds of coins.[1] The development of cashless means of payment in the form of bills of exchange, which were written orders instructing a financier to pay a certain amount of money at a specific place on a specific date, gave further impetus to the European banking sector (Kindleberger, 1984, 39–40). In particular, early bills of exchange emerged at medieval trade fairs between the thirteenth and fifteenth centuries (Denzel, 2010, ch.3; Kindleberger, 1984, pp.36–39). Reflecting the still important connection between trade and finance, the cosmopolitan Italian city states of Venice, Florence, Milan, and Genoa grew to become major banking centres during the Renaissance. Antwerp, Amsterdam, and London followed suit when the ports around the North Sea served as major European hubs for trade and finance during the seventeenth and eighteenth centuries

[1] The term "bank" originates from these currency transactions, as it refers to the benches (Italian "banca"), on which medieval money changers displayed their coins (Kindleberger, 1984, p.42).

N. Herger, *Switzerland and its Banks*, Frontiers in Economic History,
https://doi.org/10.1007/978-3-031-35904-0_3

(Kindleberger, 1984, pp.42–46; 77–82; Cassis, 2010, pp.9ff.). These merchant banks often opened subsidiaries in several financial centres and were typically organised as private partnerships with unlimited liability (Cassis, 2010, p.8). To diminish the risk of financial fraud in a world with highly incomplete information and scant possibilities of monitoring economic activities in distant places, it made sense to keep such businesses within the family by entrusting foreign subsidiaries to children, brothers, or close relatives. Famous banking dynasties included the Medici of Florence (De Roover, 1966), the Fugger of Augsburg in Southern Germany (Bergier, 1979), and the Rothschild of Frankfurt (Ferguson, 1998).

During the early modern age, banking schemes organised around a large coalition of investors with limited liability and no direct management responsibility were a major financial innovation in Europe (Ferguson, 2008, pp.69ff.). Wars and the resulting sovereign defaults had, indeed, crippled some of the most potent family banks. For example, the vast financial empire of the Medici collapsed during the 1490s after incurring a series of catastrophic defaults on loans granted to England's King Edward IV, who lost a fortune in the Wars of the Roses (1455–1485), and to Venice, which struggled to repay its debts after an expensive military campaign against the Ottoman Empire (De Roover, 1966, pp.358ff.). To better handle these types of risk, the potential of public companies was eventually realised in Holland and England, which were at the forefront of a financial revolution that helped to pave the way for their economic preeminence during the seventeenth and eighteenth centuries (Kindleberger, 1984, pp.158ff.). Among other innovations, such as stock-traded firms and insurance companies, this financial modernisation involved public schemes through which investors could jointly acquire government charters granting the right to issue paper money during a certain period. Probably, the most far-reaching example of such a banknote scheme arose with the Bank of England, which was founded in 1694 to raise additional government revenue to finance the Nine Year's War (1688–1697). This and other schemes have had a lasting legacy, because they formed the nuclei of the oldest central banks in the world (Herger, 2019, pp.9–12). However, not all attempts to issue paper money were successful. For example, during the early eighteenth century, France embarked on an ambitious reform programme to restore order in public finances. The implementation of the necessary financial reforms was entrusted to the Scottish economist and gambler John Law, who created an empire of merchant companies, including the "Compagnie du Mississippi" to exploit the French trade monopoly with North America, as well as a "Banque Royale" that issued paper money in France (Murphy, 1997; Ferguson, 2008, pp.138ff.). Although these schemes resembled those that had been successfully put in place elsewhere, John Law overused his privileges to stimulate the economy by printing massive amounts of paper money. Unsurprisingly, the corresponding monetary overhang soon began to inflate the share price of the "Compagnie du Mississippi" and reduced the value of banknotes. The outcome was a severe financial crash in 1720. Arguably, the setbacks from early French attempts to introduce paper money and joint-stock companies caused a backlash that retarded the transition towards a modern financial system and an efficient management of public debt for approximately a century. The absence of innovative financial institutions was, in turn, a source of ongoing fiscal crises and recurrent sovereign defaults, which eventually triggered the French Revolution in 1789 (Velde & Weir, 1992; Ferguson, 2008, pp.126, 154).

The cantons of the Old Confederation played no major role in the development of the European banking sector. Before the nineteenth century, the political and geographical prerequisites to sustain a leading financial centre on Swiss territory simply did not exist. To understand why this was the case, it is important to remember that waterways, including the sea, lakes, and rivers, rather than the lacklustre roads, were the preferred routes for transporting goods in medieval times. In this regard, the Alpine mountain range represented a formidable barrier that did not allow for the establishment of busy trading routes and the associated concentration of economic activities. Before industrialisation, Swiss cities, such as Bern, Basel, Zurich, and Geneva, were tiny in comparison to the leading European trade centres, such as London, Milan, Naples, Paris, and Venice (see Reinhardt, 2013, pp.50–52). In a similar vein, the landlocked cantons of the Old Confederation were barely involved in overseas trade. Regarding the development of public banking schemes, the Old Confederation remained a highly decentralised political entity, which had learned to survive by staying on the sidelines of major European conflicts (see Sect. 2.2). Owing to this decentralisation and political neutrality, there was no lavish royal court, and no need to finance a standing army. More often than not, the cantons even profited from major European wars by signing lucrative mercenary contracts with foreign monarchs or with the papacy. Contracts, such as those concluded with France in 1521, 1663, and 1777 (Thürer, 1970, pp.71–72; 186–187; Reinhardt, 2013, pp.496–498), opened up a source of foreign income in the form of the so-called pensions, which mostly ended up in the pockets of local elites (Bauer & Blackman, 1998, p.52; Bergier, 1983, pp.329ff.). Owing to these, and other, forms of capital inflows, the cities of Bern and Zurich in particular were able to accumulate substantial state treasures during the seventeenth and eighteenth centuries (Mottet, 1987a, pp.18–19). Hence, there was no need to turn to innovative financial schemes to raise funds for the government (Ritzmann, 1973, pp.16ff.). Before the nineteenth century, elites across the Swiss cantons were rather confronted with the opposite problem of finding adequate domestic and foreign investment opportunities (Ritzmann, 1973, pp.18ff.).

In premodern Switzerland, banks were, of course, not completely absent. For example, there was a substantial financial sector in Geneva with private banks devoting themselves primarily to funding the royal government in neighbouring France. On a smaller scale, early financial schemes were set up to organise the export of the aforementioned surplus capital in the cities of Bern and Zurich (see Ritzmann, 1973, p.18–22). In a similar vein, the elites of the old-established cantons required wealth management from a small number of private banks. From the seventeenth century onwards, an emerging class of entrepreneurs and merchants, especially in the textile industry, created a demand for trade finance. For the broader population, the demand for banking services arose only during early industrialisation, around 1800, in the form of the savings-bank movement (Ritzmann, 1973, pp.23ff.). The next sections provide an overview of these developments.

3.2 Geneva

Before 1800, Geneva represented "the smallest of the [...] secondary financial centres" in Europe (Cassis, 2010, p.35). However, this historical status does not necessarily provide a direct link with Switzerland's current role in international banking because Geneva did not become a full member of the Old Confederation until 1815 (see Sect. 2.2) and was even under the control of the Duchy of Savoy during the fourteenth and fifteenth centuries (Bauer & Blackman, 1998, pp.10–11). It was only after a series of wars during the reformation of the sixteenth century when Geneva allied itself with other protestant cities, especially Bern, to obtain the status of a partial member—a so-called zugewandter Ort—of the Old Confederation (Reinhardt, 2013, pp.182ff.). Furthermore, although Geneva attracted a large number of Protestant refugees who made it a remarkably cosmopolitan place, their financial relationships were heavily oriented towards France and, hence, lacked a genuinely European, let alone global, outreach (Cassis, 2010, pp.35–37; Bauer & Blackman, 1998, pp.50–53).

Geneva is located where the river "Rhône" leaves a large lake. Whereas the "Rhône" flows further downstream through the cities of Lyon and Avignon and reaches the Mediterranean Sea close to Marseilles in southern France, the lake opens up access to several Alpine crossings into Italy. Bearing in mind the importance of waterways for preindustrial transportation, the strategic location of Geneva was already recognised by ancient Celtic tribes and, later, by a Roman settlement. In medieval times, the intermediate position between major Italian and French cities turned out to be ideal for hosting annual trade fairs. These attracted prominent merchant bankers, including the Medici, during the fifteenth century (Bergier, 1983, pp.293ff.; Kindleberger, 1984, p.37; Mottet, 1987b, pp.42ff.). However, the importance of the Genevan trade fairs declined substantially during the sixteenth century as France began to promote Lyon as an own commercial entrepôt. Additionally, there was a general shift of the European centre of economic gravity away from the Mediterranean towards the North Sea (Bauer & Blackman, 1998, p.12). The political turmoil caused by the Reformation, which was officially proclaimed in Geneva in 1536, as well as the aforementioned wars with the Duchy of Savoy accelerated this commercial decline and, unsurprisingly, disrupted the development of the banking sector (Thürer, 1970, 60–62; Seitz, 1931, pp.10ff.).

Because Geneva was among the leading centres of the Reformation, the city served as a destination for Protestant refugees during the sixteenth and seventeenth centuries (Lüthy, 1959, 1961, pp.37ff.). These refugees included the so-called Huguenots from France, the most famous of whom was Jean Calvin (1509–1564). Regarding the development of the banking sector, it probably mattered that he preached a relatively business-friendly form of Christian belief without an outright condemnation of charging interest rates. Despite the prominent history of the Huguenots and Calvinism, it should not be overlooked that Geneva also became the refuge of many Protestants persecuted for their religious beliefs in places, such as Italy. That this country is nowadays known as quintessentially

Catholic also reflects the uncompromising papal inquisition, which succeeded in eradicating the reformation on the Italian Peninsula during the sixteenth century. This religious intolerance implied that many leading merchant and banking families, whose entrepreneurial ambitions may have been more appreciated by Protestant than by Catholic beliefs, were forced to emigrate. As a case in point, numerous prominent families left the Italian city state of Lucca during the second half of the sixteenth century, triggering an economic decline after the glorious era of the Renaissance (Somm, 2022, pp.83ff.). Conversely, with the influx of these families into places, such as Geneva, knowledge of some of the most advanced crafts as well as business practices arrived. In addition to new forms of Christian worship, the Protestants brought with them a range of practical skills and expertise in secular activities, such as making watches and clocks, producing silk, printing books, and double-entry accounting (Lüthy, 1959, 1961, pp.41ff.). After the turmoil of the Reformation abated, these activities provided the basis for redeveloping the Genevan economy. The increasing merchant trade laid, in turn, the foundation for a home-grown banking sector. To develop these economic and financial activities, the Protestants drew heavily on the network of their diaspora, including the personal relationships of religious refugees in Geneva with their family members and fellow believers in England, Holland, and other parts of Switzerland (Lüthy, 1959, 1961, pp.78ff.).

During the seventeenth and eighteenth centuries, the banking sector in Geneva became important in its own right (Bergier, 1983, pp.330–331). Aside from the old-established Genevan elite, many of the increasingly influential private bankers were from the French (e.g., Mallet, Mirabaud, and Naville), Italian (e.g., Butini, and Turrettini), and German (e.g., Hentsch, and Necker) Protestant diaspora.[2] Inevitably, their financial portfolios reflected these personal backgrounds. Overall, for Geneva, involvement in French government finance stood out. Despite the renewed political hostility towards the Huguenots during the seventeenth century—as reflected by the revocation of the tolerance Edict of Nantes by King Louis XIV in 1685—the kingdom of France remained faithful to their financial services (Cassis, 2010, p.35). Owing to the military backing of the Old Confederation, as well as the geographic and cultural proximity, Genevan financiers were in an ideal position to develop their "French business" (Sayons, 1937, pp.314–315; Mottet, 1987b, pp.50–51). At the time, it was quite common for Genevan banking dynasties to be represented in Paris by one of their members (Sayons, 1937, p.323). The financial market in that city was very lucrative, because France regularly undertook costly military campaigns to remain the dominant power on the European continent. Although the resulting mountain of sovereign debt attracted a large number of private financiers, it also reached dangerously high levels. Indeed, the aforementioned

[2] As a concrete example, Sayons (1935) tells the life story of Jean-Jacques Naville (1665–1743), who was born into a Protestant family in southern France and died as a wealthy and respected merchant banker in Geneva. According to his will, he had accumulated a fortune including investments in Spain as well as a large portfolio of French, English, Spanish, and Portuguese government bonds.

Banque Royale scheme and the monopolisation of French trade with America within the "Compagnie du Mississippi" represented risky attempts to stabilise public finances. Given the extraordinary financial exposure to France, it is perhaps not surprising that the Mississippi bubble around 1720 entailed dangerously high losses for several Genevan private banks (Sayons, 1937). Of course, as in any speculative cycle, there were also fortunes to be made by liquidating the inflated securities before the financial system collapsed in 1720. Of note, Geneva's banks were not only hit by the Mississippi bubble, but had also suffered from an earlier French sovereign default in 1709 as well as from the bursting of the so-called South Sea bubble in London in 1721. Nevertheless, they recovered relatively quickly from these setbacks. For Geneva, French government debt remained the most important foreign asset during most of the eighteenth century (Cassis, 2010, p.35).

Until the French Revolution of 1789, the banking business in Geneva prospered and became quite sophisticated. This development is nicely illustrated by the way in which investments were made in French life annuities during the late eighteenth century (Cramer, 1946). Through these so-called rentes viagères, investors could make outright grants against receiving a fixed annual instalment—a so-called rente—as long as a designated person was alive. Similar to a modern life insurance policy, life-contingent financial securities were originally developed to guarantee a certain level of income for a spouse, child, or a close relative (see e.g. Munro, 2003, p.519). However, medieval monarchs eventually turned to life annuities for borrowing because these types of contracts offered a way to bypass usury laws, which either fully condemned the charging of interest, or stipulated a legal maximum rate (Munro, 2003, pp.203ff.). In particular, France had begun to issue national "rentes viagères" before 1700, and towards the end of the eighteenth century, they had become a leading security for financing public debt (Velde & Weir, 1992, p.25).[3] A flaw of the policy to increase French borrowing by inconspicuously offering high effective interest rates on life annuities was that they were not priced in an actuarially fair manner and, in some cases, paid the same "rente" regardless of the age of the person, on whom they were issued (Cramer, 1946, pp.110; 114–113; Velde & Weir, 1992, p.30).[4] By being apparently better informed than the French

[3] The "rentes viagères" were the most important, but not the only form of life-contingent securities in France. Other forms included the notorious "tontines", through which the government borrowed from a group of persons by promising to pay a fixed annuity until the death of the last member of that group (Weir, 1989). This arrangement had the macabre implication of the survivors benefitting financially from the deaths of other group members.

[4] Why did France resort to complicated life annuities rather than simply offering perpetual bonds, which were successfully issued to fund the British consolidated debt at interest rates well below 5 per cent during the eighteenth century (see, e.g., Munro, 2003, pp.556ff.)? Arguably, the problem was that perpetual bonds must be backed by a long-term tax strategy, and their market interest rates will only be low, while the probability of a sovereign default remains relatively low (North & Weingast, 1989, pp.819ff.). However, in prerevolutionary France, new taxes warranted the approval of the Estates General. The French monarchs were long reluctant to summon this parliamentary assembly, because this decision would have undermined their absolute claim to power. When the public finance situation became desperate and taxes had to be raised, the opening of the Estates

monarchy about early statistical theory and mathematical methods for calculating survival probabilities, financiers began to exploit this mis-pricing by seeking, in a scientific manner, persons with long life expectancies.[5] For example, Genevan bankers found that young girls, who had survived the usual childhood illnesses and were born into the comfort of wealthy families, had, statistically, the most years left to live. Because French annuities drawn on these young "demoiselles" promised high effective interest rates, they became a popular asset (Velde & Weir, 1992, p.31). The attractiveness of these investments was further enhanced through the diversification of mortality risks by pooling life annuities across groups of typically "thirty demoiselles" (Cramer, 1946, p.116). As a result, Genevan bankers underwrote up to a quarter of French life annuities during the 1770s and 1780s, and regularly pooled them and resold the packages to local and foreign investors (Velde & Weir, 1992, pp.32–33; Mottet, 1987b, pp.58–61). By investing in these assets, even ordinary savers could earn a handsome interest rate of approximately 8 per cent (Cramer, 1946, p.117).

In contrast to the remarkable efforts to diversify the mortality risks associated with the "rentes viagères", Geneva's bankers failed to hedge themselves against French sovereign risk (Velde & Weir, 1992 p.33; Cassis, 2010, p.35). Therefore, they were critically exposed to the collapse of the "ancien régime" and the hyperinflation in the wake of the French Revolution (Cassis, 2010, p.36; Mottet, 1987b, pp.72–75).[6] The associated collapse of the French public finances was already foreshadowed by delayed "rente" payments during the 1780s (Cramer, 1946, pp.126). However, after the revolution, the republican government in Paris quickly resorted to making payments in paper money, the notorious "assignats", and eventually converted the "rentes viagères" into debased government bonds (Cramer, 1946, pp.126–128; Mottet, 1987b, pp.59–60). The corresponding losses proved catastrophic for Geneva and resulted in widespread bankruptcies during the

---

General in 1789 was indeed quickly followed by a revolutionary uprising (Velde & Weir, 1992, pp.5–10).

[5] The elaboration of early statistical methods and probability theory from the seventeenth century onwards was indeed partially motivated by the quest for pricing life annuities according to actuarially sound principles (Velde & Weir, 1992, p.20). Because these problems were not only a scientific curiosity, but had practical implications, they attracted the attention of famous mathematicians, such as Christiaan Huygens (1629–1695) in Holland, Edmond Halley (1665–1742) in England, Abraham de Moivre (1667–1754) in France, and Jacob Bernoulli (1655–1705) in Basel (see Minto, 2008). By the middle of the eighteenth century, the mathematical methods of calculating life expectancies and survival probabilities were fairly well known, but the underlying demographic data remained inaccurate and incomplete (Velde & Weir, 1992, p.20).

[6] As an irony of history, the last finance minister of the French royal government was Jacques Necker (1732–1804), who was born in Geneva and had long worked as an employee, and later as a partner, for Genevan banks in Paris before serving twice as French finance minister (Lüthy, 1959, 1961, pp.369ff.). To the present day, it remains unclear whether or not his fiscal reforms, which met much opposition from the French aristocracy, could have succeeded in stabilising the public finances (Velde & Weir, 1992, pp.2ff.). In any case, Necker was relatively popular among the ordinary public, and his dismissal on the 11th of July 1789 occurred only three days before the storming of the Bastille, which marked the official beginning of the French Revolution.

early 1790s (Cramer, 1946, pp.128ff.; Mottet, 1987b, pp.60–61; 73). The situation deteriorated further, when this economic crisis triggered the collapse of the city's political system in 1792 (Mottet, 1987b, p.73). Similar to the contemporaneous turmoil in Paris, a revolutionary committee seized power and quickly resorted to state terror in terms of handing out arbitrary punishments, extorting "patriotic taxes" depending on the personal backgrounds and political views of the payers, and sending numerous citizens to the guillotine (Mottet, 1987b, p.73). In 1798, French troops invaded and annexed Geneva (Thürer, 1970, p.91). As in other parts of Europe, political and economic stability did not return until after the Congress of Vienna in 1815, when it was decided that Geneva should join the Swiss Confederation as an ordinary canton (Thürer, 1970, p.94).

Perhaps surprisingly, some of the oldest private banks, which still exist in Geneva, can trace their roots back to the turbulent years between 1792 and 1815 (Mottet, 1987b, p.74). Apparently, the revolutionary turmoil destroyed the fortunes of the Genevan elite, but not their family structures, personal contacts, and ways of doing business (Ugolini, 2018, p.164.). However, unlike the early Genevan private bankers of the eighteenth century, the new cohort of the nineteenth century was unable to regain a leading position in funding French government debt (Cassis, 2010, p.36; Ugolini, 2018, pp.162ff.). By way of contrast, the cosmopolitan outlook survived thanks to the focus on a narrow niche of private wealth management for an international clientele (Cassis, 2010, pp.69–70, 129, 179). Taken together, these developments reflect a relative decline in comparison with other domestic financial centres, especially Zurich, and with foreign centres, such as Paris, during the industrial age (see Sect. 5.4). Nevertheless, an astonishing financial cluster still exists in Geneva today (Cassis, 2010, p.275). Some of the corresponding banks have kept ancient traditions alive, such as carrying family names, being organised as private partnerships, priding themselves on having a long-term and low-risk approach to investments, and relying on long-term business relationships with carefully selected customers around the world.

3.3 Banking Activities Within the Old Confederation

Regarding the importance of banking and finance, no city of the Old Confederation could match the status of Geneva. Although Basel was the leading financial centre in the German-speaking part of the Swiss Confederation until industrialisation, the corresponding activities barely mattered at the European level. As an exception, during a Council of the Roman Catholic Church summoned in Basel between 1431 and 1448 to debate papal supremacy and Christian unity, a cosmopolitan group of religious scholars, leading clerics, and other eminent persons gathered, with their entourage, in the city. Among other things, these dignitaries created a temporary demand for an extraordinary range of international financial services and, therefore, attracted famous bankers, including the Medici (Bauer, 1987, pp.140–143; Bauer & Blackman, 1998, pp.29–33). However, the conclusion of the council almost immediately downgraded the importance of the banking sector back to an unspectacular level (Bauer, 1987, pp.143ff.; Bauer & Blackman, 1998, pp.33ff.).[7] Benefitting from the location on the river Rhine, which provides a navigable route to the ports of the North Sea, Basel remained a regional entrepôt and hosted annual trade fairs, which underpinned a certain amount of trade and required some merchant banking and the associated exchange of coins (Bauer, 1987, pp.143ff.). However, these activities were unspectacular when compared with the contemporaneous financial progress made in, say, sixteenth-century Italy, or in seventeenth- and eighteenth-century Holland and England. As in Geneva, the influx of well-educated Protestant refugees from highly developed parts of Europe gave an economic impetus to Basel after the reformation. In particular, an outstanding silk-manufacturing cluster began to emerge. The international business networks of the corresponding merchants and the wealth of successful entrepreneurs provided, in turn, the basis for the establishment of several early private banks during the seventeenth and eighteenth centuries. Although these banks were less exposed than their colleagues in Geneva to the defaults caused by the French Revolution in 1789, Basel's trade oriented economy suffered heavily from the Continental Blockade imposed by Napoleon between 1806 and 1813.

There was an even less remarkable banking sector in the other cities and towns of the Old Confederation. Typically, a tiny class of local aristocrats, powerful guild members, and successful merchants formed the exclusive clientele of a handful of private bankers, who themselves typically belonged to the local elites. In some cantons, incomes (i.e., pensions) from recruiting mercenaries for foreign armies, as well as profits from textile manufacturing or watchmaking, created far more capital than could be sensibly invested in the local economy. This capital surplus underpinned early forms of wealth management by private banks. In addition, schemes similar to what would nowadays be called "sovereign wealth funds" were set up in several cantons. In this regard, the situation of the Canton of Bern was extraordinary. Between the seventeenth and eighteenth centuries, this city state managed to accumulate a legendary state treasure thanks to a far-sighted and thrifty government, the absence of war, substantial amounts of foreign income from mercenary contracts, and valuables expropriated from the Catholic Church during the reformation (Seelhofer, 1987, p.179–183; Schaltegger et al., 2020). Remarkably, the Bernese state treasure did not consist only of specie but also encompassed a portfolio of foreign shares, bonds, and loans. This investment strategy is even mentioned by Adam Smith in the "Wealth of Nations":

> The canton of Berne derives a considerable revenue by lending a part of its treasure to foreign states: that is, by placing it in the public funds of the different indebted nations of

[7] For Basel, the Council of the Roman Catholic Church has nonetheless left a lasting legacy, insofar as the corresponding scholarly debates provided the stepping stone for the foundation of one of the oldest universities north of the Alps (Bauer, 1987, p.143). Famous faculty members and alumni of the University of Basel, which was established in 1460, include the humanist Erasmus of Rotterdam (1466–1536), the mathematicians of the Bernoulli family, and the mathematician Leonhard Euler (1707–1783).

> Europe, chiefly in those of France and England. [...] This policy of lending money to foreign states is, so far as I know, peculiar to the canton of Berne (Smith, 1776, book V, ch.II.3).

In this way, Bern became one of the largest shareholders of the South Sea Company, which gained hold on the British trade monopoly with South America. As mentioned above, this company nearly went bankrupt amid the bursting of a speculative bubble around 1721. Nevertheless, Bern resisted the temptation to sell at the peak of the panic and was subsequently rewarded for this decision with handsome profits (Somm, 2022, p.131–133). Through these types of investments, the value of the state treasure grew to an astonishing amount of more than ten million livres tournois towards the end of the eighteenth century (Schaltegger et al., 2020, p.47).[8,9] Still, financial ruin arrived with the downfall of the Old Confederation following its defeat in 1798 by the French army, which did not hesitate to confiscate the Bernese state treasure. In particular, approximately five million livres of precious metal were carried away to Paris, and many other assets were liquidated or sold at depressed values.[10] Despite becoming the political capital of the modern Swiss confederation in 1848, Bern has not even come close to regaining its financial power during the ancien régime. Quite the opposite happened. Bern is nowadays infamous for relying on vast amounts of fiscal transfers from other, much more prosperous cantons of the Swiss Confederation.

In Zurich, a similar capital accumulation provided the economic underpinning for the foundation of the "Bank Leu" in 1755. In contrast to other cantons, the corresponding surplus resulted mainly from commercial activities rather than the foreign mercenary business, which was officially outlawed in Zurich following the preaching of the Reformer Huldrych Zwingli (1484–1531).[11] In particular, textile manufacturing provided the basis for a successful industrialisation, which took off relatively early in eastern Switzerland towards the end of the eighteenth century. However, before this industrialisation revolutionised the financial sector, the importance of Zurich's banking sector clearly lagged behind that of Geneva, Basel, and possibly even Bern. The transformation of Zurich into a major domestic and international financial centre, as we know it today, occurred only during the railway boom after the integration of Switzerland into a federal country in 1848. Chapter 5 tells this story.

---

[8] The exact value is unknown, because the Bernese treasure was treated as a state secret. Therefore, detailed accounts have not survived (Schaltegger et al., 2020, pp.22ff.).

[9] To transform this amount into modern monetary units, see footnote 4 of Chap. 2.

[10] The exact extent of these losses has again not been documented. A part of the state treasure also ended up in the pockets of French officers and civil servants stationed in Bern (Schaltegger et al., 2020, pp.45).

[11] Zwingli, who took the position of a preacher in Zurich's minster in 1519, had served as a chaplain for an army of Swiss mercenaries during the wars of the Old Confederation against the City of Milan between 1499 and 1515. In particular, he had been an eyewitness of the catastrophic defeat of the Swiss against a French force in Marignano near Milan in 1515.

3.4 The Savings-Bank Movement

During the first decades of the nineteenth century, a large number of the so-called savings banks (Sparkassen, caisses d'épargne) were founded across Switzerland (see Fig. 1.1 of Chap. 1). In several regards, these financial institutes represented a first step towards the modernisation of the banking system. In particular, they were no longer organised as family firms, but rather in the form of government-supported institutions, cooperatives, or associations under civil law (Ritzmann, 1973, pp.25–26; 29). Furthermore, savings banks introduced rudimentary financial services to the broad public, instead of focusing on an exclusive class of merchants or aristocrats, who had been the main clientele of the premodern financial sector (Ritzmann, 1973, p.36). More often than not, these banks were even dedicated to the needs of an emerging working class, or domestic servants with meagre wage incomes. For example, for 1830, the "Caisse d'épargne et de prévoyance" in Geneva reported that approximately half of its depositors were domestic servants, roughly one-third were ordinary workers within the manufacturing sector, and more than half were female (see Ritzmann, 1973, p.27). However, unlike modern commercial banks with their extensive branch networks, the savings banks of the early nineteenth century were usually small, stand-alone non-profit organisations.

The main financial product of a savings bank was, of course, the savings account, which provided a vehicle for accumulating an old-age pension, or offered a monetary safeguard against personal hardships, such as accidents or illnesses (Bauer & Blackman, 1998, p.89). As a condition for opening an account, depositors in some cases had to commit to a schedule of fixed weekly contributions. To prevent the misuse of the resulting savings for frivolous purposes, withdrawals could often be made only on specific days, required prenotification, and were subject to complicated procedures, including personal visits to the accountant, cashier, or other trustees (Ritzmann, 1973, pp.26, 29). From the bank's perspective, the provision of liquidity insurance warranted an investment in standardised and safe assets (Ritzmann, 1973, p.29). However, at the time, Switzerland had no central note-issuing bank to which small banks could turn to store their reserves (see Chap. 4). Furthermore, because the cantons were not heavily indebted, safe assets in the form of liquid government bonds, such as the consols in Britain, barely existed. Owing to the scarcity of liquid and safe public assets, Swiss savings banks often invested in specie or resorted to financing mortgages at relatively unattractive interest rates (Bauer & Blackman, 1998, p.88; Ritzmann, 1973, p.30).

Given the scant investment opportunities within the Old Confederation, why was a movement to mobilise additional savings seen as necessary? Arguably, this movement did not rest on purely economic rationales, but had strong moral and religious underpinnings in terms of supporting a thrifty lifestyle as a way to ameliorate the condition of the poor (see Bauer & Blackman, 1998, pp.88ff; Ritzmann, 1973, pp.24–31). As a case in point, this paternalistic approach to social policy lay at the heart of the so-called Städtische Dienstbotenkassen. To cater to the needs of domestic servants, members of the local elite had begun to set up these types of savings banks in, e.g., Bern and Geneva shortly before the collapse of the ancien régime. In addition to being acts of charity, they were supposed to minimise the welfare expenses of the city. Moreover, the savings-bank movement clearly predominated in Protestant areas and was, by and large, absent in Catholic parts of the country. To some degree, this pattern reflected the ideological underpinnings of the movement and concurs, of course, nicely with the theory of Max (Weber, 1930) that Protestants tend to view economic success as a divine signal for salvation, and therefore attach higher values to hard work and a thrifty lifestyle.

The savings-bank movement was not a uniquely Swiss phenomenon but had its origins in England and Scotland. Furthermore, similar projects to improve the conditions of the poor arose during the nineteenth century in other Protestant areas of the European continent, including in Holland and in parts of France and Germany (Ritzmann, 1973, p.73; Horne, 1947).[12] Although making such a profane arrangement as a bank account the centrepiece of a political movement may seem bizarre, the massive upheavals during the industrial revolution should be kept in mind. For a person born at the time, the chances of leaving one's place of birth or ending up doing a completely different type of work than that of the ancestry suddenly increased. In other words, the economic progress of the nineteenth century created employment opportunities outside the agricultural sector and, hence, dramatically enhanced the geographical and social mobility of the population. However, the industrial age not only offered new opportunities, but also created novel forms of economic risks, such as becoming unemployed during a recession. Savings accounts provided an obvious safeguard against these risks.

Recall that in Switzerland, industrialisation originated in rural areas, especially along rivers providing water power for the new type of machinery (see Sect. 2.2). As a substantial number of savings banks emerged in the countryside during the early nineteenth century, they apparently catered to the financial needs of a changing economic environment (see Ritzmann, 1973, pp.27–30). In particular, factory work gave rise to a wage-earning class receiving a regular pecuniary income. Owing to the lack of note-issuing banks (see Chap. 5), these payments were typically made in coins, which could be more conveniently and safely stored in a savings account than at home (Bauer & Blackman, 1998, pp.90–91).

[12] Advocates of a thrifty lifestyle, and active promoters of the foundation of savings banks, included well-known authors, such as Daniel Defoe (1660–1731) and Jonathan Swift (1667–1745) but also, the philosopher Jeremy Bentham (1748–1832) and the classical economist Robert Malthus (1766–1834). In Switzerland, this movement was fictionalised in the novels of the author and pastor Jeremias Gotthelf (1797–1854), who is still renowned today in German literature for his vivid descriptions of the rural living conditions and down-to-earth stories about the daily sorrows of the peasantry in the Canton of Bern. In particular, the benefits of opening an account in the local savings bank are the topic of the novel "Hans Jakob und Heiri oder die beiden Seidenweber" (i.e., John Jacob and Henry or the two silk weavers), published in 1857.

The golden age of the Swiss savings banks came to an end during the second part of the nineteenth century, when many of them were liquidated (see Fig. 1.1 of Chap. 1).[13] However, this decline does not imply that saving accounts suddenly became obsolete. Rather, they were integrated into a new type of bank specialising in the transformation of savings into various kinds of credit, such as land credit, mortgages, and commercial loans (Ritzmann, 1973, pp.30–36). The corresponding popularisation of credit led to the foundation of numerous regional, land, and dedicated mortgage banks but also relied heavily on the newly established cantonal banks during the second part of the nineteenth century (see Sects. 4.3 and 5.5).

3.5 Overview of Swiss Banking Up to 1800

This section endeavours to provide a synoptic overview of the development of Switzerland's banking sector up to 1800. Around this year, banks across Europe, including those in the Old Confederation, suffered from widespread political and social turmoil after the French Revolution. However, even before this period of upheaval, banking and finance were not particularly advanced in the area just north of the Alpine mountain range. The only outstanding financial institutes were the private family banks in Geneva, which can trace their origins back to at least the early eighteenth century and had played a major role in funding the sovereign debt in prerevolutionary France. Basel was the leading banking centre of the full members of the Old Confederation. Moreover, in the early industrialised hinterland along the streams and rivers of Switzerland, small savings banks began to emerge.

The underdevelopment of the Swiss banking sector before 1800 is underscored by the fact that the most famous bankers born in the Old Confederation had careers outside the country. As a case in point, Jacques Necker (1731–1804) began his professional life in Geneva before serving the Bourbon kings as the last finance minister before the French Revolution (see Sect. 3.2). In a similar vein, Guillaume Mallet (1747–1826) descended from a Genevan textile-merchant dynasty that later moved into banking with a branch in Paris. Guillaume Mallet was a co-founder of the Banque de France in 1800, and his son Adolphe-Jacques served as a board member of the French note-issuing bank. Antoine François Haldimand (1741–1817) from the city of Lausanne had a similar life story. In particular, he founded a successful family bank in London. His son and successor, William, served as a member of the Court of Directors of the Bank of England. Without providing an exhaustive list, another example worth mentioning is David De Pury (1709–1786), who was born in the provincial town of Neuchâtel and later had an illustrious

[13] A similar decline took place in Great Britain after 1861, when post-office savings accounts were introduced. During the subsequent decades, more than two-thirds of the savings banks disappeared (Ritzmann, 1973, pp.32–34). In Switzerland, post-office accounts were introduced a couple of decades later, at the dawn of the twentieth century.

career as an employee of the aforementioned South Sea Company in London and, thereafter, as a financier in Lisbon, where he became the court banker to the Portuguese king. After dying childless, he donated his fortune, which amounted to hundreds of millions of Swiss francs in current money, to his native city (Somm, 2022, pp.137ff.).

The story of David De Pury has gained a certain notoriety because a part of his considerable fortune resulted from financial involvement in the Portuguese slave trade (see, e.g., Fässler, 2005, pp.207ff.). These types of historical connections have recently fuelled a discussion of whether the trade in African slaves and their exploitation on cotton and sugar plantations in the former European colonies in America provided the necessary seed capital for industrialisation. Without going into the details, many European financiers, private banks, and enterprises, including the Mississippi and South Sea companies, undoubtedly profited from selling human beings as "merchandise". Recall from the discussions of Sects. 3.2 and 3.3 that the private banks in Geneva or the Canton of Bern used to be important shareholders of these companies. Nevertheless, it is unlikely that the Atlantic slave trade—although clearly immoral and beset with racism—was pivotal for the breakthrough of industrial capitalism, including the associated emergence of large-scale banking, because slavery was neither unique nor particularly pervasive in Europe and the United States when compared with societies on other continents (Sowell, 2005, pp.111–170).[14] In this regard, the Old Confederation offers an example of early industrialisation barely dependent on capital associated with the slave trade. The obvious reason is that landlocked Switzerland was neither a colonial power nor a centre for overseas trade and, therefore, lacked a direct involvement in the slave trade. Although financiers, such as David De Pury, profited indirectly from this trade, linking these investments with the emergence of mechanised forms of production or large-scale banking in Switzerland is, for several reasons, questionable. First, the importance of financial participation in overseas trading companies lagged far behind that of, e.g., the French business of Geneva's private banks, that is, the funding of the Bourbon kings' sovereign debt (see, e.g., Mottet, 1987b, pp.58–61). Second, it is doubtful whether such financial participation could be reinvested in Switzerland's industrialisation at all. Recall that the French Revolution, and the turbulent events that followed, bankrupted the banking sector in Geneva and led to the confiscation of the Bernese state treasure. Hence, most premodern financial capital was no longer around when the industrial takeoff began around 1800. Third, as emphasised above, Swiss industrialisation originated in the hinterland and was driven mainly by self-funded entrepreneurs (see Sect. 2.2). Hence, from a financial perspective, the outstanding feature was that banks were hardly involved in helping entrepreneurs to set up their early textile and machine factories. As mentioned in

[14] It is rather the case that the early centres of industrialisation played a leading role in abolishing slavery and other forms of coerced labour, such as serfdom. In particular, slavery was abolished, on a state basis, in the northern United States between 1777 and 1804 (Wright, 2022, p.131). Britain banned the slave trade in 1807 and prohibited slavery across the empire in 1833 (Ferguson, 2004, p.118).

the previous section, numerous small banks did arise in these areas, but they were designed primarily to safeguard the modest savings of the industrial workforce.[15]

In quantitative terms, the capital and foreign incomes of the mercenary business, which shares some of the ruthlessness of the slave trade, were not unimportant for the Old Confederation (see, e.g., Bergier, 1983, p.328.). Then again, this capital was not necessarily crucial for the later development of mechanised production or big banking, because the cantons closely associated with enlisting soldiers in foreign armies—namely Bern, Lucerne, and Solothurn—did not become industrial centres. Rather, Zurich emerged as the leading industrial and banking metropolis in Switzerland after 1800. Exceptionally, this canton had already outlawed the mercenary business during the reformation of the sixteenth century (see Sect. 3.3).[16]

In 1800, mechanised forms of production and financial activities to fund the novel machinery and infrastructure were still in their infancy. The social and economic upheavals of the industrial age, as well as the corresponding financial innovations to provide credit and offer modern forms of payment, occurred mainly during the nineteenth century. After 1800, the Swiss banking system underwent a massive transformation with the foundation of big financial firms to mobilise large amounts of capital, the development of universal private and cantonal banks offering a broad range of financial services across a network of branches, and the establishment of note-issuing banks. Focusing on the case of Switzerland, the next two chapters are devoted to these developments.

References

Bauer, H. (1987). Bank- und Finanzplatz Basel. In L. H. Mottet (Ed.), *Geschichte der Schweizer Banken*. Zurich: Verlag Neue Zürcher Zeitung.

Bauer, H., & Blackman, W. J. (1998). *Swiss banking–An analytical history*. Basingstoke, London: Macmillan Press.

[15] A link between slavery and the textile industry could also arise through the importation of raw materials, such as cotton. However, the early Swiss textile industry relied mainly on cotton imported from what is currently Syria, rather than the plantations in the United States (see Somm, 2022, pp.154ff.).

[16] With respect to the financial ascent of Zurich, a rather far-fetched connection with slavery has been made with Alfred Escher, who was the main promoter of the foundation of Credit Suisse in that city in 1856 (see Sect. 5.3). The connection derives from the fact that two of his uncles owned a coffee plantation on Cuba with approximately 90 slaves during the first part of the nineteenth century (Jung, 2015, pp.32–34). In 1845, this plantation was sold and the resulting revenue inherited by the father of Alfred Escher. However, it is unclear whether the Escher family profited from the Cuban coffee plantation, as its owners had led the lives of repeated bankrupts in regular need of financial support from their relatives. If anything, the corresponding profits must have been small, especially when compared with the dozens of millions of capital required to set up Credit Suisse (see Sect. 5.3). Indeed, the bulk of this capital was raised through selling equity shares to the broad public in Zurich, as well as to a commercial bank in Germany (Jung, 2000, pp.47ff.).

Bergier, J. F. (1979). From the fifteenth century in Italy to the sixteenth century in Germany: A new banking concept? In Center for medieval and renaissance studies (Ed.). *The Dawn of Modern Banking*, 105–130.
Bergier, J. F. (1983). *Die Wirtschaftsgeschichte der Schweiz: Von den Anfängen bis zur Gegenwart*. Zürich und Köln: Benzinger Verlag.
Cassis, Y. (2010). *Capital of capital. The rise and fall of international financial centres 1780–2009*. Cambridge: Cambridge University Press.
Cramer, M. (1946). Les trente Demoiselles de Genève et les billets solidaires. *Revue Suisse d'Economie politique et de statistique, 82,* 109–138.
Denzel, M. A. (2010). *Handbook of world exchange rates, 1590–1914*. Farnham: Ashgate Publishing.
De Roover, R. (1966). *The rise and fall of the Medici bank 1397–1494*. New York: Norton.
Fässler, H. (2005). *Reise in Schwarz-Weiss: Schweizer Ortstermine in Sachen Sklaverei*. Zürich: Rotpunktverlag.
Ferguson, N. (1998). *The House of Rothschild: Money's prophets 1798–1848*. London: Penguin Press.
Ferguson, N. (2004). *Empire - How Britain made the modern world*. London: Penguin Press.
Ferguson, N. (2008). *The Ascent of money: A financial history of the world*. London: Penguin Press.
Herger, N. (2019). *Understanding central banks*. Cham: Springer Nature.
Horne, O. (1947). *A history of savings banks*. Oxford: Oxford University Press.
Jung, J. (2000). *Von der Schweizerischen Kreditanstalt zur Credit Suisse Group. Eine Bankengeschichte*. Zurich: NZZ Verlag.
Jung, J. (2015). *Switzerland's success story: The life and work of Alfred Escher (1819–1882)*. Zurich: NZZ Libro.
Kindleberger, C. P. (1984). *A financial history of Western Europe*. London, New York: Routledge.
Lüthy, H. (1959, 1961). *La banque protestante en France de la Révocation de l'Edit de Nantes à la Révolution francaise* (Vol. 2). Paris: S.E.V.P.E.N.
Minto, A. (2008). Early insurance mechanisms and their mathematical foundations. *The Mathematical Enthusiast, 5,* 345–357.
Mottet, L. H. (1987a). Die Schweiz und ihre Banken. In L. H. Mottet (Ed.), *Geschichte der Schweizer Banken*. Zurich: Verlag Neue Zürcher Zeitung.
Mottet, L. H. (1987b). Die Genfer Bankiers. In L. H. Mottet (Ed.), *Geschichte der Schweizer Banken*. Zurich: Verlag Neue Zürcher Zeitung.
Munro, J. H. (2003). The medieval origins of the financial revolution: Usuary, rentes, and negotiability. *The International History Review, 25,* 505–562.
Murphy, A. E. (1997). *John Law economic theorist and policy-maker*. Oxford: Clarendon Press.
North, D., & Weingast, B. R. (1989). Constitutions and commitment: The evolution of institutions governing public choice in seventeenth-century England. *The Journal of Economic History, 49,* 803–832.
Reinhardt, V. (2013). *Die Geschichte der Schweiz* (2nd ed.). Munich: C.H. Beck.
Ritzmann, F. (1973). *Die Schweizer Banken. Geschichte - Theorie - Statistik*. Bern: Verlag Paul Haupt.
Sayons, A. E. (1935). La Fortune de Jean-Jacques Naville, d'Anduze, marchand-bankquier à Gènes, puis à Genève, d'après l'inventiare de sa sucession ouverte à Genève en 1743. *Revue d'Histoire Suisse, 15,* 40–76.
Sayons, A. E. (1937). L'affaire de Law et les Genevois. *Revue d'Histoire Suisse, 17,* 310–340.
Schaltegger, C. A., Studer, T. M., Zell, L., & Salvi, M. (2020). *Napoleons reiche Beute: Eine aktuelle Einordnung zur Bedeutung des gestohlenen Berner Staatsschatzes von 1798*. Bern: Stämpfli Verlag.
Seelhofer, H. W. (1987). Banken im alten Bern. In L. H. Mottet (Ed.), *Geschichte der Schweizer Banken*. Zurich: Verlag Neue Zürcher Zeitung.
Seitz, J. (1931). *Histoire de la Banque a Genève*. Geneva: Comptoir d'Escompte.
Smith, A. (1776). *An inquiry into the nature and causes of the wealth of nations*, London: Strahan and Cadell.

Somm, M. (2022). *Warum die Schweiz reich geworden ist - Mythen und Fakten eines Wirtschaftswunders*. Bern: Stämpli Verlag.
Sowell, T. (2005). *Black rednecks and white liberals*. New York: Encounter Books.
Thürer, G. (1970). *Free and Swiss-the story of Switzerland*. London: Oswald Wolff.
Ugolini, S. (2018). The origins of Swiss wealth management? Genevan private banking, 1800–1840. *Financial History Review, 25*, 161–182.
Velde, F. R., & Weir, D. R. (1992). The financial market and government debt policy in France, 1746–1793. *The Journal of Economic History, 52*, 1–39.
Weber, M. (1930). *The protestant ethic and the spirit of capitalism*. London: George Allan and Unwin.
Weir, D. R. (1989). Tontines, public finance, and revolution in france and england, 1688–1789. *Journal of Economic History, 49*, 95–123.
Wright, G. (2022). Slavery and the rise of the nineteenth-century American economy. *Journal of Economic Perspectives, 36*, 123–148.

Chapter 4
Free Banking and the Foundation of the Swiss National Bank (1826–1907)

4.1 Banknotes During the Nineteenth Century

This chapter discusses the role of note-issuing banks, i.e., financial institutes offering their own form of paper money to the public.[1] During the nineteenth century, a large number of Swiss banks turned to this activity or were even explicitly founded to foster the circulation of banknotes. From a modern perspective, this appears to be a very peculiar business. Today, it is more or less taken for granted that paper money is issued through a government monopoly by a central (note-issuing) bank, represents fiat money that is convertible only into itself, and has a legal-tender status by serving as an officially recognised, albeit increasingly technologically outdated, means of payment.[2] However, at the dawn of the nineteenth century, the situation was very different; banknotes were a quite novel form of money and represented a claim to receive from their issuer, upon demand, a clearly defined amount of monetary metal. After they were first introduced in Europe during the seventeenth century, these written claims on gold or silver gradually became a convenient substitute for coins in settling large payments.[3] Moreover, paper money was initially quite illiquid, meaning that it was not broadly accepted in everyday transactions. In most countries, the corresponding popularisation began, sooner or later, during the nineteenth century with the foundation of officially supported central banks, which issued uniform and more liquid banknotes with legal-tender status in small as well as large denominations.[4]

---

[1] This chapter draws on Herger (2021) and Herger (2022).

[2] Only a handful of commercial banks in Scotland, Northern Ireland, and Hong Kong have retained their traditional right to issue their own banknotes.

[3] For a historical discussion of the development of paper money in Western Europe, see Kindleberger (1984, pp.49ff.).

[4] For an extensive discussion of the transition from private note-issuing banks to central banking in Belgium, England, France, Germany, Scotland, and the United States, see Smith (1936).

N. Herger, *Switzerland and its Banks*, Frontiers in Economic History,
https://doi.org/10.1007/978-3-031-35904-0_4

As in many other areas of banking and finance, Switzerland was a latecomer to this development. In particular, as one of the last foundations of its kind in Western Europe, the Swiss National Bank (SNB) opened its doors in 1907, after central note-issuing banks had already been set up in neighbouring France in 1800, Austria-Hungary in 1816, Germany in 1876, and Italy in 1893 (see Capie et al., 1994, p.6). Furthermore, the introduction of broadly accepted forms of paper money was hampered by the highly decentralised political system and the corresponding economic fragmentation across the cantons. Until the middle of the nineteenth century, there was not even a common national currency. As illustrated by Fig. 4.1, the consequence was that for almost a century, a large number of private and publicly supported financial institutes competed in the market for paper money. Overall, nineteenth-century Switzerland was a rare case of a free-banking system, which is characterised by the broad absence of regulations, and other forms of government interference regarding the private supply of banknotes.[5]

In other parts of the world, competitive paper-money systems also existed in Scotland between 1716 and 1844 (see, e.g., White, 1995, ch.3 and 4), and in the United States during the decades before the Civil War (see, e.g., Rockoff, 1991). However, Switzerland's case is unique, insofar as it can be subdivided into a period with more or less unfettered competition between 1826 and 1881, and a strongly regulated regime after 1881, when federal legislation was introduced to, among other things, impose minimum-reserve requirements and a mutual-conversion rule of all Swiss banknotes at par value (Baltensperger & Kugler, 2017, ch.8).

Free-banking systems are still of interest today, because they illustrate how private money and currency competition worked in practice, and explain why government monopolies in paper money have prevailed around the world. Furthermore, although private note issuing has not survived, commercial banks still compete in offering close substitutes for cash, such as bank deposits. Owing to recent technological breakthroughs with digital currencies, it is conceivable that a genuinely competitive money supply will reappear. Finally, when the reputation of central banks has been damaged by high levels of inflation, as during the 1970s, private competition has occasionally been advocated as a remedy for unstable money (see Hayek, 1978).

In Switzerland, the transition from private to central note issuing was accompanied by fierce political debates about the adequate role of government in monetary affairs. The introduction of the Swiss franc and, more than half a century later, the foundation of the Swiss National Bank are legacies of these debates. To uncover the origins of these important components of the current monetary system, the following sections review the history of the corresponding free-banking period across the abovementioned regimes of unfettered competition, and strict banknote regulation.

[5] For a theoretical discussion of currency systems with a competitive money supply, such as free banking, see Selgin and White (1994).

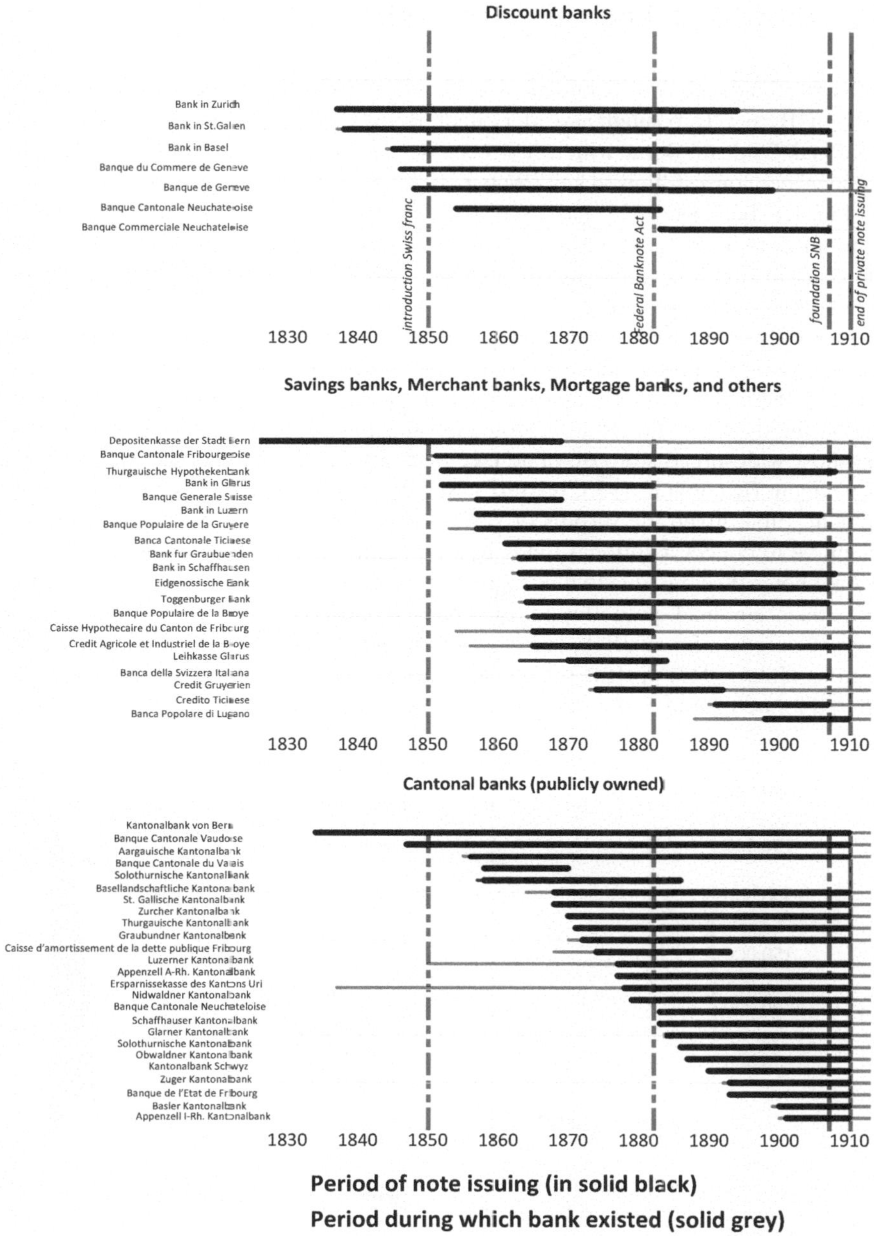

Fig. 4.1 Swiss note-issuing banks (1826–1913) (own figure based on Jöhr, 1915, p.521)

4.2 Unfettered Banknote Competition (1826–1881)

In Switzerland, the first banknote was issued in 1826 by the deposit bank of the City of Bern ("Depositenkasse der Stadt Bern").[6] In 1834, the publicly owned Cantonal Bank of Bern, which had been set up as a political vehicle to support the local economy, followed suit (Weber, 1988, pp.464–466). Moreover, as reported by Fig. 4.1, between 1837 and 1846, several private discount houses, such as the Bank in Zurich, the Bank in St. Gallen, the Banque du Commerce de Genève, and the Bank in Basel, began to supply nearby households and firms with paper money (see Weber, 1988, pp.466ff.).

Not only were Swiss banknotes introduced much later than elsewhere, but their early development was also remarkably slow. More specifically, as shown in Fig. 4.2, there was virtually no growth in the corresponding amount in circulation during the decades after 1826. Throughout this period, savings accounts remained the most widespread store of value (see Sect. 3.4), and coins the dominant means of payment (Ritzmann, 1973, pp.39ff.). Several factors explain this sluggish development. First, given the surplus of savings mentioned earlier, banks often had no incentive to collect additional funds by issuing innovative financial products, such as banknotes. Second, due to the fragmentation of the Swiss monetary system at the time, they remained quite illiquid. In particular, until the foundation of the modern Swiss Confederation in 1848, currency and money fell under the jurisdiction of the cantons (Jöhr, 1915, pp.15ff.). Until the mid-nineteenth century, Switzerland even offered a rare example of a genuine currency competition in the sense that various

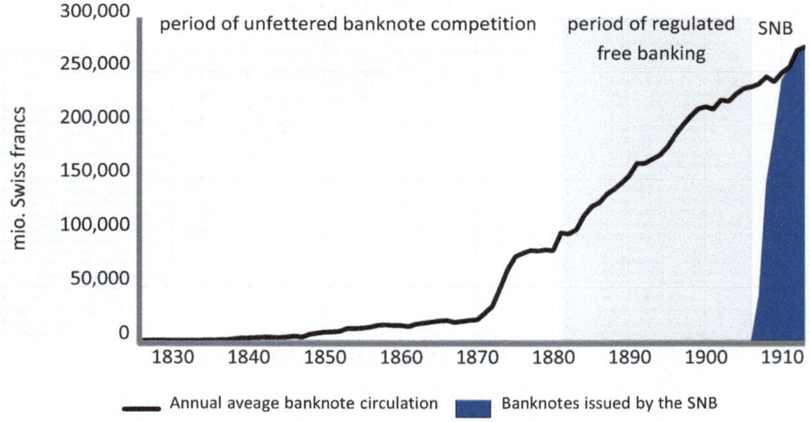

Fig. 4.2 Banknote circulation in Switzerland (1826–1913) (own figure based on Herger (2021, p.3). Data source: Jöhr (1915, pp.496, 497))

[6] A comprehensive history of note-issuing banks in Switzerland can be found in Jöhr (1915). See also Baltensperger (2012, pp.37ff.), and Baltensperger and Kugler (2017, ch.8).

coins circulated alongside each other, and banks were essentially free to choose the type of money into which their notes should be converted (see Baltensperger & Kugler, 2017, pp.134–135). Owing to the lack of a national currency as well as the inferior quality of the cantonal monetary systems, early Swiss banknotes were often convertible into foreign units, such as the French franc or the Brabant thaler (Weber, 1988, p.460).

In connection with the popularisation of classical liberal ideas in politics and economics, including the call for laisser-faire and nationally integrated markets, the Swiss Constitution of 1848 introduced a uniform currency, but preserved the freedom of enterprise in banking (Weber, 1992). During the subsequent decades, it became clear that the combination of a standardised national currency and a free-banking system encapsulated policy conflicts that dominated the money-and-banking debate until the foundation of the Swiss National Bank.

Reflecting an important step towards financial modernisation, the Swiss franc was introduced in 1850 and soon became an official replica of the bimetallic system of France. Hence, one franc was convertible into 4.5 grams of silver or 0.29 grams of gold, implying a silver-to-gold exchange rate of 15.5 to 1 (see Baltensperger & Kugler, 2017, p.27). Initially, the Swiss franc was conceived as a pure silver currency (Baltensperger, 2012, pp.82–83). However, the reduction of the market price for gold relative to silver during the 1850s set Gresham's law in motion. On the one hand, the officially undervalued gold coins flooded into circulation in France. On the other hand, it became prohibitively costly to mint silver coins at the prevailing market prices in Switzerland and elsewhere. To preserve the traditional monetary links with France, the Swiss currency had to officially adopt the corresponding bimetallic system in 1860 (Paillard, 1909, p.20). In 1865, this monetary alignment was internationally institutionalised, when Switzerland joined the "Latin Monetary Union", which constituted a multilateral agreement with Belgium, France, and Italy (later Greece also joined). These countries agreed to share their currencies through the mutual acceptance of coins based on a common silver-to-gold mint-par of 15.5 to 1 (Baltensperger & Kugler, 2017, pp.26–29). Because French and Swiss franc coins were equivalent, the official exchange rate between them stood at one-to-one. This international monetary cooperation even extended to most Swiss coins being actually minted in France (Baltensperger, 2012, p.82).

In contrast to the standardisation of coinage, Switzerland's paper-money system remained highly fragmented and competitive. Although the introduction of a national currency abolished competition regarding denomination, as banknotes convertible into Swiss francs became the norm, none of the note-issuing discount, savings, merchant, or cantonal banks managed to gain a share in excess of 25 per cent within the paper-money market (Weber, 1992, p.191). Moreover, numerous entries into and some exits from this market occurred after 1850 (see Fig. 4.1). Reflecting a liberal licensing policy by the cantons, which had retained jurisdiction over banking, the number of note issuers actually increased to more than thirty—publicly supported as well as purely private—institutes.

Even after the nationalisation of the currency, the underdevelopment and fragmentation of the market for paper money continued to be the Achilles heel of the more or less unregulated free-banking system in Switzerland (Herger, 2022, pp.2ff.). In particular, banknotes were still a quite illiquid asset, the value of which depended on the reputation of the issuer. With their relatively high denominations, they circulated mainly locally and offered a store of value rather than a convenient means of payment (Paillard, 1909, p.190; Jöhr, 1915, pp.80ff.).

Despite the rapid industrialisation and integration of the Swiss economy after the mid-nineteenth century, it was not until the 1870s, when paper money began to circulate more widely. The Franco-Prussian War between 1870 and 1871 served as catalyst for the dramatic increase in the corresponding amount in circulation, as depicted in Fig. 4.2. Within Switzerland, this war triggered a short, but severe, liquidity crisis, because domestic banks found themselves suddenly cut off from the French money market and the currency reserves of the Banque de France (Baltensperger, 2012, pp.86–87). However, for the increased popularity of banknotes, it was the developments following the war that mattered. In particular, the years after 1871 were characterised by an economic boom, referred to as the "Gründerjahre" (i.e., foundation years), across German-speaking countries (Weber, 1992, p.202). This boom was closely intertwined with a monetary expansion that resulted from Germany's decision to employ the indemnity received from France after the swift victory in the Franco-Prussian War to create a gold-based currency, called the "mark". As several important countries soon followed in the footsteps of Germany, the years after 1871 witnessed the advent of the classical gold standard as an international currency system (Eichengreen, 2008, pp.15ff.). For the remaining bimetallic currencies, including the Swiss franc, the demonetisation of silver, and the resulting reduction of the corresponding price, reactivated Gresham's law. However, in contrast to the conditions around two decades earlier, it was now the relatively cheaper silver coins—according to the mint-par—that flooded into circulation. Of note, silver coins are heavy compared with their value. Hence, they did not lend themselves for settling large transactions. Taken together, these developments fostered the popularity of Swiss banknotes, which offered a close substitute for heavy coins, across the last decades of the nineteenth century (Paillard, 1909, p.191; Ritzmann, 1973, p.42).

4.3 Regulated Free Banking (1881–1907)

The liquidity crisis in Switzerland caused by the Franco-Prussian War also acted as a catalyst for monetary reforms (Jöhr, 1915, pp.133ff.; Ritzmann, 1973, pp.92–93). However, during the political debates that followed, it became clear that the time was not ripe for a banknote monopoly and the foundation of a central bank. In a first attempt, even the much more modest project of regulating the free-banking system was rejected in a referendum in 1872. The required amendment of the Swiss constitution was endorsed by the voters only in 1874, after a clause had been added that explicitly prohibited a government monopoly in paper money (Jöhr, 1915, pp.137–138). Further political conflicts, especially regarding the definition of the minimum-reserve requirement, the privileges of cantonal banks, and the organisation of the federal supervision of note-issuing banks, retarded the introduction of the corresponding legislation for another seven years (Jöhr, 1915, pp.138–143). Eventually, the Federal Banknote Act became law in 1881. This piece of legislation was a landmark for the reformation of the free-banking system because it essentially replaced unfettered banknote competition with a strictly regulated regime (Baltensperger, 2012, pp.95–97). The corresponding government interventions endeavoured to integrate the paper-money market by introducing commonly accepted, standardised, and secure Swiss-franc notes (Paillard, 1909, p.195). A key element in enhancing the liquidity of paper money was a mutual-conversion rule forcing note issuers to convert every Swiss banknote at par value. Furthermore, to maintain a minimum standard of quality, they were required to cover at least 40 per cent of their note circulation by metallic reserves, and at least 50 per cent by equity capital (Baltensperger & Kugler, 2017, pp 37–38). Finally, the Federal Parliament obtained the right to limit the total amount of paper money in circulation (see Jöhr, 1915, 143ff.). In contrast, legal-tender status for banknotes was not introduced (Baltensperger, 2012, p.100).

The regulatory restrictions imposed after 1881 changed the nature of banknote competition (Herger, 2022, pp.3ff.). In particular, although the common acceptance fostered through the mutual-conversion rule was merely supposed to make banknotes more liquid, it also weakened the public's incentive to discriminate among different types, or brands, of paper money (Neldner, 2003). Why should anyone care about the quality of notes when they could be converted, by law, at par value in any bank? A lack of brand loyalty could, in turn, undermine the self-discipline against overissuing, as all note-issuing banks jointly bore the liquidity risks of an indiscriminate paper-money supply.[7]

According to Neldner (2003), this type of overissuing was manifested in a monetary overhang and, in turn, a conspicuous depreciation of the Swiss franc after the introduction of the Federal Banknote Act in 1881. Consistent with this view, especially during the 1890s, the exchange rate between Switzerland and its most important foreign financial market in Paris stood well above the official value, according to which Swiss and French francs should have been equivalent (see Fig. 4.3). Given the current status of Switzerland's currency as one of the strongest in the world, this tendency towards depreciation during the last part of the nineteenth century is remarkable.

Of course, the exchange-rate movements depicted in Fig. 4.3 are small when compared with the conditions during the current era of more or less free floating. Nevertheless, this "volatility" became a major topic in the monetary debate around 1900, because for some banks, the weakness of the Swiss franc gave rise to notorious problems with the so-called silver drainage. Especially between 1896 and 1902, the

[7] For a formal analysis of this problem, see Klein (1974).

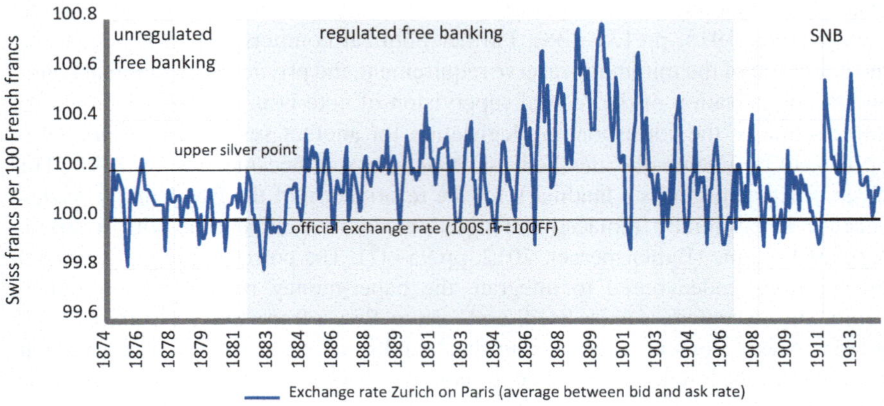

Fig. 4.3 Exchange rate between the Swiss and French franc (1874–1913) (own figure based on Herger (2021, p.4). Data sources: Kalkmann (1900) and NZZ Archiv)

Swiss exchange rate on Paris stood well above the upper specie (or silver export) point of approximately 100.25 Swiss per 100 French francs. This implied that exchanging 100 French francs into, say, 100.25 Swiss francs, approaching a note-issuing bank in Switzerland to convert this amount at the mint-par into 100.25×4.5 grams $= 451.125$ grams of silver (coins), and exporting this amount back to end up with 100.25 francs at the mint-par in France yielded an arbitrage profit in excess of the fees and transportation costs associated with the transaction. Owing to the restrictions imposed by the Banknote Act of 1881, the note-issuing banks located sufficiently close to the French border (especially in Geneva) could do little to prevent the resulting loss of silver reserves. Annoyingly, some note issuers, such as the Banque du Commerce in Geneva, were occasionally forced to reimport, at a higher price, the very silver money they had paid out shortly before. Towards the end of the 1890s, silver drainage reached an unsustainable level and inflicted severe losses on some note-issuing banks (Paillard, 1909, pp.223–224; Ritzmann, 1973, p.97).

The Swiss-franc depreciation was not the only, and perhaps not even the most important, caveat against the regulated free-banking system (Herger, 2021, pp.6ff.). In particular, contemporary observers also complained about the lack of flexibility, or what used to be called "elasticity", of the banknote supply to cope with demand fluctuations.[8] As in modern monetary environments, the volume of nineteenth-century payments, and hence the demand for money, varied considerably across the seasons as well as according to the ups and downs of the business cycle. For example, in Switzerland, the demand for paper money usually increased around June and November, when many financial securities matured (Paillard, 1909, pp.198–

[8] Examples of such complaints are Kalkmann (1900, pp.28ff.), Gygax (1901), Paillard (1909, pp.199ff.), and Jöhr (1915, pp.308ff.).

199; Kalkmann, 1900, p.54). In this regard, the rigidities associated with the regulated free-banking regime gave rise to major frictions in terms of regularly creating an oversupply of paper money during the first half of the year, and a shortage during the second half (see, e.g., Kalkmann, 1900, p.29, Nüscheler, 1912, pp.3ff.). Unsurprisingly, this "inelasticity" and the associated shortages of means of payment were seen as unnecessary impediments to trade and investment (Paillard, 1909, p.225: Baltensperger, 2012, p.103).

Other concerns about a system with unchecked currency competition are associated with the risk of instability and outright fraud. In this regard, sceptics of banknote competition have often pointed to the experiences of the United States during the decades before the Civil War (1861–1865). Arguably, this free-banking system suffered from notorious—although perhaps over-romanticised—practices of the so-called wildcat banking, where criminals simply printed paper money without holding any monetary metal in reserve (see, e.g., Rockoff, 1974, pp.145ff.). Furthermore, failures of note-issuing banks were relatively frequent (Rolnick & Weber, 1984, pp.5–8). However, Switzerland's experiences with free banking were completely different in terms of giving rise to a highly stable system and, even during the period of unfettered competition, virtually no defaults. In particular, between 1826 and 1907, there were only two cases of panicky banknote conversions in Switzerland involving the "Banque Générale Suisse" in 1859, and the "Eidgenössische Bank" in 1869. Moreover, there was one failure involving the publicly supported "Banque Cantonale du Valais" in 1870 (Weber, 1992, pp.202–203). However, even in these cases of instability, no banknote holder was harmed. Swiss banknotes issued during the free-banking system were, arguably, always redeemed at par value (Jöhr, 1915, p.92).

4.4 The Role of the Cantonal Banks

Owing to the restrictions and regulatory costs of the Federal Banknote Act, several banks renounced their right to issue paper money after 1881 (Jöhr, 1915, p.186). However, as shown in the overview of Fig. 4.1, this decline was largely offset by the foundation of a series of the so-called cantonal banks (Kantonalbanken, banques cantonales) during the last part of the nineteenth century. Typically, they were set up as publicly owned institutes (i.e., state banks) to support the local economy. In addition to offering loans and mortgages as well as accepting deposits and savings, this support included the issuing of paper money during the free-banking era (Weber, 1992, pp.195–197).

Cantonal banks are not an invention of the regulated free-banking era after 1881, as illustrated by the much earlier foundations in Bern in 1834 (see also Sect. 4.2), and in Vaud in 1845. However, only the former provides an early example of a bank publicly owned through the canton; elsewhere, mixed ownership, with a minority stake by the canton, predominated (Jöhr, 1915, p.73). Reflecting a broader trend away from the laisser-faire policies of the proponents of classical liberalism towards more government intervention in the economy during the so-called democratic movement, cantonal banks with full public ownership became much more common during the last decades of the nineteenth century (see Sect. 2.3). A case in point of this transition is the Cantonal Bank of Zurich, which was founded amid an intensive debate shortly after the democratic movement had managed to win a majority in the parliamentary elections of that canton in 1869 (Nüscheler, 1912, pp.5ff.). Similar developments elsewhere implied that the number of cantonal banks increased during the following decades.[9]

The regulatory environment of the Federal Banknote Act of 1881 favoured cantonal banks in terms of partially exempting them from paying taxes on issuing banknotes or relaxing the rules regarding the type of securities, against which paper money could be issued. Nevertheless, the share of these publicly owned banks in the market for paper money barely increased from 43 per cent in 1880, to 47 per cent in 1890 (Weber, 1992, p.196). This share increased only to 60 per cent towards the end of the nineteenth century, when it had become clear that the era of free banking would soon be over. Consequently, purely private banks began to leave the paper-money market. Despite the regulatory advantages and the state guarantee, the cantonal banks never managed to obtain a factual banknote monopoly.

4.5 Foundation of the Swiss National Bank

Around the world, systems with a competitive paper-money supply were sooner or later replaced by a government monopoly, which automatically gives rise to standardised banknotes that are broadly accepted, unless a country suffers from rampant inflation. As mentioned earlier, Switzerland was a latecomer to this development. The Swiss National Bank did not open its doors until 1907, and private note issuing was not completely outlawed until 1910.[10] The only major country, where the corresponding transition occurred even later, was the United States, with the passage of the Federal Reserve Act in 1913.

Although central banks have today almost everywhere obtained the exclusive right to issue paper money denominated in the national currency, their triumphant advance was by no means a forgone conclusion. Rather, public banknote monopolies were initially met with widely held concerns regarding the increasing government

---

[9] In 1906, only three cantons had no publicly owned cantonal bank. In particular, there was no cantonal bank in Valais, as a short-lived state-owned bank had collapsed in 1870 producing a financial and political scandal. In a similar vein, in Geneva, the high-flying ambitions of the local government to establish a so-called Banque Générale, which was also supposed to issue banknotes, quickly ended in failure in 1869 (see Sect. 5.4). Finally, in Ticino, entrenched political conflicts between the conservative and liberal parties had long prevented the permanent establishment of a government-supported bank. See Jöhr (1915, p.189).

[10] An extensive discussion of the events that led to the foundation of the Swiss National Bank can be found in Baltensperger and Kugler (2017, ch.3).

power in monetary affairs. These concerns still resonate today, especially when failed monetary policies are seen as the main culprit in economic instability.

In Switzerland, the political conflicts surrounding the establishment of a central bank were aggravated by the decentralisation of political power across the cantons. Obviously, they did not easily give up their privileges in money and banking, let alone the revenue accruing to the cantonal banks from note issuing. Hence, early proposals to underpin the Swiss franc with a central monetary authority were doomed to failure. However, the increasing popularity of government interventions in the economy during the late nineteenth century, together with the notorious impotence of the regulated free-banking system to stabilise the exchange rate, was crucial in overcoming the opposition to central note issuing (Baltensperger & Kugler, 2017, pp.42ff.; Herger, 2021, p.10). Concretely, a constitutional amendment seeking a banknote monopoly for the Swiss Confederation was passed in 1891. However, a draft law to establish a state-owned central bank was defeated in a referendum in 1897 (Jöhr, 1915, pp.251ff.). Further to the discussion above, opponents had successfully invoked the dangers of the centralisation of government power in monetary affairs (Jöhr, 1915, pp.259ff.). During the following years, political debates continued to rage about the adequate legal framework (public or private) of the planned central note-issuing bank, its head-office location, and finding a way to compensate the cantons for losing part of their fiscal revenue. Finally, a compromise was reached in 1905 with a law proposing a stock-traded company that is under the supervision of the federal government and offers only severely curtailed voting rights to the shareholders. The administrative headquarter of the Swiss National Bank is located in Bern, and the seat of the Governing Board ("Direktorium") in Zurich. To render the loss of monetary privileges acceptable to the cantons, they received two-fifths of the shares, with a further fifth being allocated to the former note issuers (including many cantonal banks). The remaining shares were sold to private investors. As a legacy of the free-banking era, the cantons are the largest shareholders of the Swiss National Bank to this day.

Given the historical problems with the free-banking system, it is perhaps not surprising that the original legal mandate instructed the Swiss National Bank to regulate the money market, to facilitate payments, and to supply Swiss-franc banknotes in a flexible manner (Paillard, 1909, pp.231ff.; Baltensperger & Kugler, 2017, pp.45ff.). Hence, as in the United States, the central bank of Switzerland was originally set up to facilitate the money supply and to improve the payments system, rather than to raise revenue for the central government, which was a key consideration for the foundation of the first central banks, including the Bank of England in 1694 (Bordo, 2018, p.104; Jöhr, 1915, p.302). In any case, as shown in Fig. 4.2, there was indeed ample demand for centrally issued Swiss-franc notes, which successfully replaced their private counterparts within a couple of years.

The right to issue private forms of paper money in Switzerland was finally abolished in 1910. For the banking sector, the corresponding restructuring of the money market was not innocuous, but rather triggered a consolidation process (see Wetter, 1918). Above all, as shown by Fig. 4.1, the discount houses that were dedicated to issuing banknotes were either acquired, or liquidated between 1907 and

1910 (Ritzmann, 1973, p.110). The government banknote monopoly had additional knock-on effects. In particular, as the Swiss National Bank imposed relatively high quality standards for discounting bills of exchange, the liquidity costs for obtaining Swiss francs increased. After 1910, this increase caused severe losses at some regional banks. As a result, dozens of them were acquired by larger rivals, including some cantonal banks, which managed the transition away from note-issuing relatively well. From the second decade of the twentieth century onwards, they became more or less conventional commercial banks, although with a state guarantee, but without the right to issue paper money (Ritzmann, 1973, p.107).

References

Baltensperger, E. (2012). *Der Schweizer Franken - Eine Erfolgsgeschichte*. Zürich: NZZ Libro.

Baltensperger, E., & Kugler, P. (2017). *Swiss monetary history since the early nineteenth century*. Cambridge: Cambridge University Press.

Bordo, M. D. (2018). Currency competition in Switzerland. *Aussenwirtschaft, 68*, 101–108.

Capie, F., Goodhart, C., Fisher, S., & Schnadt, N. (1994). *The future of central banking—The tercentenary symposium of the Bank of England*. Cambridge: Cambridge University Press.

Eichengreen, B. (2008). *Globalizing capital: A history of the international monetary system*. New Jersey: Princeton University Press.

Gygax, P. (1901). *Kritische Betrachtungen über das Schweizerische Notenbankwesen mit Beziehung auf den Pariser Wechselkurs*. Zürich: Müller.

Hayek, F. A. (1978). *Denationalisation of money - The argument refined*. London: The Institute of Economic Affairs.

Herger, N. (2021). Regulated free banking in Switzerland (1881–1907). *Swiss Journal of Economics and Statistics, 157* (9), 1–12.

Herger, N. (2022). Unregulated and regulated free banking: Evidence from the case of Switzerland (1826–1907). *Explorations in Economic History, 83*, 101,423.

Jöhr, A. (1915). *Die Schweizerischen Notenbanken, 1826–1913*. Zürich: Orell Füssli.

Kalkmann, P. (1900). *Untersuchungen über das Geldwesen der Schweiz und die Ursachen des hohen Standes der auswärtigen Wechselkurse*. St. Gallen: Zollikofersche Druckerei.

Kindleberger, C. P. (1984). *A financial history of Western Europe*. London: Routledge.

Klein, B. (1974). The competitive supply of money. *Journal of Money, Credit and Banking, 6*, 423–53.

Neldner, M. (2003). Competition necessarily tends to produce excess: The experience of free banking in Switzerland. *German Economic Review, 4*, 389–408.

Nüscheler, H. E. (1912). *Die Zürcher Kantonalbank 1870–1904*. Zürich: Verlag E. Speidel.

Paillard, G. (1909). *La Suisse et L'Union Monétaire Latine*. Lausanne: Imprimeries Réunies.

Ritzmann, F. (1973). *Die Schweizer Banken. Geschichte - Theorie - Statistik*. Bern: Verlag Paul Haupt.

Rockoff, H. (1974). The free banking era—A reexamination. *Journal of Money, Credit, and Banking, 6*, 141–164.

Rockoff, H. (1991). Lessons from the American experience with free banking. In Capie, F., & Wood, G. (Ed.), *Unregulated banking: Chaos or order?* London: Macmillan.

Rolnick, A. J., & Weber, W.E. (1984). The causes of free bank failures: A detailed examination. *Journal of Monetary Economics, 14*, 267–91.

Selgin, G. A., & White, L. H. (1994). How would the invisible hand handle money? *Journal of Economic Literature, 32*, 1718–49.

Smith, V. (1936). *The rationale of central banking and the free banking alternative*. Indianapolis: Liberty Fund.

Weber, E. J. (1988). Currency competition in Switzerland, 1826–1850. *Kyklos, 41*, 459–78.

Weber, E. J. (1992). Free banking in Switzerland after the liberal revolutions in the nineteenth century. In Dowd, K. (Ed.), *The experience of free banking*. London: Routledge.

Wetter, E. (1918). *Bankenkrisen und Bankenkatastrophen der letzen Jahre in der Schweiz*. Zurich: Orell Füssli.

White, L. H. (1995). *Free banking in Britain: Theory, experience, and debate, 1800–1845* (2nd ed.). London: Institute of Economic Affairs.

Chapter 5
Railway Boom, the Big Banks, and the Ascent of Zurich as Financial Centre (1848–1914)

5.1 The Ascent of Zurich in Industry and Finance

The decision to host the main activities of the Swiss National Bank (SNB) in Zurich reflected a broader story of economic success that gradually transformed this city into a "little financial giant" (Straumann, 2006). At the dawn of the twentieth century, the presence of two big banks, the largest stock market in Switzerland, a federal polytechnical college, and important national and international railway connections was a further unmistakable sign of this success (Cassis, 2010, p.127). The corresponding concentration of banking and industrial activities foreshadowed later developments, which first made Zurich a national financial hub, and subsequently a leading offshore centre for wealth management during the twentieth century.

Before the modern Swiss Confederation was inaugurated in 1848, the hierarchy was very different. Although the Canton of Zurich experienced early industrialisation in textile production and machinery, which obviously required some banking services to settle payments, exchange currencies, and arrange loans, Geneva and Basel at the time were clearly the leading financial centres within Switzerland (see Chap. 2). How did Zurich manage to catch up with, and eventually surpass, its rivals? This chapter tells the story, which is closely related to the integration of the Swiss economy and political system into a federal state, the subsequent industrial boom, and the construction of the national railway network. Similar to developments elsewhere, the new age of mass production and transportation gave rise to monumental social and economic changes, including financial modernisation within a couple of generations.

N. Herger, *Switzerland and its Banks*, Frontiers in Economic History,
https://doi.org/10.1007/978-3-031-35904-0_5

5.2 Banking in Zurich before 1848

Zurich officially joined the Old Confederation in 1351 and, together with Basel, Bern, and Lucerne, belonged to the group of city cantons, which often had political views at odds with those dominating in the Alpine hinterland (see Sect. 2.2). Tensions reached dangerous levels during the reformation, which prevailed in Zurich owing to the theological influence of the locally popular priest Huldrych Zwingli (1481–1531), but also created almost insurmountable conflicts with the Catholic cantons during the sixteenth and seventeenth centuries (Reinhardt, 2013, pp.171ff.). Nevertheless, in many cities across Switzerland, the era of the reformation coincided with an expansion of premodern trade and industry. This economic progress, in turn, bolstered the power of the craft guilds, which became the dominant political force in Zurich. Moreover, by securing the position of the so-called Vorort, i.e., the canton that summoned and chaired the diet meeting of the Old Confederation, Zurich managed to further strengthen its political profile from the fifteenth century onwards.

At the economic level, a textile-manufacturing cluster gradually began to take shape in eastern Switzerland—especially in the Cantons of St. Gallen, Glarus, and Zurich—during the seventeenth century. In the early stages of this development, production was typically organised in the form of a cottage industry, with, e.g., individual weavers working at home rather than in dedicated factories. Specialised brokers (called "Verleger") acted as suppliers of the necessary raw materials, merchants of the final product, and financiers for the numerous self-employed textile workers. During the eighteenth century, this brokerage system (or "Verlagssystem") was gradually replaced by integrated "manufactories". These rudimentary mass-production facilities represented a kind of preindustrialisation, insofar as they began to split the production process into different stages and to rely on basic types of machinery, the output of which was destined for the foreign market. Of note, small companies established with the financial means of individual entrepreneurs still dominated the scene. Moreover, by relying on running water as the main source of power for these rudimentary production facilities, Switzerland's textile-manufacturing sector emerged along the rivers, and hence in a highly dispersed manner across rural areas (see Sect. 2.2). Zurich is a case in point of this development, as the first textile manufactories sprang up around a town called Winterthur, which is located next to a river called "Thur", rather than in the lakeside city that gave the canton its name (Wehrli, 1987, pp.207–208).

The profits accruing from textile manufacturing, combined with the thrifty protestant lifestyle, led to large savings in preindustrial Zurich. As a result, an entrenched capital surplus arose, which was associated with a relatively low interest-rate level when compared with that in other European cities (Keller, 1955, pp.18ff.; Wehrli, 1987, pp.207–208). These differences, in turn, offered possibilities for international arbitrage transactions. To better organise the capital export, through which the higher interest rates abroad could be exploited, the "Bank Leu" was founded in 1755 (see, e.g., Bauer and Blackman, 1998, pp.55–59; Keller, 1955).

Named after the city councillor in charge of public finances at the time, Johann Jakob Leu (1689–1768), this bank invested first and foremost in relatively high-yielding sovereign bonds and shares in foreign financial markets, such as London, Paris, or Vienna, against issuing own bonds (called "Rathausobligationen"), which were held by local investors in Zurich (Wehrli, 1987, p.108). However, after suffering from heavy losses due to the wave of defaults sweeping across Europe after the French Revolution, the Bank Leu changed its strategy from being a state-supported vehicle for foreign investments to an ordinary commercial bank (Keller, 1955, pp.64ff.). Reflecting this transformation, the Bank Leu was converted into a stock-traded company in 1854, fully privatised in 1869, and was finally acquired by Credit Suisse in 1990. Complete integration into the parent company followed in 2011, implying that the Bank Leu had disappeared more than 250 years after its foundation.

In general, the development of the banking sector before 1848 was slower, and less spectacular in Zurich than in Geneva, let alone in the leading European financial centres of the ancien régime, i.e., Amsterdam, London, and Paris. As in other Swiss cities, several private banks catered, of course, to the financial needs of a monied elite, while numerous small savings banks appeared in the early industrialised hinterlands around the City of Zurich (Wehrli, 1987, p.207–210; and Ch.3.4). Furthermore, the free-banking system eventually warranted a note issuer, which appeared in 1837 in the form of the "Bank in Zurich" (see Fig. 4.1 of Sect. 4.1). Remarkably, this was the first bank in Switzerland organised as a joint-stock company. Following the broad trends at the time, the Bank in Zurich renounced the right to issue paper money in 1892 and became a mere discount house, before being acquired by Credit Suisse in 1905 (see Sects. 4.4 and 4.5).

5.3 Railways and the Big Banks

The transition from an incoherent group of cantons to a politically and economically much more integrated country had far-reaching implications for Switzerland during the nineteenth century (see Sect. 2.2). Zurich had been a forceful advocate of this federal integration and, accordingly, found itself on the winning side of the brief civil war that paved the way for the creation of the modern Swiss Confederation in 1848 (see Sect. 2.3). However, Bern was chosen as the capital city and permanent seat of the federal government and parliament, which replaced the politically much less potent diet meeting. Reflecting the still decentralised organisation of the country, the newly established federal institutions were spread across various cities. In particular, the Federal High Court was installed in Lausanne in 1874, and the Federal Insurance Court in Lucerne in 1902. Conversely, until the foundation of the Swiss National Bank in 1907, Zurich managed to attract, in terms of political power, only a relatively unimportant federal institution, the polytechnical college (Eidgenössische Technische Hochschule (ETH)), established in 1855.[1]

Despite—or perhaps because of—the lack of privileged status within the Swiss Confederation, Zurich embarked on a rapid industrialisation process and, as a result, emerged as the economic and financial powerhouse of the country during the second part of the nineteenth century. At the heart of this spectacular boom lay the railway industry (Bauer & Blackman, 1998, pp.79–81; Reinhardt, 2013, pp.383–393). In Switzerland, the political and economic fragmentation across the cantons, as well as the mountainous terrain, had long been insurmountable obstacles to this revolutionary mode of transportation. While Britain had begun to export steam engines and other parts of rail technology to countries, such as Belgium, Austria, Germany, and France during the 1830s, the first bits of track on Swiss ground were built only in 1844 to connect the City of Basel with Strasbourg across the nearby French border. A short railway line linking Zurich with Baden soon followed in 1847 (see Fig. 5.1). As of the year 1850, thousands of kilometres of railway lines had been built in Germany and France, compared with a meagre 25 kilometres in Swiss territory. However, after the political and economic integration of 1848, Switzerland caught up rapidly. Concretely, during both the 1850s and the 1860s, approximately a thousand kilometres of new tracks were laid (Ritzmann, 1973, pp. 53–56). Backed by the early industrialisation mentioned earlier, which had also given rise to a pro-business political elite, Zurich became the centre of this boom, which culminated—literally and metaphorically—when the first railway line surmounting the Swiss Alps was built through the Gotthard. For Zurich, this monumental infrastructure project, completed in 1882, opened a direct north–south link with Germany and the plain of Lombardy as well as the rest of Italy (see Fig. 5.1). However, both technologically and financially, construction was a daunting task. In particular, it took eight years to dig the longest tunnel in the world at the time (measuring more than 15 kilometres) at substantially higher cost than initially planned (Jung, 2015, pp.77ff.).[2]

There are obvious interrelationships between industrial and financial modernisation, because innovative ways were needed to raise the tremendous amounts of capital required for the era of mechanised production and mass transportation. The prime example of these interrelationships was the railways themselves, which not only represented a major technological breakthrough, but also initiated a profound transformation within the banking industry during the nineteenth century (Kindleberger, 1984, pp.199ff.; Cassis, 2010, pp.54ff.). From a financial point of view, the main challenge of the railway age was how to fund the necessary construction. The unprecedented scale of the corresponding infrastructure far

[1] Another "école polytechnique" was set up in the French-speaking part of Switzerland, in Lausanne.

[2] This old railway link is not to be mistaken for the much more recently built Gotthard "base tunnel", which was completed in 2016 and at 57 kilometres in length, is currently the longest railway tunnel in the world.

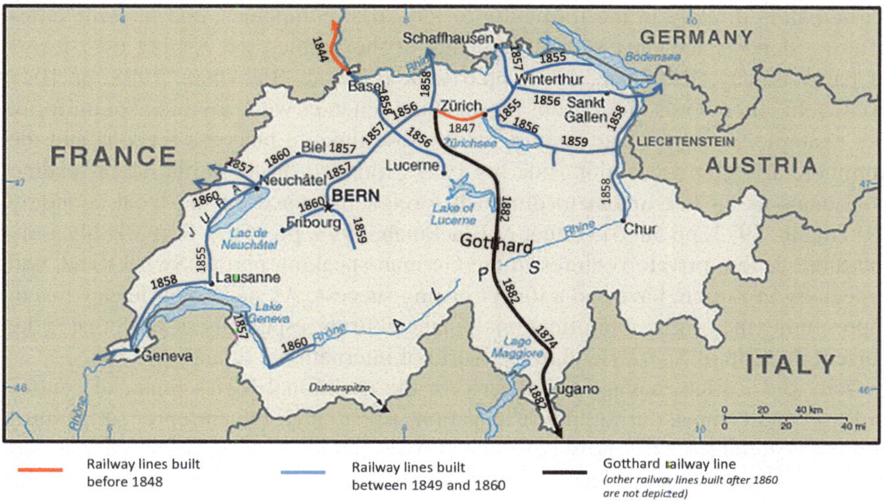

Fig. 5.1 Overview of the early development of the Swiss railway network (own figure)

exceeded the funding capabilities of any individual entrepreneur or private family bank (Kindleberger, 1984, p.187). Solutions to this financial challenge included the formation of broad coalitions of private investors through joint-stock companies, which were important vehicles for the early development of the English railways, or relying on public investments and the funding power of national governments, which was the approach chosen by, e.g., Belgium (Kindleberger, 1984, pp.199–202, pp.207–209; Cassis, 2010, pp.54–59.). In the area of commercial banking, the railway revolution was closely intertwined with the emergence of large banks, which were typically organised as joint-stock companies and provided a vehicle for mobilising savings from across the population, and bundling them into large projects (Cassis, 2010, pp.42ff.). In different countries, these "steam engines of credit" appeared in slightly different forms and under different names, including the "credit mobilier" in France (Cassis, 2010, p.47–49), the "universal bank" in Germany (Cassis, 2010, pp.51–52), the "investment bank" in the United States (Cassis, 2010, p.60), and last but not least the so-called big bank (Grossbank; grande banque) in Switzerland.

Regarding the just mentioned approaches, the construction of Switzerland's railways occurred, by and large, under a private regime with several competing companies (Thürer, 1970, pp.131–132). The necessary capital was raised partially abroad and, hence, led to an upsurge in foreign investment, which caused a certain consternation in a country accustomed to having a capital surplus (Bauer & Blackman, 1998, p.129; Ritzmann, 1973, p.72–73). Furthermore, the domestic savings were tapped through the establishment of several big banks. In addition to railway financing, they often engaged in a broad range of other activities, including the subscription of shares and bonds, asset trading on secondary markets, participating directly in the formation of industrial companies, and in some cases offering deposit accounts as well as loans to the public, and issuing own forms of paper money (Ritzmann, 1973, pp.61–69; Bauer & Blackman, 1998, pp.104–105ff.). In other words, the various big-banking schemes were anything but uniform. For example, purely private ventures with close links to business tycoons and the commercial sector arose alongside big banks founded on the initiative of leading politicians as an instrument to diminish foreign influence on the local economy (Ritzmann, 1973, pp.58–61; Bauer & Blackman, 1998, pp.75ff.). Remarkably, only the more or less private ventures in the German-speaking part of Switzerland, and especially in Zurich, have had a longer lasting success. As such, their legacy lies in representing the origin of multinational financial firms, especially of UBS that is the current flagship of Switzerland in the world of international finance.

Why did Zurich manage to outperform the traditional Swiss financial centres in Basel and Geneva during industrialisation. Apparently, the entrepreneurial spirit and seed capital from the early-developed textile and machine industry, and perhaps also the absence of an ancient private banking sector trying to obstruct the financial innovations associated with the railway age, provided fertile ground for the corresponding ascent. Furthermore, this ascent received a major impetus from the forceful personality of Alfred Escher (1819–1882), who was the leading industrialist and a dominant local politician in Zurich, and later also on the national stage of Switzerland, during the heyday of the industrial boom.[3] Born into an ancient and influential family of the City of Zurich in 1819, Escher was elected for the liberal party to the cantonal parliament at the age of 25 and became a member of the cantonal government in 1848. During the same year, he also embarked on a phenomenal political career at the national level by becoming a member of the newly established Federal Parliament, over which he presided during 1849, 1856, and 1862. For Escher, gaining access to all levels of government and being a doyen of the liberal party, which dominated the political scene at the time, provided the basis for his industrial enterprises, especially for building his empire of railway companies in and around Zurich. In particular, he spearheaded the opposition to a government-led approach to developing a national network. Eventually, the concentration of economic and political power, unusual for Switzerland, encountered increasingly strong political opposition. The broad public began to denounce Escher as a "railway king", which is a strong insult in a republican country. Reflecting this growing hostility, during the 1860s and 1870s, a so-called democratic movement arose, which gradually dismantled the "System Escher" by defeating the liberal party at the ballot box as well as fostering the expansion of direct democracy at the cantonal and federal levels (see Sect. 2.3). In particular, the introduction of the constitutional initiative as a new political instrument opened the way to nationalising the main railway lines, which was approved in a popular vote in 1898 (Thürer, 1970, pp.131–132; Bauer & Blackman, 1998, pp.155–164).

[3] For an overview of Escher's life, political career, and economic legacy, see Jung (2015).

In banking and finance, Alfred Escher acted as the main figure behind the early development of Credit Suisse, which opened its doors in 1856 under the name "Schweizerische Kreditanstalt".[4] A key motive for setting up this bank was to prevent foreign investors, above all the Parisian "hautes banques", from gaining a controlling stake in Switzerland's railway companies (Jöhr, 1956, p.15; Jung, 2000, pp.47–49). Given this goal, it is perhaps ironic that roughly half of the 15 million Swiss francs that capitalised this large-scale credit institute had to be raised abroad, namely, in Germany, while the remaining shares were sold to Swiss industrialists and the general public. During the following decades, Escher left his mark on the "Kreditanstalt" by acting as its first president of the board: a position he held, with a brief interruption, until his death in 1882. Aside from raising capital for domestic railways, such as the abovementioned Gotthard project, activities included providing loans for industrial ventures (especially in machinery and electric engineering), discounting bills of exchange, and participating in the formation of new companies (Jung, 2000, pp.49ff.).[5] In particular, Credit Suisse took the initiative to set up several financial ventures in Zurich, including the life insurance company "Schweizerische Lebensversicherungs- und Rentenanstalt" (today "Swiss Life"), founded in 1857, and the reinsurance company "Schweizerische Rückversicherungsgesellschaft" (today "Swiss Re"), founded in 1863. During the 1870s and 1880s, this diversification across several industries was, probably, crucial for the survival of the "Kreditanstalt", which suffered from multiple setbacks, including the liquidity crisis during the Franco-Prussian War (see Sect. 4.2), the following postwar boom-and-bust cycle in Germany and the surrounding countries, and losses incurred from the large cost overruns of the Gotthard railway project (Bauer & Blackman, 1998, p.131).

Credit Suisse was not the only big commercial bank that emerged in the Canton of Zurich during the nineteenth century. However, in several regards, the early history of the second major example, the Union Bank of Switzerland ("Schweizerische Bankgesellschaft"), was quite different.[6] In particular, its origins lay in two regional financial institutes located outside the City of Zurich. The first was essentially a highly specialised merchant bank founded in 1862 to provide trade finance, foreign-exchange transactions, and warehousing facilities in the town of Winterthur, which was an early centre of textile manufacturing and the machine industry (see Sect. 5.2). This "Bank in Winterthur" almost immediately proved its worth to the local business community as aggravated price fluctuations and shortages in supply arose on the cotton market due to the US Civil War (1861–1865) (Bauer & Blackman, 1998, p.133). However, as soon as the transatlantic cotton trade returned to normal, the storage and warehousing business declined.

[4] The rebranding from "Schweizerische Kreditanstalt" to the internationally more recognisable name of "Credit Suisse" occurred in 1997. For a detailed overview of the history of the "Kreditanstalt", see Jöhr (1956) and Jung (2000).

[5] However, Credit Suisse was never a note-issuing bank.

[6] For a detailed overview of the history of the Union Bank, see Strehle et al. (1987).

Nevertheless, until the beginning of the twentieth century, the "Bank in Winterthur" gradually, and with major setbacks from failed adventures into the financing of railways, broadened its business by providing mortgages, insurance policies, and loans to local industry (Ritzmann, 1973, p.66–67). The second bank was founded in 1863 in the Toggenburg Valley in northeastern Switzerland to serve as a savings and loan institute for local textile manufacturers and the broader population. This task required a network of subsidiaries, which expanded during the following decades across the region of St. Gallen and, subsequently, into the neighbouring Cantons of Thurgau, Zurich, and Schwyz (Wehrli, 1987, p.218). In reaction to the general downturn of the textile industry in Switzerland, as well as to the financial restructuring after the end of the free-banking system in 1910 (see Sect. 4.4), the "Bank in Toggenburg" joined forces with the "Bank in Winterthur" in 1912 to form the "Union Bank of Switzerland" (Wehrli, 1987, p.218). That the head office of this merged financial firm was moved to the City of Zurich further enhanced its status as a financial centre (Wehrli, 1987, p.216).

5.4 Big Banks Outside Zurich

At the dawn of the industrial age, Basel was in an excellent position to become the leading financial centre in Switzerland. After all, this city could look back on a considerable banking tradition and benefitted from an ideal location next to the river Rhine, which provides a navigable access to neighbouring France, the industrial heartland of Germany, and ultimately the North Sea port of Rotterdam (see Sect. 3.3). As mentioned earlier, after 1844, Basel also had Switzerland's first international railway link. Last but not least, several innovative chemical and pharmaceutical companies were founded in the city during the second part of the nineteenth century (Bauer, 1972, pp.77ff.). Taken together, the scene was set for a straightforward transition to larger forms of banking suitable for the industrial age. However, in Basel, this transition ran into the opposition of the old-established private banks, which did everything possible to forestall the emergence of a large credit institute among them (Bauer, 1987, pp.156ff.). To this end, they reacted to the new economic environment by forming what would today be called financial joint ventures (Bauer, 1972, pp.18ff.; Bauer & Blackman, 1998, pp.102–104). At the time, the corresponding forms of cooperation, through which larger amounts of credit could be issued, had the legal status of a so-called Verein, i.e., an association (or a syndicate). These associations, in turn, left a lasting legacy by representing one of the forerunners of the multinational firms that dominated the Swiss financial sector during the second part of the twentieth century.

In Basel, a particularly successful association was formed in 1854 among six private banks, which agreed to arrange regular meetings to discuss and organise the joint subscription of shares for railway projects, or the issuance of bonds on behalf of the canton or local governments (Bauer, 1972, pp.27ff.). This group, which quickly became known as the "Bankverein", joined forces in approximately 40 ventures during the following decades, including a financial stake in the transalpine Gotthard railway. In 1871, the "Bankverein" was converted from a loose association into a proper stock-traded company.[7] The resulting "Basler Bankverein" shared many similarities with the early history of Credit Suisse, in terms of having an equivalent amount of initial share capital (50 million Swiss francs) and suffering from heavy losses during the economic downturn in the German-speaking part of Europe during the late 1870s, but also by prospering thereafter through participation in lucrative domestic railway projects and other thriving industrial ventures. A next step taken in 1897 involved the acquisition of several banks not only in Basel, but also in Zurich and St.Gallen (Bauer, 1972, pp.116ff.). The relabelling of the resulting enlarged financial firm as the "Schweizerischer Bankverein", or under its official English name, the "Swiss Bank Corporation", reflected this geographical expansion.[8] Furthermore, the Bank Corporation soon adopted a pioneering role in terms of opening the first foreign branch of a big Swiss bank in London in 1898 (Bauer, 1972, pp.139–140).

The "Bankverein" did not encompass the entire financial community of Basel. Rather, a second group of private bankers had set up their own association during the 1850s and strengthened this collaboration in 1862 through the foundation of a dedicated joint-stock company, called the "Basler Handelsbank" (or "Basel Merchant Bank") (Ritzmann, 1973, pp.65–66; Bauer, 1987, p.159). From the outset, the activities of this financial firm were quite broad and included not only the joint subscription of financial securities, but also the provision of commercial loans and, obviously, merchant banking (Bauer, 1987, p.159). Unlike the clear focus of the early "Bankverein", this broader strategy inevitably gave rise to overlaps with the business of the sponsors of the "Handelsbank", which arguably hampered its early development (Bauer & Blackman, 1998, p.102). Later, during the Great Depression of the 1930s, the "Handelsbank" became embroiled in scandals and suffered from heavy losses and other setbacks, from which it never managed to recover. Hence, it was integrated in 1945 into the Swiss Bank Corporation, which had by then become the dominant financial player in Basel (see Ch.6.3 and Bauer, 1987, pp.169–170). To anticipate the further development, the Bank Corporation merged, in turn, into the UBS during the 1990s (see Fig. 8.3 of Chap. 8).

Concerning the situation in Geneva, several attempts failed to successfully adapt its remarkable financial heritage to the era of the big bank. Probably the most serious attempt to enter this segment was undertaken with the "Banque Générale Suisse de Credit Internationale Mobilier et Foncier", which was founded in 1853 with a quite lavish equity capital of 60 million francs (Ritzmann, 1973, pp.61–62). The lengthy name alludes to the high ambitions pursued by means of this

---

[7] For a comprehensive overview of the history of the "Bankverein", see Bauer (1972).

[8] Initially, the English translation was simply "Swiss Bankverein". However, when German expressions were met with increasing hostility in the Anglo-Saxon world during World War I, the name "Swiss Bank Corporation" was introduced in 1917 (Bauer, 1972, p.228). Unfortunately, the term "corporation" disguises the origin in an association, i.e., a "Verein".

venture, which combined an extraordinarily broad range of financial activities, including all kinds of domestic and international investments, retail banking, the provision of mortgages, discounting bills of exchange, issuing paper money (see Fig. 4.1 of Chap. 4), and even offering life insurance policies and pension plans (Ritzmann, 1973, p.62). However, the risks of an overexpansion soon hit home, as the "Banque Générale" suffered from large losses within its Paris branch in 1859. The corresponding uncertainty immediately led to panicky banknote conversions back in Geneva in a rare event of instability within Switzerland's free-banking system (see Sect. 4.3). To some degree, this instability also reflected that the "Banque Générale" was not a purely economic project, but also served as a political tool to undermine Geneva's moneyed elite. More specifically, during the mid-nineteenth century, the political landscape of Geneva, and indeed of large parts of Switzerland, was characterised by deep-seated conflicts between a conservative establishment and the so-called liberals with their progressive agenda of fostering economic freedom, introducing new industrial technologies, such as railways, and reforming the banking sector accordingly (see Sect. 2.3). In Geneva, the liberal movement was headed by the journalist and politician James Fazy (1794–1878), who launched projects, such as the "Banque Générale", with an eye to weakening the Genevan private banks.[9] Against this background, the fate of Fazy's banking projects became closely intertwined with that of the liberal movement, whose dominance began to decline in Geneva and in the rest of Switzerland during the 1860s. Reflecting the diminishing political support, the "Banque Générale" was liquidated in 1869, e.g., only 15 years after its foundation. In addition, private banks had also begun to rise to the financial challenges of the industrial age by jointly setting up a discount house in 1855. This "Comptoir d'Escompte de Genève" gradually grew into a bigger bank but eventually failed during the Great Depression (see Sect. 6.3). Overall, Geneva was unable to keep up with the financial ascent of Zurich during the nineteenth and twentieth centuries.

Bern, which was designated the capital city of the modern Swiss Confederation in 1848 (see Sect. 2.3), also had some hopes of playing an important role in industry and finance. To fulfil these hopes, the "Eidgenössische Bank" was founded in 1864 on the initiative of the local liberal politician, Jakob Stämpfli (1820–1879). The activities of this ambitious big-banking scheme included issuing paper money, discounting bills of exchange, and offering merchant-banking services (Ritzmann, 1973, pp.67–69). However, things did not get off to a good start, as the bank suffered from a rare case of panicky banknote conversions in Switzerland in 1869 (see Sect. 4.3). In the longer term, Bern simply lacked a sufficiently strong industrial base to become Switzerland's financial or economic capital. Restricted by the modest size of the local economy, the high ambitions of the "Eidgenössische Bank" were never fulfilled. That it renounced the right to issue paper money in 1882 and relocated its head office to Zurich in 1892 bear testimony to this development. The final decline of the "Eidgenössische Bank" began during the Great Depression (see Sect. 6.3).

[9] Of note, in Geneva, the liberals appeared under the name the "radicaux" ("radicals").

5.5 Overview of Swiss Banking During the Nineteenth Century

Towards the end of the nineteenth century, industrialisation was well under way in many parts of the world. Furthermore, the volume of cross-border trade and capital flows had grown to unprecedented levels in what would later be recognised as the first wave of globalisation (Obstfeld & Taylor, 2004, pp.24ff., 126ff.). These developments had also sustained a global expansion of the banking sector with a concentration of the corresponding activities across leading financial centres around the world. Accordingly, large banks organised as stock-traded companies had replaced the ancient private banks, which rested on family networks, as the most potent financial firms. On the European continent, they typically combined a broad range of activities, such as collecting vast amounts of savings and channelling them into industrial projects, subscribing of shares and bonds, discounting bills of exchange, providing mortgages, and in some cases even offering deposit and savings accounts.

As one of the earliest industrialised countries on the European continent, albeit a latecomer to building the novel railway infrastructure, Switzerland participated in this development. In particular, to facilitate investments in mechanised forms of production and the new modes of mass transportation, several big banks were founded during the second part of the nineteenth century. Not least because of the benign conditions for these increasingly large financial firms, the Swiss banking sector grew, on average, at a real annual rate of roughly 5 per cent between 1890 and 1913 (Mazbouri et al., 2012, pp.470–471).

The monumental changes during industrialisation were also closely intertwined with the ascent of Zurich as the economic and financial powerhouse of Switzerland. Before the outbreak of World War I in 1914, this city became the head-office location of two big banks as well as the main location of the National Bank, i.e., Switzerland's central bank. Nevertheless, reflecting the decentralised character of the country, Zurich has never completely dominated the scene. Reflecting a long financial tradition, Basel, and especially Geneva with its private banks dating back to the ancien régime, have remained important players within Switzerland's banking sector.

During the second part of the nineteenth century, the popularisation of credit also gave rise to marked financial developments at the local level. In particular, according to the statistics that have become available since the nineteenth century, hundreds of regional banks (i.e., savings, land, and other local banks) that had been founded across Switzerland before the end of the nineteenth century accounted for approximately half of the combined balance sheet of the entire sector in 1900 (see also Fig. 1.1a of Chap. 1). Equipped with a branch network, they gradually replaced savings banks as the key financial institutes for the broad public. The 25 cantonal banks, which were typically also equipped with a state guarantee, accounted for another third. Thus, the domestically oriented cantonal and regional banks were clearly the dominant players at the time.

Of note, these statistics do not capture the situation of private banks, which began to publish aggregate balance-sheet data only from the mid-twentieth century onwards (see again Fig. 1.1a of Chap. 1). Traditionally, the business of these banks is oriented towards international financial activities. However, especially when compared with the spectacular growth of the wealth-management business during the twentieth century, Switzerland was not yet a fully fledged offshore banking centre before the outbreak of World War I. In particular, the big banks funded primary domestic industrial ventures but lacked the global outlook of the current flagships of the Swiss banking sector. Around 1900, Switzerland's joint-stock banks were only "big" at the domestic level but did not appear on the list of the twenty largest banks around the world before the outbreak of the Great War (Cassis, 2010, p.92). Correspondingly, foreign representation was limited to one branch of the Swiss Bank Corporation in London (Cassis, 2010, p.128). It is remarkable that the foreign representation of Credit Suisse began only with an affiliate in Argentina that opened in 1910 (Jöhr, 1956, p.30; Cassis, 2010, p.128). Finally, despite being a quite cosmopolitan banking centre, Geneva remained strongly oriented towards its traditional business relationships with France (Cassis, 2010, pp.128–129).

References

Bauer, H. (1972). *Schweizerischer Bankverein 1872–1972*. Basel: Schweizerischer Bankverein.

Bauer, H. (1987). Bank- und Finanzplatz Basel. In Mottet, L.H. (Ed.), *Geschichte der Schweizer Banken*. Zurich: Verlag Neue Zürcher Zeitung.

Bauer, H., & Blackman, W.J. (1998). *Swiss banking—An analytical history*. Basingstoke: Macmillan Press.

Cassis, Y. (2010). *Capital of capital. The rise and fall of international financial centres 1780–2009*. Cambridge: Cambridge University Press.

Jöhr, A. (1956). *Schweizerische Kreditanstalt 1856–1956*. Zurich: Conzett and Huber.

Jung, J. (2000). *Von der Schweizerischen Kreditanstalt zur Credit Suisse Group. Eine Bankengeschichte*. Zurich: NZZ Verlag.

Jung, J. (2015). *Switzerland's success story : The life and work of Alfred Escher (1819–1882)*. Zurich: NZZ Libro.

Keller, T. (1955). *Leu & co*. Zürich: Denkschrift zum zweihundertjährigen Bestehen der Aktiengesellschaft Leu & Co.

Kindleberger, C. P. (1984). *A financial history of Western Europe*. London and New York: Routledge.

Mazbouri, M., Guex, S., & Lopez, R. (2012). Finanzplatz Schweiz. In Halbeisen, P., Müller, M., & Veyrassat, B. (Eds.), *Wirtschaftsgeschichte der Schweiz im 20. Jahrhundert* Basel: Schwabe Verlag.

Obstfeld, M., & Taylor, A. (2004). *Global capital markets integration, crisis, and growth*. Cambridge: Cambridge University Press.

Reinhardt, V. (2013). *Die Geschichte der Schweiz* (2nd ed.). Munich: C.H. Beck.

Ritzmann, F. (1973). *Die Schweizer Banken. Geschichte - Theorie - Statistik*. Bern: Verlag Paul Haupt.

Straumann, T. (2006). Der kleine Gigant: Der Aufstieg Zürichs zu einem Internationalen Finanzplatz. In Institut für Bankhistorische Forschung (Ed.), *Europäische Finanzplätze im Wettbewerb*. Stuttgart: Franz Steiner Verlag.

Strehle, R., Trepp, G., & Weyermann, B. (1987). *Ganz oben - 125 Jahre Schweizerische Bankgesellschaft*. Zurich: Limmat Verlag.
Thürer, G. (1970). *Free and Swiss—The story of Switzerland*. London: Oswald Wolff.
Wehrli, B. (1987). Banken und Bankiers in Zürich. In Mottet, L.H. (Ed.), *Geschichte der Schweizer Banken*. Zurich: Verlag Neue Zürcher Zeitung.

Chapter 6
A Safe Haven in an Unstable World (1914–1945)

6.1 The Safe-Haven Status and Its Origin

World War I (1914–1918) undoubtedly marked a significant historical turning point. On the European continent, the terrible loss of human life and the colossal destruction caused by four years of military conflict on an industrial scale ended with a revolution in Russia, the collapse of the Austrian–Hungarian empire, and the frightening destabilisation of Germany. Unfortunately, the more or less complete disintegration of the traditional political and economic order, and the turmoil that followed, provided a breeding ground for totalitarian ideologies, including communism in Russia, fascism in Italy, and national socialism in Germany.

In the realm of international economics and finance, World War I crippled the classical gold standard and put an end to a free-trade era with largely unhindered cross-border capital flows (Eichengreen, 2008, pp.43ff.). Indeed, across a range of measures, the pre-1914 level of economic and financial globalisation was not restored until the end of the twentieth century (Obstfeld & Taylor, 2004, pp.126ff.). Despite widely held aspirations during the interwar years (1919–1939) to bring back a certain degree of stability by reinstalling an international financial system based on gold, these plans were probably doomed to failure due to the massive amounts of debt accumulated by the belligerent countries. In particular, Britain had been financially weakened by forfeiting large parts of its foreign assets and, as a result, the ability to play a stabilising role within the international monetary system. In Germany, the situation was much worse, as the democratic system of the so-called Weimar Republic remained fragile, and the country suffered from the burden of having to scrape together the war reparations imposed by the victorious Allied powers. It is perhaps not surprising that this fragmented international environment gave rise to two decades characterised by entrenched political conflicts, a series of unusually severe economic and financial crises during a peacetime period, and, as a reaction, more and more extensive government interventions intended to remedy the corresponding adverse effects. Particular events of this interwar instability include

N. Herger, *Switzerland and its Banks*, Frontiers in Economic History,
https://doi.org/10.1007/978-3-031-35904-0_6

the German hyperinflation of 1923, the stock-market crash on Wall Street in 1929, and the Great Depression of the 1930s with its pervasive bank failures, mass unemployment, entrenched deflation, and cascade of currency devaluations.

Ironically, the Swiss banking sector benefitted, at least in relative terms, from the international instability during the first half of the twentieth century (Fior, 2002; Perrenoud et al., 2002, pp.44ff.). By remaining an island of stability in a sea of political and economic turmoil during the interwar years, Switzerland began to emerge as an international financial centre with a particular focus on offshore wealth management (Cassis, 2010, pp.176ff.). A comparison of the situations before World War I and after World War II is striking. In 1914, Switzerland was not one of the leading financial centres, and none of its banks appeared on the list of the twenty largest financial firms around the world (Cassis, 2010, p.92). Conversely, the decades after 1945 are often considered the golden age of Swiss banking (see Chap. 7). During these years, Zurich was by some measures the third-largest financial centre in the world, in complete disproportion to the size of the country given that the top positions were occupied by London and New York, i.e., the cities representing the superpowers of the nineteenth and the twentieth centuries, respectively (Cassis, 2010, pp.232ff.). In a similar vein, World War I also marked the historical conversion of the Swiss franc into a safe-haven currency (Baltensperger & Kugler, 2016). During the decades after its introduction in 1850, the franc was not particularly strong (see Sect. 4.3). However, the fact that Switzerland belonged to only a handful of European countries that survived the turmoil after 1914 more or less intact altered this pattern. After World War I, a Swiss "interest island" began to emerge with lower nominal rates than abroad (Kugler & Weder, 2002).[1] Furthermore, since around the 1920s, episodes of international economic and political instability have tended to give rise to substantial capital inflows into Switzerland. The resulting appreciation in times of crisis reflects, in turn, an outstanding feature of a so-called safe-haven currency (Ranaldo & Söderlind, 2010).

The safe-haven status of the Swiss franc is usually attributed to the stability of the underlying political and economic system, including relatively sound monetary and fiscal policy (see e.g. Auer, 2015). However, this comparatively stable environment did not emerge until the interwar years. During this period, Switzerland's democratic institutions proved to be sufficiently strong to resist the temptation for autocratic government, which was widely seen at the time as a remedy for political instability and a prerequisite for curing economic ills, such as pervasive levels of deflation and unemployment (see Sect. 2.3). In the international comparison for the century between 1918 and 2018 shown in Table 6.1, Switzerland's economic stability is reflected in a range of variables, including relatively low levels of inflation and nominal interest rates, the absence of a hyperinflation or cases of sovereign default,

[1] Due to the vagaries of constructing robust measures of (expected) inflation and gauging the extent of the risk premium, it is more difficult to establish the corresponding pattern of the real interest rate. However, according to Hauzenberger et al. (2021), a Swiss interest island also existed with respect to real rates, especially around the years of the Bretton Woods System.

Table 6.1 Economic stability and instability (1918–2018)

	France	Germany	Italy	United Kd.	USA	Switzerland
ø inflation	7%	19%	8%	4%	3%	2%
ø interest rate (nom)	6%	6%	7%	6%	5%	4%
# hyperinflations	0	1	0	0	0	0
# sovereign defaults	0	2	0	0	0	0
# devaluations (1918–73)	14	2	6	6	1	1
# revaluations (1918–73)	0	2	2	0	0	1
Appreciation ag. $ (1973–2018)	−25%	38%	−182%	−46%	0%	70%

Notes: Data on inflation and nominal interest rates (referring to long-term rates) are taken from the Jordà–Schularick–Taylor Macrohistory Database (www.macrohistory.net). For some countries, the corresponding data are missing during a war or during a severe economic crisis. The number of sovereign defaults refers to outright defaults and cases of a debt rescheduling as reported by Reinhart and Rogoff (2009, p.96). The number of devaluations and revaluations has been taken from Vogler (2006, p.40). The appreciation of the local currency unit against the US dollar refers to the annual average of the nominal exchange rate in 1973 and 2018

and a stable currency in terms of a small number of parity adjustments under the system of fixed exchange rates before 1973, and an appreciation of the franc against the US dollar thereafter. Of note, these comparisons are relative and do not imply that Switzerland did not suffer from widespread economic problems, such as unstable prices around World War I, the severe and long-lasting economic downturn during the Great Depression, harmful upsurges in inflation around the 1970s, and instability within the banking sector after the Global Financial Crisis of 2008. However, the safe-haven status refers to the fact that these problems were, typically, less severe at home than abroad.

For the Swiss economy, the safe-haven status has had far-reaching implications. In general, the tendency of the franc to appreciate during aggravated international political conflicts and times of economic instability has posed a major challenge for the domestic export industry. The problem of being confronted with a simultaneous decline in international demand and an increase in product prices, after they have been converted into foreign currency units, arose, e.g., during the Great Depression and more recently during the Global Financial Crisis. However, the capital inflows associated with a stable currency have also provided the basis for Switzerland's flourishing offshore banking business (Cassis, 2010, pp.178–179). Since around the interwar period, this development has also given rise to the question of whether these capital inflows originate from legitimate motives to protect foreign savings from inflation or confiscation by autocratic governments, or from illegitimate activities, such as tax evasion (Farquet, 2012). The remaining part of this chapter discusses the effects of the unstable period between 1914 and 1945 on the Swiss banking sector in greater detail.

6.2 World War I and the Postwar Period

As a neutral country, Switzerland had not formed an alliance with either the Entente (Britain, France, and Russia) or the Central Powers (Austria–Hungary and Germany) and, hence, did not go to war in August 1914. Nevertheless, the army was mobilised to secure the border, and the nearby military conflict resulted in economic and financial hardships comparable with those in other parts of Europe (see Baltensperger & Kugler, 2017, pp.54ff.). In particular, the quite unexpected outbreak of World War I triggered a panic-driven liquidity crisis, as the general public rushed to convert savings into banknotes and gold. Furthermore, the stock market crashed reflecting the anticipation that many companies would suffer from a war in Europe. Finally, the collapse of free trade had immediate knock-on effects on the international monetary system, which, at the time, was organised mainly around discounting bills of exchange as a cashless means of payment. For the banking sector, these combined crises obviously posed a serious threat. In Switzerland, the big banks in particular had been deeply involved in international trade finance and, therefore, found themselves suddenly stuck with large portfolios of illiquid bills of exchange with aggravated risks of default. For example, in 1914, these types of bills accounted for approximately twenty per cent of the balance sheet of the Swiss Bank Corporation (Bauer & Blackman, 1998, pp.185–186). Furthermore, some of the smaller banks located in the border town of Basel had to be restructured or even failed because they suffered from unsustainable losses on mortgages issued on properties in neighbouring France and Germany (Bauer, 1987, p.167). However, thanks to the resolute interventions of the government and the Swiss National Bank (SNB), including the suspension of banknote redemption in gold, an increase in the official discount rate, the introduction of small-denomination banknotes as legal tender, and the closure of the stock market, the initial panic abated relatively quickly (Bauer & Blackman, 1998, p.185). After overcoming the initial shock, the financial and banking system managed to adjust to a new wartime normal in the autumn of 1914.

In contrast to the initial, short-lived, financial panic, the fact that Switzerland could not survive without importing certain amounts of vital goods became a pressing problem throughout the war years between 1914 and 1918. Above all, it was crucial to secure the supply of commodities, above all coal without which it would have been impossible to operate the railways as the main transportation system. However, due to the economic disruptions of World War I, the overall volume of imports into Switzerland, as measured in tonnes, fell dramatically (Bauer & Blackman, 1998, p.186). To manage scarce foreign goods and commodities, the system with more or less private transactions of the pre-1914 gold standard was replaced by government planning. This type of war economy, which was applied by most countries at the time, implied that the organisation and distribution of strategically important goods, including the corresponding financial contracts and payments, was placed under the control of dedicated public agencies. Tellingly, in Switzerland, the agency responsible for trade finance with the Central Powers—

especially with Germany—was called the "Coal Central" (Kohlezentrale), reflecting the crucial role of this commodity. Conversely, the agency handling the payments for imports from the Entente—especially from France and Britain—was called the "Swiss Financial Society" (Schweizerische Finanzgesellschaft). Between 1914 and 1918, the commercial freedom of the banking sector was severely curtailed. In particular, some foreign assets were blocked by the belligerent countries, and commercial banks were, by and large, relegated to the role of supporting the war effort by issuing guarantees and loans according to the instructions of the government (Jöhr, 1956, pp.34–35; Jung, 2000, pp.70–71).[2]

Another financial challenge arose in terms of providing additional funds for the government, whose financial situation deteriorated dramatically due to the massive increase in public expenditure on national defence, social benefits, and food subsidies to support low-income households. Additionally, the breakdown of free trade led to a collapse in customs revenue, which was an important source for funding the federal government at the beginning of the twentieth century (Baltensperger & Kugler, 2017, p.57). As it was impossible to completely cover the resulting public deficits by collecting additional taxes, the Swiss government turned to debt finance.[3] In particular, at the federal level, nine tranches of the so-called mobilisation bonds (Mobilitätsanleihen) were issued between 1914 and 1918 (Schaltegger & Schmid, 2021). The banking sector was given the task of placing some of these bonds on the capital market (Jöhr, 1956, pp.36–37; Jung, 2000, p.71). However, as the amount of domestic savings could not cope with public deficits that continued to increase the longer the war dragged on, the interest-rate level began to increase. Furthermore, towards the end of the war, the federal government resorted to monetising the debt through the Swiss National Bank (Baltensperger & Kugler, 2017, pp.57ff.). As shown in Fig. 6.1, the unsurprising result of this expansionary fiscal and monetary policy was a marked upsurge in inflation, which reached levels similar to those in other European countries.

The war legacy of an inflationary money supply and the underlying public debt overhang gave rise to nasty economic dilemmas after the armistice in November 1918 (Herger, 2019, pp.25ff.). In particular, to deal with the economic consequences of the war, Britain pursued a deflationary policy involving a reduction of public debt through tax increases, austerity programmes in the public sector, and the

[2] The war-induced government restrictions on international finance also opened the door to illegal arbitrage activities. For example, Bauer and Blackman (1998, p.197) report an example of clandestine transactions by an employee of the "Basler Handelsbank", who travelled anonymously to Paris to convert financial assets, such as securities or gold, into Swiss francs amid fears of a looming devaluation of the French currency. At the time, exports of capital and gold were restricted by the French government.

[3] Several new taxes were, of course, introduced during the war, including a federal income and wealth tax in 1915. This tax at the time was conceived of as a temporary measure, and, according to the federal constitution, has to be renewed every 15 years through a popular vote. To the present day, the population has always approved this renewal meaning that the "emergency taxes" of World War I have survived. Hence, they are a good example of Milton Friedman's ironic dictum that "nothing is so permanent as a temporary government programme".

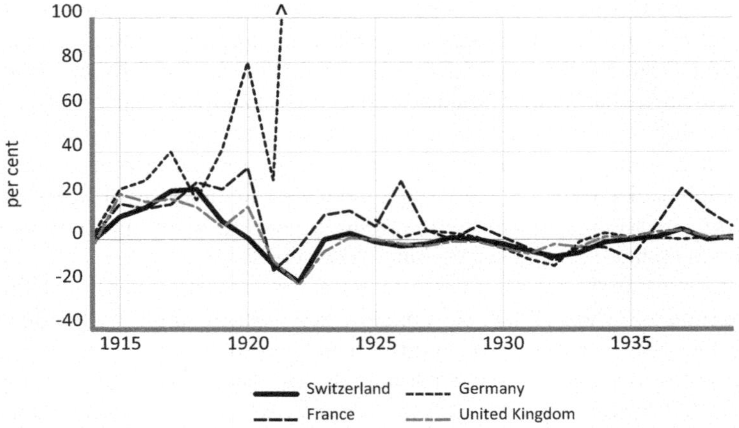

Fig. 6.1 Inflation in Switzerland and in other European countries (1914–1939) (own figure. Data: calculated from the price index reported in Mitchell (1992, Tab. H2))

mobilisation of additional savings by means of a temporary hike in interest rates. Although these measures typically created a severe economic downturn, they were necessary to shrink the money supply and, hence, to pave the way for returning to a currency that was convertible at the traditional gold parity. Despite the economic cost, this deflationary policy was widely seen as desirable at the time because the prewar gold standard was generally associated with economically benign and stable conditions. A second option was to inflate the war debt away. This inflationary policy, of course, posed a serious risk by undermining trust in a country's currency. In extreme cases, a complete collapse could happen, as during the hyperinflations in Austria in 1922, and in Germany in 1923 (see Fig. 6.1).

Compared with the belligerent countries, Switzerland was in a less miserable situation. For example, public expenditure had increased only from 11 per cent of GDP in 1913 to 15 per cent in 1920, while this share had increased from 13 to 25 per cent in France, and from 13 to 28 per cent in Britain during the same period (Farquet, 2012, p.6). The extent of the government's expansion mattered because it sooner or later was mapped onto an increasing tax burden as well as the temptation to resort to an "inflation tax". Despite the relatively benign conditions in Switzerland, a deflationary policy was warranted during the postwar years to reverse price increases dating back to World War I (Bauer & Blackman, 1998, pp.191ff.; Baltensperger & Kugler, 2017, pp.62ff.). This tightening of monetary policy was manifested in the sharp reduction of the consumer price index by an astonishing 40 per cent between 1920 and 1922 (see also Fig. 6.1) and in a severe, but short-lived, recession with a dramatic upsurge in unemployment and a downturn in industrial output around 1922. After going through this painful "stabilisation crisis", and following the example of Great Britain, Switzerland went back on the gold standard in 1925 (Bordo & James, 2007, pp. 46–48; Baltensperger & Kugler, 2017, p.66.).

The return of the Swiss-franc exchange rate to traditional parity during the following years became a potent symbol of economic and political stability. The banking sector, including the big banks, was a major beneficiary of this development.

During the first part of the twentieth century, the Swiss banking sector underwent a profound structural transformation that was associated with a reduction in the number of banks by approximately twenty per cent (see Figure 1.1 and Ritzmann, 1973, pp.108–115). In addition to the aforementioned collapse of the savings-bank movement since the second part of the nineteenth century (see Sect. 3.4), and the elimination of dedicated note-issuing banks after the introduction of a public banknote monopoly in 1907 (Sect. 4.4), the financial and economic turmoil during the war and postwar years was a major factor of this transformation. The corresponding beneficiaries included the cantonal banks, which managed to increase their market share from approximately 30 per cent in 1901 to 40 per cent in 1929. However, in both absolute and relative terms, the rise of the eight big banks at the time—Bank Leu, Basler Handelsbank, Comptoir d'Escompte de Genève, Credit Suisse, Eidgenösssiche Bank, Swiss Bank Corporation, Swiss Volksbank, and Union Bank—was even more spectacular. Their market share rose from approximately 15 per cent in 1901 to 40 per cent in 1929. During the decade after World War I, they managed to almost double the size of their combined balance sheet, from 4.2 billion Swiss francs to 8.2 billion. Domestically, expensive infrastructure projects, including the electrification of the railway network to reduce its dependency on coal imports, were an important driver of this growth (see e.g. Jöhr, 1956, p.39). Furthermore, the success of the big banks was a result of the internationalisation of Switzerland's financial sector. Due to looming currency devaluations and the hightax burden of the belligerent countries, an inflow of securities and gold had already occurred during World War I (Bauer & Blackman, 1998, p.188; Baltensperger, 2012, p.147). In response to the political and monetary chaos in nearby Germany as well as in parts of Eastern Europe, these capital inflows continued after 1918. Especially during the second part of the 1920s, the stability of the Swiss franc also acted as a magnet for substantial amounts of capital from France and, to a lesser extent, Britain and Italy (Fior, 2002, p.6). In addition to the private banks, the big banks began to attract substantial amounts of foreign capital, which, in turn, provided the basis for issuing foreign bank loans, making short-term investments (especially in Germany), and offering all kinds of offshore wealth-management activities (Fior, 2002, pp.9–10; Cassis, 2010, pp.177ff.). Especially, the latter were destined to become an iconic feature of Switzerland's banking sector. Reflecting these developments during the interwar years, Zurich also began to replace Berlin and Vienna as the leading financial centre in the German-speaking part of Europe (Cassis, 2010, pp.143–144).[4]

[4] Other small, neutral countries in Europe benefitted from a similar development. For example, the Netherlands, especially Amsterdam, became a leading European financial centre during the 1920s (Cassis, 2010, pp.176–177).

Of note, owing to the lack of comprehensive balance-of-payments statistics, it is impossible to quantify the amount of capital imports and exports during the 1920s and, in turn, the exact development of the wealth-management business (Cassis, 2010, p.178; Farquet, 2012, p.4).[5] However, the patchy evidence that is available suggests that the internationalisation of Switzerland's big banks during the interwar period was modest compared with the multinationalisation that would take place during the second part of the twentieth century. In particular, their foreign activities were heavily focused on a small number of countries, especially neighbouring Germany and France.

Although Switzerland was not involved in the peace negotiations that took place in Versailles in 1919, one of the thorniest issues of the resulting treaty, the payment of war reparations, had a lasting effect more than a decade later by leading to the establishment of the Bank for International Settlements (BIS) in Basel (Kindleberger, 1984, p.304). More specifically, although Germany had in principle agreed to pay compensation for the economic damage caused during World War I, the precise amount of these reparations, as well as the way in which they were to be settled, became a source of ongoing tensions between Germany, Britain, France, and the United States. After a series of renegotiations during the 1920s, a final attempt was made in 1929 and 1930 to resolve this issue through the so-called Young Plan, which was conceived under the leadership of the US representative on the Reparations Committee, Owen D. Young. His plan intended to limit German war reparations to the payment of 121 billion gold marks over the next fifty-nine years. Furthermore, it stipulated the winding up of the Reparations Agency in Berlin, by means of which the Allies had overseen the government finances of Germany and arranged the collection and the distribution of the amounts due (Kindleberger, 1984, p.304). After Germany regained fiscal autonomy, it was agreed to transfer the remaining war reparations through a dedicated "Bank for International Settlements". Under the joint ownership of the major European countries and Japan, this bank was supposed to administer these payments and, when possible, "securitise" them by issuing its own bonds (Liaquat, 2009, p.336). Basel was chosen as the location for the BIS due to the excellent international railway connections, but also as a compromise between Britain (and its bids for either London or Amsterdam) and France (and its bids for either Paris or Brussels) (Cassis, 2010, pp.177–178). Ironically, the original raison d'être for the BIS soon vanished because the war reparations were first postponed by the Hoover Moratorium imposed during the German banking crisis of 1931 and then halted altogether with the conclusion of the Lausanne Agreement in 1932. However, by quickly becoming an indispensable hub and meeting point for central bankers, the BIS was not dismantled, despite the increasing tensions among its members during the Great Depression and World War II (Kindleberger, 1984, p.305). Today, the BIS still serves as a forum for discussions among central bankers, as a counterparty and trustee for their financial transactions,

[5] Reliable statistics on the amount of domestic and offshore assets accepted and managed by Swiss banks have only become available since the 1990s (Vogler, 2006, p.59).

and as a research centre for questions on monetary policy and financial stability (Toniolo, 2007).

6.3 The Effects of the Great Depression

Although it is well known that the Great Depression of the 1930s was one of the most devastating downturns in economic history, it is nevertheless impressive to recall the actual extent of this crisis. Within a couple of years after the US stock market had crashed in 1929, global industrial output had fallen by approximately one-third, and trade measured by volume by one-quarter (Kindleberger, 1973, pp.171ff.; Feinstein et al., 1997, pp.103ff.). Moreover, pervasive levels of deflation with average prices declining by twenty per cent and more were the rule rather than the exception (see e.g. Friedman & Schwarz, 1963, pp.299ff.). Last, but for the broader population not least, unemployment became a massive problem. In the worst-hit countries, including the United States and Germany, roughly one-third of the workforce was without a job at the bottom of the downturn during the first half of the 1930s (Feinstein et al., 1997, pp.125ff; Cassis, 2010, p.182).

In Switzerland, the Great Depression manifested primarily in a sharp reduction in international trade as well as increasingly volatile cross-border capital movements. In particular, the export of goods, including watches, machinery, and textile products, declined by approximately 30 per cent between 1929 and 1932.[6] Conversely, as shown in the top panel of Fig. 6.2, industrial output destined for domestic consumption remained remarkably stable throughout the 1930s. Owing to this resilience of the domestic economy, (official) unemployment increased from less than one per cent in 1929 to "only" six per cent in 1936, which was low compared with the situation elsewhere.[7] As illustrated by the international comparison of industrial output shown in the bottom panel of Fig. 6.2, although the downturn was relatively moderate, it took Switzerland quite a long time to overcome the Great Depression. For example, the level of unemployment did not peak until 1936, and the industrial sectors closely connected with international trade typically did not return to their precrisis output levels until after World War II. The main culprit in this sluggish recovery was, arguably, the reluctance to devalue the Swiss franc against gold. Sterling was devalued in 1931, and the US dollar followed suit in 1933 (Eichengreen, 2008, pp.78–86). Conversely, together with Belgium, France,

[6] Zurlinden (2003) provides a comprehensive overview of the Swiss economy during the Great Depression, including a broad range of economic data.

[7] These figures should be taken with a grain of salt because they refer to the number of persons officially registered as unemployed. However, as there was no compulsory unemployment insurance at the time, for many workers, there were scant incentives to report the loss of a job because this would not create an entitlement for collecting social benefits. Therefore, as in other countries, the figures of the 1930s in Switzerland certainly underestimate the true share of the workforce looking for a job.

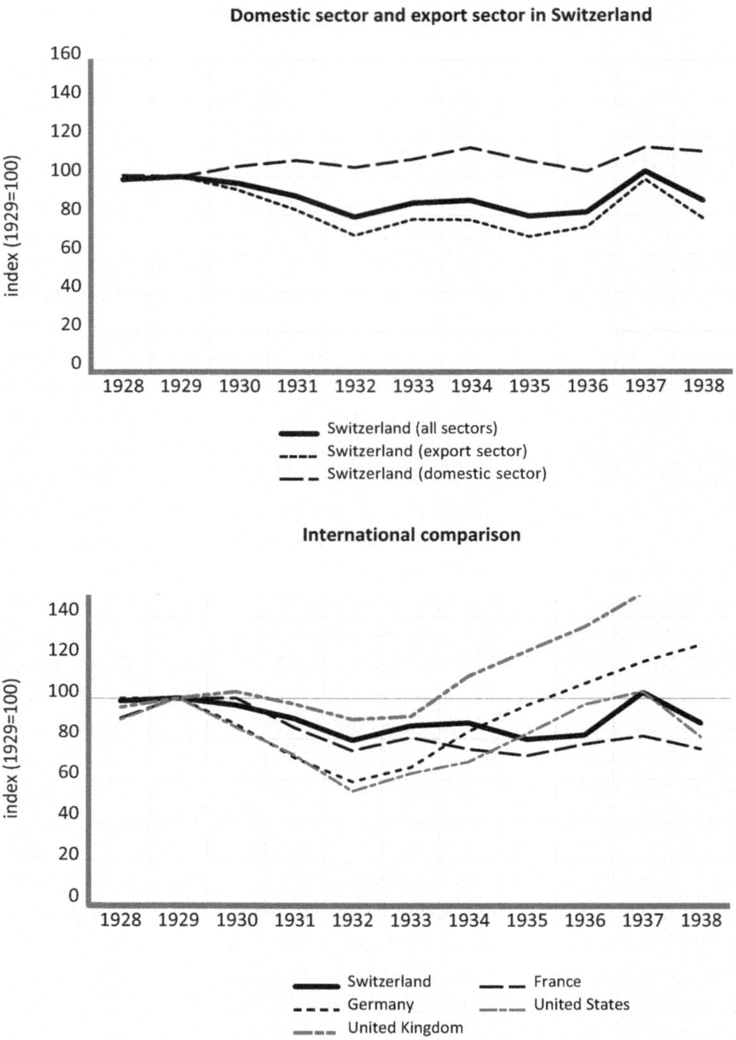

Fig. 6.2 Industrial production during the Great Depression (own figure. The data have an annual frequency and refer to an index of (real) industrial production (with 1929 = 100). See Zurlinden (2003, pp.88, 95) for an exact definition and the original sources)

and the Netherlands, Switzerland belonged to a loose alliance called the "gold-block countries", whose monetary policy was characterised by a strong desire to adhere to the principles of the classical gold standard (Feinstein et al., 1997, pp.156ff.). Reflecting this policy stance, the Swiss franc was devalued by 30 per cent against gold only in September 1936, one day after France had finally abandoned the restrictions of the established parities (Baltensperger & Kugler, 2017, pp.82ff.).

During the years before 1936, this strict monetary policy implied that the Swiss economy suffered from a chronic loss of international competitiveness, as was reflected by high real wages and export prices when expressed in non-gold-block currencies, such as pounds or dollars. Furthermore, by honouring the traditions of the gold standard, it was impossible to stimulate economic activity by pursuing a policy of cheap money (Bordo & James, 2007). Taken together, the entrenched economic downturn in Switzerland was a reflection of the widely documented phenomenon that countries did not recover economically from the Great Depression until after the devaluation of their currency (Choudhri & Kochin, 1980; Eichengreen & Sachs, 1986; Bemanke & James, 1991).

Pervasive problems with financial instability, including recurrent waves of bank failures, provide a prominent explanation of why the economic troubles of the 1930s were exceptionally severe and why the corresponding downturn lasted much longer than most recessions before and thereafter.[8] Several aspects of this instability in banking can be mapped, indeed, onto some of the outstanding features of the Great Depression, such as the collapse of the amount of money and credit in circulation, which gave rise to deflation, and the sharp decline in domestic and international investment (see e.g., Friedman & Schwarz, 1963, pp.351ff.). In a similar vein, the economic downturn in Europe began in earnest with two large bankruptcies in 1931, namely, that of the Austrian "Creditanstalt" and the German "Darmstädter und Nationalbank" (or Danat) (Feinstein et al., 1997, pp.107ff.). In Germany, the widespread fear of further bank failures triggered a liquidity crisis with panicky withdrawals by depositors in July 1931, and a sudden stop in international lending. As a reaction to this twin crisis in domestic banking and international lending, capital controls were imposed and not lifted until after the end of World War II. These restrictions to contain the outflow of gold, assets, and currency from Germany inflicted painful losses on foreign banks, including some of the leading merchant banks in London. Their financial problems, in turn, gave rise to a further destabilisation of the British financial system, which was already exposed to gold outflows caused by adverse balance-of-payments trends, an overvaluation of sterling, and an unsustainable combination of high interest and unemployment rates. In an event that shook the world, sterling was devalued in September 1931 (Eichengreen, 2008, pp.78–83). Concerning the US economy, the hope that the downturn would be short-lived was shattered by several waves of financial instability during the tragic years of 1932 and 1933, when literally thousands of banks failed across the country (Friedman & Schwarz, 1963, pp.324ff.). The US dollar was devalued in April 1933. Taken together, these shocks reflected an increasing disintegration of the global trade and payments system. For example, in addition to the protectionist capital controls imposed by Germany, and

[8] It is generally agreed that there is no single cause for the severity and long duration of the Great Depression. Rather, various explanations have been considered, including the overexpansion and the money-and-credit boom of the late 1920s (Hayek, 1931), the lack of a fiscal stimulus (Keynes, 1936), protectionism (Kindleberger, 1973), and a misguided monetary policy (Friedman & Schwarz, 1963). These explanations are, of course, not necessarily mutually exclusive.

subsequently by Austria, Hungary, and Poland, the global economy was increasingly divided into a sterling area around the United Kingdom and the abovementioned gold block under the leadership of France (Feinstein et al., 1997, pp.146ff.). Even though these devaluations and administrative controls were originally introduced as emergency measures to shield the domestic economy from the adverse shocks of the Great Depression, the international disintegration became deeply entrenched. In particular, controls on the exchange of currencies, restrictions of gold transactions, and high import tariffs implied that cross-border capital flows remained low when the world economy began to recover during the second part of the 1930s. That the exchange and capital controls were not dismantled reflected widespread scepticism regarding the benefits of an open financial system, foreign investments, and even international trade. In particular, it was commonly thought that many private cross-border transactions rested on dubious motives, including speculation to avoid losses from looming currency devaluations or the desire to evade taxes imposed by highly indebted governments (Cassis, 2010, p.193; Jöhr, 1956, p.43).

As in the real economy, the Great Depression initially affected the Swiss financial sector mainly through its international connections with countries at the core of the crisis. In this regard, the main exposure occurred via the big banks that had benefitted from the instability in the neighbouring countries and the economic boom of the roaring twenties by attracting substantial amounts of foreign capital, which was usually reinvested abroad (see Sect. 6.2). After the tide turned at the beginning of the 1930s, for some Swiss banks, the exposure to bad foreign debt led to critical situations.[9] Although there were no waves of banking panics comparable to those in, e.g., the United States, a major source of financial instability was the economic downturn and deteriorating political situation in Germany, where roughly one billion Reichsmarks (equivalent to approximately 240 million dollars or 1.2 billion Swiss francs at the time) of short-term loans were held by Swiss banks at the beginning of the 1930s (Ehrsam, 1985, p.87; Bauer & Blackman, 1998, pp.210–211). These loans, as well as other assets, were blocked, or became "frozen", when Germany introduced capital controls during the summer of 1931 (Feinstein et al., 1997, p.110; Perrenoud et al., 2002, pp.154ff.). Switzerland accounted for about one-sixth of these frozen assets and hence ranked as one of the largest creditor nations behind the United States and the United Kingdom (Raff, 1962, p.108). The situation deteriorated further after the national socialists under Adolf Hitler came to power in 1933 and quickly resorted, by means of a series of "patriotic" laws, to even stricter controls of cross-border transactions (Perrenoud et al., 2002, pp.173ff.). These increasingly extreme economic policies were enforced through draconian punishments, including imprisonment, and, after 1936, even the possibility of being sentenced to death for failing to declare foreign assets, or refusing to repatriate them through authorised German foreign-exchange banks (Perrenoud et al., 2002, pp.66ff., pp.78ff.). Unsurprisingly, this severe form of financial repression led to the

[9] For an overview of these developments, see Ehrsam (1985), Bänziger (1985, pp.54ff.), and Perrenoud et al. (2002, Ch.2–3).

closure of a large number of German bank accounts in Switzerland during the 1930s (Perrenoud et al., 2002, pp.66–81).

Frozen assets in Germany after July 1931 did not necessarily imply a total loss for the lender. Rather, negotiations were quickly opened with the affected banks to achieve a debt restructuring that resulted in the so-called Stillhalteabkommen, or Standstill Agreement, concluded in Basel in August 1931 (Zurlinden, 2003, p.91). Although initially only a six-month moratorium on the repayment of short-term loans was agreed upon, the standstill of payments was subsequently renewed on an annual basis, because Germany was clearly insolvent (Kindleberger, 1984, p.390; p.46). For Switzerland's banks, these early arrangements paved the way for collecting at least part of the interest on the outstanding short-term German loans (Perrenoud et al., 2002, pp.173ff.). However, throughout the 1930s, Germany moved further and further away from the freedom of capital movements to a system with rigid exchange controls organised around government-to-government payments based on bilateral clearing agreements as well as direct settlements against German exports (Kindleberger, 1984, pp.390–391; Feinstein et al., 1997, pp.161–163). Thanks to a high creditworthiness and non-negligible import power, Switzerland was able to reach an agreement with Germany to arrange these types of payments (Perrenoud et al., 2002, pp.177ff.). They enabled the Swiss banks, in turn, to liquidate substantial parts of their foreign loan portfolio (Perrenoud et al., 2002, pp.219ff.). However, the corresponding financial repatriations were complicated and typically occurred at a great loss. For example, payments based on the Standstill Agreement were usually made through a dedicated currency for cross-border transactions, the so-called Registermark, which traded at a large discount relative to the official German currency, the "Reichsmark" (Zurlinden, 2003, p.110).

On top of the difficulties caused by the German capital controls, the cascade of currency devaluations, especially those of sterling in 1931 and the US dollar in 1933, resulted in significant write-downs on the foreign asset portfolio of the Swiss banking sector (Baltensperger & Kugler, 2017, pp.81ff.). Furthermore, recurrent speculations about imminent devaluation by the gold-block countries, as well as political instability in countries, such as France, gave rise to volatile capital movements. For example, French capital flight increased dramatically after the government of the so-called Popular Front took office in 1936. This coalition of the radical, communist, and socialist parties under the leadership of Léon Blum endeavoured to implement a French New Deal. However, as a fiscal stimulus was incompatible with maintaining the established gold parties, it paved the way for the devaluation of the French franc and, soon thereafter, the Swiss franc in September 1936 (Feinstein et al., 1997, pp.159–160). This devaluation, and the collapse of the Blum government in 1937, reversed the capital flows. Although comprehensive statistics are unavailable to document this volatility, it is possible to focus on the example of Credit Suisse, where the amounts held by nonbank French customers increased from approximately 45 million Swiss francs in 1935 to 90 million Swiss francs in 1936, and dropped to approximately 60 million in 1939 (Perrenoud et al., 2002, p.94).

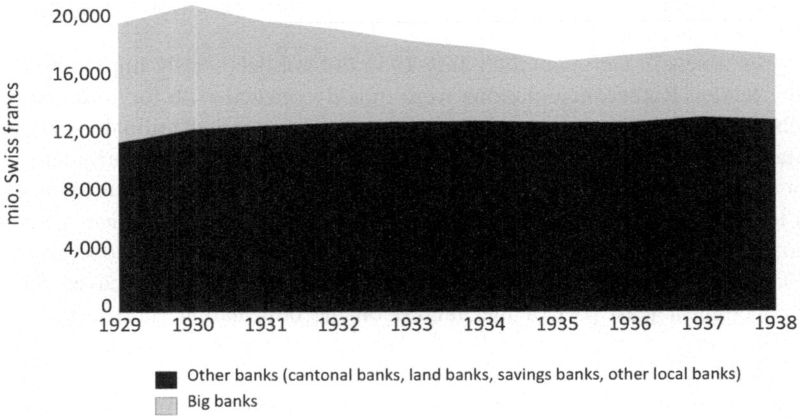

Fig. 6.3 Balance sheet total of the Swiss banking sector during 1930s (own figure. The data have an annual frequency. See Fig. 1.1b for the corresponding long-term overview and definition of the data. See also Zurlinden (2003, p.110))

The increasing financial disintegration in Europe and in other parts of the world undermined the internationalisation of Switzerland's banking system during the second part of the interwar years. As shown in Fig. 6.3, the aggregate balance sheet of all Swiss banks combined decreased, in nominal terms, from 21 billion Swiss francs in 1930, to 17 billion in 1935. Of course, these years were also characterised by a marked deflation of roughly 20 per cent (Zurlinden, 2003, p.98). These average price decreases imply that in real terms, the development of the aggregate balance sheet more or less stagnated during the 1930s, which nonetheless represented a structural break from the vigorous growth of the 1920s. When contemplating the structure of this balance sheet, it is perhaps not surprising to observe a flight towards safer and more liquid assets, especially reserves in the form of cash (Zurlinden, 2003, pp.109–110). In the case of Switzerland, this rearrangement reveals the widely observed collapse of the money-and-credit multiplier within the banking sector during the Great Depression.

The freezing of foreign assets, the associated losses, the capital outflows, and other challenges resulting from the difficult economic and political environment of the 1930s affected Switzerland's banks in a highly uneven manner. As mentioned above, by incurring losses worth millions, the big banks suffered heavily, especially when they had built up a sizable short-term loan portfolio in Germany, France, or Eastern Europe. Overall, they experienced a nominal reduction of their joint balance sheet by approximately one-half and saw a virtual collapse of their profits by two-thirds between 1930 and 1935 (Bänziger, 1985, p.57; Cassis, 2010, p.186). Given a contemporaneous deflation of roughly 20 per cent, even in real terms, these reductions were substantial. As shown in Fig. 6.3, the big players accounted essentially for the entire nominal reduction in the balance sheet of Switzerland's banks during the Great Depression.

At the individual level, as summarised by Table 6.2, five big banks had to be restructured during the 1930s. Only Credit Suisse and the Swiss Bank Corporation managed to stay afloat without additional support. Although there were no imminent doubts that their capital buffers could absorb the losses from the Great Depression, the associated financial problems were anything but negligible. For example, the Swiss Bank Corporation had to deal with a deposit decline from almost 1.2 billion Swiss francs in 1930, to 700 million in 1935. Short-term drafts and acceptances quickly fell from 205 million in 1929, to about 50 million in 1930 (Bauer & Blackman, 1998, pp.212–213). In a similar vein, for Credit Suisse, the dramatic deterioration of the economic and political situation in Germany warranted almost complete withdrawal from this market. Concretely, the assets held in Germany declined from almost 300 million Swiss francs in 1933 to approximately 60 million in 1939 and only 10 million at the end of World War II (Jung, 2000, pp.76–77). More often than not, it was possible to wind down these positions only at a substantial loss, which amounted to approximately 90 million Swiss francs for the German asset portfolio of Credit Suisse. In addition to suffering from heavy losses, the Union Bank had recourse to its shareholders (see Strehle et al., 1987, p.70–71). In particular, they agreed to a reduction of their equity stake by 40 million Swiss francs to stabilise the bank (see Table 6.2). Despite the severe financial problems, these three big banks weathered the financial instability of the Great Depression relatively well. In the longer term, this resilience provided the stepping stone for a spectacular rebound after World War II (see Chap. 7).

Conversely, for several big financial institutes, the Great Depression represented a massive setback, or even a fatal blow. In particular, both the "Eidgenössische Bank" and the "Basler Handelsbank" had no option but to approach their shareholders for a substantial equity capital reduction during the 1930s (see Table 6.2). These banks never fully recovered from this panicky restructuring and, after struggling for more than a decade, were finally taken over in 1945 (see Sect. 6.6). Moreover, to arrange a relatively large recapitalisation of 64 million Swiss francs, the "Bank Leu" had recourse to its shareholders and to its creditors (see again Table 6.2). Although it ultimately recovered from the Great Depression, this ancient bank in Zurich was unable to match the spectacular development of its local rivals during the second part of the twentieth century.

The Great Depression had particularly serious repercussions for Geneva's banking sector (Cassis, 2010, pp.186–187, Ehrsam, 1985, pp.93–97). At the beginning of the crisis in Europe during the summer of 1931, destabilising withdrawals and large losses on foreign assets triggered the closure of the "Banque de Genève", which had been established by the cantonal government in 1848, e.g., at the time when the so-called liberals under James Fazy had embarked on their financial modernisation programme (see Sect. 5.4). This background of a semipublic institute was probably one reason why the "Banque de Genève" fell prey to the crisis at an early stage, in 1931: entrenched political conflicts with the increasingly strong socialist opposition in Geneva prevented a bailout by the cantonal government (Bänziger, 1985, pp.57–58). During the following years, and in several waves, the instability was propagated through Geneva's financial system, and, above all, crippled the only big bank in

Table 6.2 Restructuring of the big banks during the 1930s (in mio. Swiss francs)

	From shareholders	Other	Total	Balance sheet 1930	Total as % of balance sheet	Comments
Credit Suisse	–	–	–	1785	0 %	No restructuring required.
Bank Corporation	–	–		1636	0 %	No restructuring required.
Union Bank	40	–	40	983	4 %	Equity capital reduction in two stages in 1933 in 1936 by a total amount of 40 mio.
Eidgenössi- sche Bank	33	–	33	854	4%	Equity capital reduction in two stages in 1933 and 1936 by a total amount of 33 mio. Loan by the federal government in 1935.
Basler Handelsbank	55	–	55	835	7%	Restructuring in several stages between 1933 and 1937, which led to a nominal share price reduction from 500 to 100 Swiss francs. Overall, equity capital was lowered by 55 mio.
Bank Leu	33	31	64	416	15%	Equity capital reduction of 13 mio. in 1932, and of 10 million in 1934. Request for a grace period under the Banking Act in 1935 followed by an equity capital reduction of 10 mio. and losses of 65 per cent imposed on creditors and depositors.
Comptioire (or Banque) d'Escompte	165	85	250	677	37%	Merger with the "Union Financière de Genève" and contribution of 30 mio. by other banks in 1931. After this merger, the bank is renamed to "Banque d'Escompte Suisse". Federal government aid and merger with "Banque de Dépôts et de Crédit" in 1933. Failure in 1934.
Volksbank	195	–	195	1680	12%	In 1933, loan from the federal government of 100 mio. followed by a reduction of the cooperative's capital by one-half in 1933 and by another half in 1937. 1936 liquidation of the entire foreign portfolio.

Notes: Adapted from Ehrsam (1985, p.90) and Zurlinden (2003, p.111). Comments based on Bauer (1987, p.168), Cassis (2010, p.187), Keller (1955, pp.234ff.), and Raff (1962, p.114; pp. pp.125ff.)

the French-speaking part of Switzerland, the "Comptoir d'Escompte" (see also Sect. 5.4). Its financial troubles originated mainly in large exposures to investments in Central and Eastern Europe, where capital controls and asset freezes were widely introduced after 1931. Despite a broad range of measures, including emergency liquidity support by the Swiss National Bank, an injection of private equity capital jointly arranged by the big banks, a series of mergers with other commercial banks in Geneva, and, last but not least, a bailout by the federal government in 1933, bankruptcy could not be avoided in the following year (Bänziger, 1985, pp.66–67). This bankruptcy essentially ended Geneva's long-held ambition to create a large, home-grown commercial bank.

A second bailout by the federal government during the 1930s involved the Swiss Volksbank, whose name of a "peoples bank" reflected its original purpose of providing financial services to the broad public. However, since the foundation as a cooperative in Bern in 1869, i.e., at the time of the "democratic movement" when hostility towards the industrial and financial empires of the business tycoons reached its climax (see Sect. 5.3), the "Volksbank" had itself become a big financial institute with supposedly lucrative foreign investments. Owing to vigorous domestic and international expansion during the 1920s, and with a balance sheet of 1.7 billion francs (see Table 6.2), the "Volksbank" even became the second-largest Swiss bank for a short period around 1930. Unsurprisingly, this overexpansion was a serious liability when the Great Depression broke out in Europe (Ehrsam, 1985, pp.97–101). In particular, despite two large reductions in cooperative capital, a bankruptcy could be avoided only through a bailout worth 100 million Swiss francs from the federal government in 1933 (Bänziger, 1985, pp.71–72). Thereafter, the "Volksbank" was no longer on equal terms with the big players. Several decades later, in 1993, it was finally taken over by one of them, Credit Suisse, after incurring another round of heavy losses from the Swiss real-estate crisis in the early 1990s (see Sect. 8.3).

Thanks to the relatively benign conditions within the Swiss economy, most domestically oriented banks managed to survive the Great Depression. Above all, the cantonal banks, which were the backbone of Switzerland's financial system at the time, typically did not suffer from dangerous levels of instability. Unsurprisingly, the few exceptions in this situation resulted from extraordinarily large interconnections with the international economy (Zurlinden, 2003, p.111; Ehrsam, 1985, pp.115–117). For example, the state guarantee had to be invoked by the cantonal bank in Neuchâtel, where the economic downturn hit the internationally oriented watchmaking industry particularly hard. Similar problems arose in Bern and Graubünden, which are important international tourist destinations. Moreover, between 1930 and 1938, only two of the hundreds of regional and savings banks failed, while approximately three dozen were liquidated (Ritzmann, 1973, pp.357–361). Overall, these recapitalisations, government bailouts, failures, and liquidations represented a severe crisis, but never propagated into a complete collapse of the financial system. Fortunately, no systemically important financial institute went bankrupt, as in, e.g., Austria and Germany. For this, and other, reasons, Switzerland managed to avoid the kind of economic and political chaos that beset these neighbouring countries during the Great Depression.

6.4 Federal Banking Act of 1934

Systemic financial crises tend to undermine trust in the market mechanism and are, therefore, often followed by an expansion of government regulation. The Great Depression was no exception to this tendency. Within the banking system, several regulatory instruments and numerous supervisory authorities indeed trace their origins back to the events of the 1930s. For example, in the United States, commercial and investment banking activities were separated under the Banking Act of 1933 (also known by the names of its main sponsors in the US Congress as the "Glass-Steagall Act"),[10] and the Federal Deposit Insurance Corporation (FDIC) was established in 1934 to protect the savers from financial losses resulting from bank failures.

The tendency of severe financial crises to open the door to new regulatory interventions also unfolded in Switzerland during the Great Depression. Although there had been several plans to introduce government supervision of the banking sector at the federal level before that time, especially during the turmoil of World War I, they had never been implemented (Bänziger, 1985, pp.28ff.). In this regard, the abovementioned public bailouts of the "Banque d'Escompte" and the "Volksbank" in 1933 acted as the necessary catalyst for reform, as it became impossible to explain to the broad public that bankers could draw on the financial support of the taxpayer without having to face consequences in terms of a tighter government oversight (Vogler, 2001, p.83; Vogler, 2006, pp.24ff.). Given this political climate, the "Federal Act on Banks and Savings Banks", or in short the "Banking Act" (Bankengesetz, Loi sur les banques), was adopted by Switzerland's parliament within an unusually short period of time in 1934 and entered into force at the beginning of the next year (Bänziger, 1985, pp.66ff.). The relevant sections of this law forced all Swiss banks to undergo regular audits by independent accounting agencies, established the supervisory Federal Banking Commission, introduced liquidity and capital requirements to protect creditors and depositors, and specified various procedures (deferral of debt repayments, a debt-restructuring moratorium, filing for bankruptcy) to deal with banks that had run into serious financial difficulties. These procedures were almost immediately put into practice, as between 1935 and 1938, 12 banks approached the newly established Federal Banking Commission to ask for a deferral of debt repayments, 46 requested a debt moratorium, and 8 filed for bankruptcy under the new law (Ehrsam, 1985, p.84; Zurlinden, 2003, p.111).

Compared with the regulatory reforms in other countries, the Swiss Banking Act was based on quite broadly defined principles, and the corresponding regulatory interventions and restrictions were generally more moderate than elsewhere (Cassis, 2010, p.190; Keller, 1955, pp.240ff.). For example, universal banking was not out-

[10] This policy of essentially prohibiting universal banking, i.e., combining the savings and loan business with the issuing, distribution, and subscription of shares and other financial instruments, was revoked in the United States during the 1990s.

lawed, and no compulsory deposit insurance scheme was introduced. However, one clause of this act later became very famous, both domestically and internationally: the codification of banking secrecy in Article 47.

6.5 Origins of Banking Secrecy—Myths and Reality

Article 47 of the Federal Banking Act of 1934 said:

> Whosoever, as an executive, official, or employee of a bank, as auditor or assistant to an auditor, as member of the Banking Commission, as official or employee of the Banking Commission's Secretariat intentionally discloses confidential information or infringes banking secrecy, induces or tries to induce others to do so, shall be punished by fine not exceeding twenty thousand francs or up to six months imprisonment (see Vogler, 2001, p.73).[11]

It is probably no exaggeration to say that this is the most notorious sentence in the history of Swiss banking. In plain words, Article 47 made the disclosure of financial information to domestic and foreign government authorities that are not conducting an official investigation, or to a private individual without the consent of the bank customer, a criminal offence. Since the introduction during the 1930s, this type of banking secrecy has been widely condemned (see e.g. Waller, 1972; Clarke & Tigue, 1975; Faith, 1982). Arguably, it severely obstructs the ability of fiscal authorities to combat money laundering and tax evasion. Moreover, these types of illegal activities are often thought to represent the main pillar of the international success of Switzerland's banks. Staunch critics even go so far as to claim that foreign bank accounts are almost per se dubious, as they are allegedly opened for no other reason than to hide money. Conversely, by means of attaching an overwhelming importance to financial privacy and data protection, banking secrecy has also been glorified as an indispensable safeguard against expropriation, above all the confiscation of assets by kleptomaniac dictatorships around the world. As a case in point, it has been claimed that Article 47 was introduced primarily to help members of the Jewish community rescue their financial assets from confiscation by the German Nazis (see, e.g., Büchenbacher, 1977, pp.77ff.; Vogler, 2001, pp.73–74; Guex, 2000, p.239). Of course, this glorification almost deliberately ignores potential abuses of

[11] In the latest edition of the Federal Banking Act, the corresponding section of Article 47 says:

> Whosoever intentionally does the following shall face imprisonment of up to five years or be fined accordingly:
>
> a. Disclose confidential information entrusted to that person in his or her capacity as a member of an executive body or supervisory authority, employee, representative, or liquidator of a bank [...] or as a body or employee of an audit company [...].
> b. Attempts to induce another person to infringe banking secrecy.
> c. Disclose confidential information to third parties or abuses this information to obtain personal benefits or benefits for others.

banking secrecy to cover up financial transactions associated with tax evasion, fraud, organised crime, and terrorism. However, the actual historical path leading to Article 47 is barely compatible with both the demonising and the glorifying narrative. Given the fierce debate during the decades after the 1930s, it is certainly astonishing to hear that the Federal Banking Act of 1934 was passed almost unopposed, and that Article 47 was more or less unanimously supported across the political spectrum at the time (Guex, 2000, pp.243ff.; Vogler, 2001, pp.82ff.; Vogler, 2006, pp.26ff.). The following paragraphs endeavour to shed light on why this consensus emerged.

The codification of banking secrecy into federal law occurred long after the leading Swiss banks were founded, and their gradual rise in international wealth management began somewhere between the eighteenth and early twentieth centuries (Vogler, 2001, p.73; Vogler, 2006, pp.11ff.). However, this absence of explicit rules with respect to the handling of financial information did not imply that the corresponding issues did not matter. Rather, according to an "unwritten law", bankers in Switzerland, and elsewhere, were generally expected to treat financial information obtained through accepting deposits or safeguarding assets as confidential (Tobler, 2019, p.36).[12] In principle, bank customers could bring infringements of this type of "professional secrecy" to court under civil law. Furthermore, some Swiss banks stipulated their own forms of confidentiality rules through internal guidelines (Guex, 2000, p.240; Vogler, 2006, p.13–14). At the time, confidentiality vis-à-vis the bank customer caused little concern, given that the size of the government, and hence the direct burden of taxation, was much smaller than it is today. For example, in Switzerland in 1900, the total taxes collected across the federal, cantonal, and municipal levels of government amounted to only about 5 per cent of national income.[13] Hence, low-tax governments had only scant incentives to gather all kinds of financial information.

The government expansion around the interwar period exacerbated the conflict between protecting and penetrating financial privacy. As mentioned earlier, World War I created mountains of public debt in many countries. Welfare programs, which were continued after the war to support the poor and the sick, as well as the payment of war reparations added to the fiscal burden in countries, such as Austria and Germany, during the 1920s. In summary, this dramatic expansion of the public sector sooner or later had to be matched by additional taxes (including inflation taxes). The Great Depression further aggravated this development through the additional debt resulting from bank bailouts, social benefits to support the unemployed masses, and the adoption of primitive fiscal-stimulus programmes.

As emphasised throughout this chapter, during the interwar years, Switzerland found itself in a relatively benign situation by inheriting a manageable public debt increase from World War I. Accordingly, the tax burden "only" doubled from

[12] Until today, this type of professional conduct is expected from medical doctors, lawyers, or priests

[13] These figures are taken from the Historical Statistics of Switzerland (www.hsso.ch) Table U.15 and Table Q.1.a. and Mitchell (1992, pp. 825, 896).

roughly 5 per cent before the war to 10 per cent thereafter, compared with an increase by factor three observed in some belligerent countries (Farquet, 2012, p.37). Hence, it was unnecessary to resort to a pervasive inflation tax, let alone to run the risk of destroying the currency through hyperinflation, as in Austria and Germany. Quite the opposite happened, as the Swiss franc belonged to only a handful of currencies that returned to the Gold Standard at prewar parities during the 1920s. Over the next decade, Switzerland's domestic sector also proved to be remarkably resilient to the economic shocks of the Great Depression, and the Swiss franc was devalued only in 1936, one of the last major currencies to succumb (see Sect. 6.3). Taken together, the relatively lowtax burden, the stable currency system, and the attractive fiscal environment acted as a magnet for foreign capital. The corresponding inflows of all kinds of assets from abroad during the first part of the interwar years, in turn, provided the basis for a marked internationalisation of Switzerland's banks. Due to the entrenched political problems of the Weimar Republic, Germany was particularly exposed to this type of capital flight. After the national socialists seized power in 1933, the widespread oppression of political opponents, including members of the communist party and the Jewish community, added a dimension of evil to this phenomenon. At about the same time, the fiscal situation in France also deteriorated markedly as successive governments struggled with large budget deficits (see, e.g., Feinstein et al., 1997, pp.84ff.; pp.157ff.). Against this background, capital flight became a major problem in both France and Germany during the 1930s, regardless of whether the underlying motives are deemed immoral, such as evading democratically imposed taxes to address an economic crisis, or respectable, such as depriving a rogue regime of the possibility of confiscating property.

With the transformation of Switzerland into a financial safe haven, capital flight became a source of recurrent tensions and political conflicts with neighbouring countries. As early as World War I, the belligerent countries did not hesitate to resort to methods, such as bribing Swiss bankers or turning to foreign espionage to gather valuable information on financial transactions in Switzerland designed to avoid high war taxes at home (Vogler, 2001, pp.81ff.). These methods partially continued after 1918 and were used by, e.g., France to estimate the amount of German assets held in Switzerland and in the Netherlands. This type of information was quite useful in reinforcing the demand for high war reparations (Vogler, 2006, p.19). With the increasing economic problems during the Great Depression, it was again in France, but also in (Weimar and Nazi) Germany, that government authorities turned to heavy-handed methods to enforce capital controls, combat tax evasion, and confiscate property from political opponents. Although it is inherently difficult to determine the true extent of these clandestine activities, several cases of bank espionage by foreign agents were documented in Switzerland during the 1930s. A spectacular case was the so-called Paris affair, which started with a raid on the offices of the Basler Handelsbank by the French authorities in 1932 (Guex, 2000, pp.249ff.). This raid uncovered undeclared assets held in Switzerland by prominent French politicians, entrepreneurs, senior clerics, and generals. Subsequently, the French government announced that this type of fiscal fraud would be suppressed by "by all means available to a government" (Guex, 2000, p.250). These means included not only the bringing of charges against several Swiss banks and the freezing of their assets held in France, but also the extraordinary request that the accounts of the Handelsbank in Basel be examined by French officials. When two members of the board of administration of the Handelsbank, who had been summoned to Paris by the French authorities, refused to comply with this request, they were immediately arrested. During the "Paris affair", the Swiss government was alerted to several cases of suspected bank espionage by agents of the French government in Switzerland. In a similar vein, during the 1930s, a series of cases of German bank espionage in Switzerland was revealed. For example, in 1931, a German agent, who had approached Union Bank employees to hand over information on accounts of German clients, was caught and expelled from the country (Vogler, 2006, p.19). A year later, the revelation that an employee of the Cantonal Bank of Zurich had accepted bribes to pass information about hundreds of depositors to the German tax authorities hit the headlines (Perrenoud et al., 2002, pp.106ff.). After the transformation of Germany into a notorious dictatorship, indiscretions, such as that of a Credit Suisse employee after 1941, could have terrible consequences, as the fiscal crime of holding undeclared foreign assets could lead to imprisonment, or even to the death sentence (Jung, 2000, p.83; Perrenoud et al., 2002, pp.122ff.; Vogler, 2001, p.81–82).

Given these blatant violations of Swiss sovereignty, making foreign bank espionage a criminal offence became politically very popular during the 1930s (Bänziger, 1985, pp.74–76). Hence, Article 47, which actually added this offence to the Federal Banking Act, was not the subject of major debates in parliament, and the new banking legislation was unanimously supported in the chamber representing the cantons (i.e., the Council of States), and by 119 votes to 1 vote in the second chamber (i.e., the Council of Nation). Perhaps, the support of the social democrats is somewhat surprising, as around a decade earlier, they had launched a popular initiative calling for the exact opposite, namely, the introduction of a wealth tax and, to enforce it, far-reaching obligations to disclose financial information to the fiscal authorities. However, this so-called wealth-tax initiative had been rejected by almost 90 per cent of voters in 1922 (Guex, 2013). In addition to remembering this crushing political defeat, it was perhaps the aggressive steps taken against the labour movement in Germany that helped to change minds on the political left during the 1930s (Guex, 2000, pp.254–255; Vogler, 2001, p.84). According to an anecdote told by a leading figure of the Swiss communist movement at the time, Walter Bringolf (1895–1981), the German trade unions, which were broken up in 1933, indeed managed to rescue some of their financial assets by moving them across the border into Switzerland (Vogler, 2006, p.28). Insofar as the political left would later become a staunch critic of the lack of financial transparency and half-hearted combat against fiscal fraud around the world, it is perhaps ironic that German trade unions, together with the Jewish community, were among the first beneficiaries of Switzerland's banking secrecy laws.

Taken together, the introduction of Swiss banking secrecy was a byproduct of the regulatory reforms caused by the financial, economic, and political upheavals of the 1930s. However, the broad consensus on Article 47 was later replaced by intense domestic debates and international criticism. Further to these controversies, the myths that banking secrecy was introduced for humanitarian reasons or as a disgraceful policy to help foreigners evade taxes were born. Unfortunately, these myths have often prevented a sensible debate on how financial information should be shared among commercial banks, their customers, and the government. For example, similar to data protection issues in other areas, there is a question regarding what procedures and limits should be imposed on a public authority's efforts to obtain access to personal information in banking and finance. Are there legitimate reasons for tax evasion when, say, a state turns to confiscatory levels of taxation or authorities routinely twist their own tax laws? Should governments be allowed to turn to bribery, or even "to all means available", to fight money laundering and fiscal fraud? Are these means effective, or do they merely set a bad example and, hence, undermine the public's trust in the government? Is it possible to give financial asylum to protect assets from confiscation, in similar way as to give political asylum to persons oppressed by totalitarian governments? These, and other, questions about banking secrecy became strongly pertinent for Switzerland during the decades after 1945. However, until that year, these issues lay largely dormant, as World War II severely curtailed the international activities of banks.

6.6 World War II: Gold Transactions and Dormant Accounts

With the outbreak of World War II in 1939, Switzerland was again confronted with challenges similar to those of 1914. In addition to the military clashes between the Axis Powers—led by Germany, Italy, and Japan—and the Allies—including Britain, France, the Soviet Union, and the United States—the second global conflict during the twentieth century was also fought with the means of economic warfare. Hence, the exchange of goods and assets became more or less separated between the spheres of influence of the Axis and the Allied camps (Cassis, 2010, pp.193ff.). Neutral countries, such as Switzerland, had to find a way to navigate between these camps.

In both the belligerent and neutral countries, goods rationing, price controls, and government planning of domestic production and international trade became commonplace. Within the financial system, public and private banks were typically tasked with mobilising savings for the government and ensuring that the necessary amounts of foreign currency and gold reserves were available to pay for vital imports. Capital controls, which had already been put in place in Germany during the 1930s, became so widespread during the war that international financial transactions could often be made only through central banks. For example, the Swiss National Bank became heavily involved in cross-border payments, and the corresponding foreign trade was largely managed by the so-called Office Suisse de Compensation (Perrenoud et al., 2002, p.183). The commercial banks, whose international business had expanded during the interwar period, suffered obviously from these restrictions, economic disruptions, and state interventions. In

Switzerland, it was above all the private and the big banks that faced a very difficult environment with a further decline in business and profits from the already meagre levels of the 1930s.

Switzerland was very fortunate to be one of only a handful of European countries that had escaped the destruction and horrors of direct involvement in World War II (see Sect. 2.3). Apart from luck, the economic preparations for the outbreak of a major international conflict were much better in 1939 than in 1914. In particular, the opening of hostilities with Germany's invasion of Poland in September 1939 neither came as a surprise nor triggered a domestic liquidity crisis or bank runs. To some extent, this relatively calm reaction of the banking sector reflected that large parts of international trade and the corresponding cross-border payments had already been paralysed by the economic and political instability of the 1930s. However, there were also lessons that had been learned from the experiences of World War I, such as avoiding the monetisation of war expenditures and, hence, the social conflicts that could result from rampant levels of inflation (Baltensperger & Kugler, 2017, p.88). Rather, the massive increase in government expenditure between 1939 and 1945 amounting to approximately 12 billion Swiss francs—of which 8 billion were spent on national defence—was covered, in more or less equal parts, through additional taxes and public borrowing (Bauer & Blackman, 1998, pp.224–225).

The changing war fortunes nevertheless posed a formidable challenge to a neutral and landlocked country in the centre of Europe. Above all, after the surprisingly rapid defeat of France in May and June of 1940, the situation within Switzerland became quite precarious. For more than four years, the country was surrounded by Nazi Germany, its puppet regime of Vichy France, and Fascist Italy. The fates of, e.g., the Netherlands and Belgium, which were annexed during the military campaign against France, revealed that Adolf Hitler would not respect the neutral status of countries that stood in his way. Trade was, henceforth, possible only through territories and ports controlled by the Axis Powers. In addition to this isolation, in June 1940, the United States froze all dollar assets from countries on the European continent (Jöhr, 1956, p.53; Bauer & Blackman, 1998, p.225). This blockage seriously limited the ability of Swiss banks to make dollar payments. Overall, for Switzerland, the political, logistical, and financial challenges of securing the supply of vital foreign goods were probably more severe during World War II than during World War I.

Nevertheless, the import and export of goods continued, although at a lower level than before the war. However, as mentioned above, the corresponding payments were now typically settled not through private channels, but rather on the basis of bilateral clearing agreements between the Swiss National Bank, the German Reichsbank, and other central banks. Furthermore, gold began to fulfil its function as an ultimate means of payment in times of an international emergency. Because Switzerland had a trade surplus with Germany, and during the first part of the war also with the Allies, this type of wartime financial system inevitably gave rise to gold inflows, which essentially reflected the high foreign demand for Swiss francs (Baltensperger & Kugler, 2017, pp.88ff.). In summary, between 1939 and 1945, gold inflows worth approximately 1.5 billion Swiss francs were recorded from both

Germany and the United States, and approximately 700 million from the United Kingdom (Baltensperger & Kugler, 2017, pp.91–92). Although these amounts were modest when compared with, e.g., the financial transfers under the US "lend-lease" programme, which was worth approximately 50 billion US dollars between 1941 and 1945 (equivalent to more than 200 billion Swiss francs), the transactions with the German Reichsbank were controversial both during the war and thereafter (Bordo & James, 2007, pp.76ff.; Kindleberger, 1984, pp.424–427). In particular, at an early stage, the Swiss National Bank was apparently aware that the corresponding gold could have been confiscated from central banks, or even stolen from private persons in occupied countries (Baltensperger & Kugler, 2017, pp.91). Conversely, owing to the limited role in international payments, Switzerland's commercial banks were much less exposed to this type of transaction. For example, the Swiss Bank Corporation recorded a gold inflow in the range of 150 million francs between 1939 and 1945, while Credit Suisse recorded only 7 million francs (Jung, 2000, p.86).

The encirclement of Switzerland by the Axis Powers naturally had detrimental effects on the commercial banking sector. Above all, the suspension of free trade and cross-border payments, the freezing of foreign assets, and severe disruptions in international travel and communication brought the offshore wealth-management business almost to a standstill (Jung, 2000, pp.77ff.; Cassis, 2010, p.198). Often, international payments could simply not be made, and tasks that were routine in peacetime, such as communicating with a foreign customer by mail, became difficult or even impossible to fulfil. After 1940, only a handful of international business relationships, especially with German banks and companies, remained open. For example, Credit Suisse was able to maintain some commercial links with the Deutsche Bank, and the Swiss Bank Corporation with the Dresdner Bank (Cassis, 2010, p.198). At the domestic level, the big banks and cantonal banks were tasked with raising money for the government. Therefore, they quickly turned into the main creditors of the Swiss government by holding large portfolios of the so-called federal bonds (Bundesanleihen; obligations fédérales), which were issued to finance the wartime expenditures. Compared with the returns of foreign investments before the war, the return on these bonds was relatively low. Consequently, profits within the commercial banking sector declined (Raff, 1962, p.120).

In addition to the aforementioned gold transactions, the extraordinarily unstable international environment of the 1930s and 1940s left other delicate historical legacies for the Swiss banking sector, including cases of bank espionage and outright blackmail to force German citizens to repatriate assets on foreign bank accounts, stolen property that ended up in bank safes, and accounts held by members of the German National Socialist Workers Party (see, e.g., Jung, 2000, pp.81–87).[14] However, the handling of dormant accounts of the numerous victims of the conflict,

[14] Despite recurrent claims to the contrary, there is little evidence that leading German Nazis were able to move large amounts of money to Swiss banks before the collapse of Hitler's regime (Vogler, 2006, p.62). The wartime restrictions on cross-border payments and international travel as well as the tight surveillance of the German police state likely left only scant possibilities of making such transfers (see also Jung, 2000, pp.84–85).

especially of the holocaust, became the most notorious issue (Perrenoud et al., 2002).

In general, it can be quite difficult to trace foreign bank customers, when contacts with them have been interrupted for years or even decades. Concerning offshore deposits in Swiss bank accounts before and during World War II, these difficulties were obviously aggravated by the chaos at the time. As mentioned above, the international exchange of information became very patchy. Furthermore, widespread deportations, atrocities, and all kinds of violence implied that a large number of bank-account owners unfortunately did not survive the war. Their financial claims should, of course, have been inherited by the surviving descendants. However, given the turmoil, documents for the corresponding accounts often no longer existed (Perrenoud et al., 2002, p.17). Last but not least, it was not uncommon for bank accounts of holocaust victims to be identified only through a specific number to restrict information on the depositor's identity to a small circle of trusted bank employees (Roethenmund, 1980, p.56). Although Swiss banks are neither the inventor nor the exclusive provider of the "numbered account", they began to popularise them during the 1930s to address the problems with foreign espionage mentioned earlier (Vogler, 2006, pp.55–56).[15] Obviously, the resulting anonymity provided an additional safeguard against the risk of indiscretions and denunciations and, hence, a better protection of financial privacy. On the downside, numbered accounts complicated the search for the legal owner or the identification of claims on dormant accounts by their rightful heirs.

During World War II, Switzerland's banks, by and large, fulfilled their primary task of diligently safeguarding their (domestic and foreign) clients' assets. However, it was mainly the behaviour after 1945 that became a target of recurrent criticism (see Sects. 7.1 and 8.4). As a result of several intensive debates during the second part of the twentieth century, the criticism that dormant accounts dating back to World War II were not dealt with in an adequate manner is now commonly accepted. In particular, various Swiss banks differed in their efforts to trace the owners of these accounts (ICEP, 1999, p.11). While some private banks initiated active searches for surviving clients or their heirs, others, especially the big banks, lacked the due diligence to do so. For example, at Credit Suisse, the search for assets belonging to potential holocaust victims was long treated as a routine matter, rather than a problem that could not be dealt with via normal procedures and internal guidelines (Jung, 2000, p.79). Switzerland also failed to adopt a law about the handling of dormant accounts until the beginning of the twenty-first century (Perrenoud et al., 2002, p.199). Hence, the banks were more or less left alone to find a way to address

[15] Before World War II, numbered accounts existed also in, e.g., Italy. In Austria, they are quite common to the present day. It may well be worthwhile to address several popular misconceptions about numbered accounts. In particular, they cannot offer complete anonymity, because somebody within the bank must have access to information on the identity of the depositor to, e.g., authorise withdrawals. Furthermore, in Switzerland, numbered accounts, and the assets deposited in them, neither are especially protected by banking secrecy nor receive privileged treatment under the banking law (see, e.g., Büchenbacher, 1977, pp.91–92; Vogler, 2006, p.55).

these delicate questions. In many cases, the usual paperwork for providing access to dormant accounts was requested. Although these requests can be necessary to prevent fraud, they failed to account for the extraordinary circumstances of dormant accounts dating back to World War II (ICEP, 1999, p.21).

Nevertheless, there is no evidence of systematically careless dealings with dormant accounts (ICEP, 1999, pp.19ff.). In a similar vein, the recurrent claims about dozens of billions in holocaust money lingering on Swiss bank accounts far exceed the amounts that have actually been uncovered. Early, selective, and informal searches during the 1940s and 1950s identified less than 1 million Swiss francs in accounts potentially belonging to holocaust victims (ICEP, 1999, pp.89–90). The so-called Meldebeschluss (or "reporting decision") that was passed in 1962 to initiate a systematic search for dormant accounts from before 1945 uncovered about 6 million Swiss francs in more than 700 accounts (ICEP, 1999, pp.91–92). To date, the most comprehensive search for dormant accounts, covering the entire period between 1933 and 1945, was conducted in 1997 following a reopening of the debate about the role of Switzerland during World War II (see Sect. 8.4). The corresponding investigations in that year found approximately 5500 dormant accounts held by foreign owners with unclaimed amounts worth slightly less than 75 million Swiss francs (ICEP, 1999, pp.92–97). To put these numbers into perspective, during the period under investigation, there were roughly 7 million Swiss bank accounts, of which more than 50,000 were identified as offshore accounts (ICEP, 1999, pp.58, 70). Moreover, as shown in Tables C.1 and C.2 of the appendix, the combined balance sheet of all Swiss banks amounted to slightly less than 20 billion Swiss francs during the 1930s and early 1940s, and more than 1700 billion Swiss francs in 1997.

References

Auer, R. A. (2015). *A safe haven: International demand for Swiss francs during the euro area debt crisis*. Zurich: SNB Quarterly Bulletin 2/2015.

Baltensperger, E. (2012). *Der Schweizer Franken - Eine Erfolgsgeschichte*. Zürich: NZZ Libro.

Baltensperger, E., & Kugler, P. (2016). The historical origin of the safe haven status of the Swiss franc. *Aussenwirtschaft, 67*, 1–30.

Baltensperger, E., & Kugler, P. (2017). *Swiss monetary history since the early nineteenth century*. Cambridge: Cambridge University Press.

Bänziger, H. (1985). Vom Sparerschutz zum Gläubigerschutz—die Entstehung des Bankengesetzes im Jahre 1934. In *50 Jahre eidgenössische Bankenaufsicht*. Zürich: Schulthess.

Bauer, H. (1987). Bank- und Finanzplatz Basel. In Mottet, L.H. (Ed.), *Geschichte der Schweizer Banken*. Zurich: Verlag Neue Zürcher Zeitung.

Bauer, H., & Blackman, W. J. (1998). *Swiss banking—An analytical history*. Basingstoke: Macmillan Press.

Bemanke, B., & James, H. (1991). The gold standard, deflation, and financial crisis in the great depression: an international comparison. In *National Bureau of Economic Research (ED.)*, Financial Markets and Financial Crises, pp 33–68.

Bordo, M., & James, H. (2007). From 1907 to 1946: Happy childhood or troubled adolescence? In SNB (Ed.), *The Swiss National Bank 1907–2007*. Zurich: NZZ Libro.

Büchenbacher, C. (1977). *Tatsachen über das schweizerische Bankgeheimnis*. Zurich: Nova Press.
Cassis, Y. (2010). *Capital of capital. The rise and fall of international financial centres 1780–2009*. Cambridge: Cambridge University Press.
Choudhri, E., & Kochin, L. (1980). The exchange rate and the international transmission of business cycles: Some evidence from the Great Depression. *Journal of Money, Credit, and Banking, 12*, 565–574.
Clarke, T., & Tigue, J. J. (1975). *Dirty money: Swiss banks, the mafia, money laundering, and white collar crime*. London: Simon and Schuster.
Ehrsam, P. (1985). Die Bankenkrise der 30er in der Schweiz. In Eidgenössische Bankenkommission (Ed.), *50 Jahre eidgenössische Bankenaufsicht*. Zürich: Schulthess.
Eichengreen, B. (2008). *Globalizing capital: A history of the international monetary system*. New Jersey: Princeton University Press.
Eichengreen, B., & Sachs, J. (1986). Competitive devaluation and the Great Depression: A theoretical reassessment. *Economics Letters, 22*, 67–71.
Faith, N. (1982). *Safety in numbers: The mysterious world of Swiss banking*. London: Hamish Hamilton.
Farquet, C. (2012). The rise of the Swiss tax haven in the interwar period: An international comparison. In *EHES Working Paper in Economic History No. 27*.
Feinstein, C. H., Temin, P., & Toniolo, G. (1997). *The European economy between the wars*. Oxford: Oxford University Press.
Fior, M. (2002). Le rôle de l'Entre-deux guerres dans le dévelopement de la place financière suisse. In *Contributions à l'histoire de la finance Cahier No.3*. Association pour l'Histoire de la Finance Suisse et Principauté Lichtenstein.
Friedman, M., & Schwarz, A. (1963). *A monetary history of the United States, 1867–1960*. Princeton: Princeton University Press.
Guex, S. (2000). The origins of the Swiss banking secrecy law and its repercussions for Swiss federal policy. *Business History Review, 74*, 237–266.
Guex, S. (2013). Conflicts and bargaining about banking secrecy in Switzerland in the aftermath of the first world war. *L'Année Sociologique, 63*, 157–187.
Hauzenberger, N., Huber, F., Kaufmann, D., Stuart, R., & Tille, C. (2021). Interest rates in Switzerland 1852–2020. In *Grundlagen für die Wirtschaftspolitik Nr. 24*. Bern: State Secretariat for Economic Affairs SECO.
Hayek, F. A. (1931). *Prices and production*. London: Routledge.
Herger, N. (2019). *Understanding central banks*. Cham: Springer Nature.
ICEP (1999). Report on dormant accounts of Nazi Prosecution in Swiss banks. Geneva.
Jöhr, A. (1956). *Schweizerische Kreditanstalt 1856–1956*. Zurich: Conzett and Huber.
Jung, J. (2000). *Von der Schweizerischen Kreditanstalt zur Credit Suisse Group. Eine Bankengeschichte*. Zurich: NZZ Verlag.
Keller, T. (1955). *Leu & Co*. Zürich: Denkschrift zum zweihundertjährigen Bestehen der Aktiengesellschaft Leu & Co.
Keynes, J. M. (1936). *The general theory of employment, interest and money*. London: Macmillan.
Kindleberger, C. P. (1973). *The world in depression 1929–1939*. Berkeley: University of California Press.
Kindleberger, C. P. (1984). *A financial history of Western Europe*. London: Routledge.
Kugler, P, & Weder, B. (2002). The puzzle of the Swiss interest rate island: Stylized facts and a new interpretation. *Aussenwirtschaft, 53*, 49–63.
Liaquat, A. (2009). *Lords of finance*. London: Penguin Books.
Mitchell, B.R. (1992). *International historical statistics. Europe 1750–1988*. New York: Stockton Press.
Obstfeld, M., & Taylor, A. (2004). *Global capital markets integration, crisis, and growth*. Cambridge: Cambridge University Press.
Perrenoud, M., Lopez, R., Adank, F., Baumann, J., Cortat, A., & Perers, S. (2002). La place financerère et les banques suisses à l'époque du national-socialisme. In *Publication de la Commission Indépandante d'Experts Suisse-Seconde Guerre Mondiale*. Zurich: Chronos.

Raff, H. (1962). *Schweizerische Bankgesellschaft 1862 - 1912 - 1962*. Zurich: Orell Füssli.

Ranaldo, A., & Söderlind, P. (2010). Safe haven currencies. *Review of Finance, 10*, 385–407.

Reinhart, C., & Rogoff, K. (2009). *This time is different—eight centuries of financial folly*. Princeton: Princeton University Press.

Ritzmann, F. (1973). *Die Schweizer Banken. Geschichte - Theorie - Statistik*. Bern: Verlag Paul Haupt.

Roethenmund, R. (1980). The Swiss banking handbook. In *A complete manual for practical investors*. New York: Books in Focus.

Schaltegger, C. A., & Schmid, L. A. (2021). Public perceptions and bond markets during the Great War: the case of a neutral country. *Public Choice, 186*, 537–561.

Strehle, R., Trepp, G., & Weyermann, B. (1987). *Ganz oben - 125 Jahre Schweizerische Bankgesellschaft*. Zurich: Limmat Verlag.

Tobler, S. (2019). *Der Kampf um das Schweizer Bankgeheimnis. Eine 100-jährige Geschichte von Kritik und Verteidigung*. Zurich: NZZ Libro.

Toniolo, G. (2007). *Central bank cooperation at the bank for international settlements, 1930–1973*. Cambridge: Cambridge University Press.

Vogler, R. U. (2001). The genesis of Swiss banking secrecy: Political and economic environment. *Financial History Review, 8*, 73–84.

Vogler, R. U. (2006). *Swiss banking secrecy: Origins, significance, myth. contributions to financial history* (Vol. 7). Zurich: Association for Financial History.

Waller, L. (1972). *The Swiss bank connection*. New York: Signet.

Zurlinden, M. (2003). *Gold standard, deflation and depression: The Swiss economy during the Great Depression*. Zurich: SNB Quarterly Bulletin 2/2003.

Chapter 7
The Golden Age (1946–1970s)

7.1 Washington Agreement as a Turning Point

Owing to the pervasive instability, if not chaos, the years between the beginning of the Great Depression in 1929 and the end of World War II in 1945 represented a severe setback in the development of the international financial system, including the banking sector (Obstfeld & Taylor, 2004, pp.97ff.). Against this background, it seems inappropriate to claim that the Swiss banks "did well out of the war" (Faith, 1982, pp.100ff.). Actually, they suffered, as did other financial firms around the world, from the entrenched economic instability, the massive government interventions and restrictions, and the heavy losses caused by the war. Above all, Switzerland's banks were heavily impacted by the freezing of foreign assets, the severe impediments to international wealth management, and the losses on assets held in Germany before 1945 and in Eastern Europe during the rise of communism thereafter. For the "Basler Handelsbank" and the "Eidgenössische Bank", which had long featured among the leading financial firms of the country, the corresponding losses became unbearable. By 1945, these banks were critically weakened and, as a result, destined for being taken over by the Swiss Bank Corporation and the Union Bank, respectively.

As a neutral country that had clung to political and economic connections with the surrounding Axis Powers until almost the end of World War II, Switzerland found itself isolated after 1945 (Frei, 1969, pp.580ff.; Baltensperger & Kugler, 2017, p.97). In particular, its diplomatic relationships with the postwar French government, which disapproved of countries that had made common cause with the Vichy regime, became quite tense. In a similar vein, the United States government reckoned at the time that neutral countries had unjustly benefitted from the war. Reflecting these views, approximately five billion francs' worth of Swiss assets in the United States were not unfrozen in 1945 (Frei, 1969, pp.577, 587). For Switzerland's banks, this blockage implied that trade and payments on the basis of

N. Herger, *Switzerland and its Banks*, Frontiers in Economic History,
https://doi.org/10.1007/978-3-031-35904-0_7

the US dollar standard, which had begun to dominate the world, remained heavily restricted.

The abovementioned questions about the legitimate origin of the gold acquired by the Swiss National Bank from the German Reichsbank became a major source of the diplomatic conflict with the Allies (Bordo & James, 2007, p.90; Baltensperger & Kugler, 2017, p.97). Moreover, they insisted on gaining access to the foreign assets of German citizens, including their deposits in offshore bank accounts, to pay for the postwar reconstruction of Europe (Frei, 1969, pp.576ff.). By doing so, the Allies were reacting to the situation following the Peace Treaty of Versailles when private offshore wealth had provided Germany with a source for rebuilding capabilities in strategically important industries (Frei, 1969, p.572). Hence, after World War II, pressure was exerted on Switzerland to hand over control over these types of assets.

Because Switzerland could ill afford an economic conflict with the victorious Allies, a series of negotiations was opened to restore normal relationships in international trade and payments with countries in Europe as well as with the United States. Of outstanding importance was the so-called Washington Agreement, which was signed in May 1946. After several rounds of intense negotiations, the Swiss delegation in Washington agreed to hand over 250 million Swiss francs, including a contribution of 100 million by the Swiss National Bank, to the Allies as compensation for accepting gold that had probably been stolen by Germany during World War II (SNB, 2007, p.90, pp.133–134; Baltensperger & Kugler, 2017, pp.91–92). Furthermore, it was agreed to liquidate the frozen assets of German citizens living in their native country and to transfer the corresponding revenue—totaling approximately 400 million francs—to the Allied Control Council for the reconstruction of Europe (Frei, 1969, p.599; Bauer & Blackman, 1998, p.241).[1]

For Switzerland's banking sector, the conclusion of the Washington Agreement marked a turning point. The following slow, but steady, transition to an international economic and financial order characterised by increasingly free trade and payments ended two decades of stagnation and decline and opened the door to what was later called the "golden age" (Cassis, 2010, p.232). During the early phase of this transition, deblockage of Switzerland's dollar assets after the conclusion of the Washington Agreement was a stepping stone to the expansion of international banking (Bauer & Blackman, 1998, p.241; Cassis, 2010, pp.218–219). At the same time, Switzerland's political isolation ended rather abruptly with the beginning of the Cold War between the free Western world led by the United States and the Eastern hemisphere controlled by the Soviet Union (Frei, 1969, pp.608ff.). Quite suddenly, a stable democracy with a market-based economy, an intact political

[1] Of note, the dormant accounts that became a notorious legacy of World War II during the second part of the twentieth century were no more than a side issue during the Washington negotiations. In particular, the Allies merely asked the Swiss delegation to look into the matter and, if the rightful owner of a dormant account was no longer alive, to transfer the corresponding money as financial aid to the governments of France, Great Britain, and the United States (Perrenoud et al., 2002, pp.239–241). Moreover, a bilateral agreement dealing with the legacy of dormant accounts was, e.g., concluded with Poland in 1949 (Perrenoud et al., 2002, pp.244ff.).

system, and a healthy financial sector became a much-appreciated partner in the reconstruction of Western Europe. For Switzerland's banks, the postwar boom at home as well as in neighbouring countries, together with the regained freedom to manage foreign assets and to issue loans across the Western hemisphere, provided the basis for several decades of spectacular growth.

7.2 Glorious Years and Growth Miracle in Swiss Banking

The years after 1945 are known in France as "les trentes glorieuses" (the glorious thirty), and (Western) Germany refers to them as the period of the "Wirtschaftswunder" (economic miracle). Despite worries reflecting the bitter experiences after World War I that the transition to a peacetime economy would yet again be accompanied by pervasive levels of instability, high unemployment, and rampant inflation, the liberalisations after 1945 actually gave rise to a long-lasting boom in Western Europe. For example, between 1950 and 1973, Germany grew on average at a real per-capita rate of roughly 5 per cent and France at roughly 4 per cent (Cassis, 2010, p.200). Owing to this vigorous economic growth, incomes recovered rapidly and soon surpassed the depressed levels of the 1930s. The establishment of a European customs union between Belgium, France, Germany, Italy, Luxembourg, and the Netherlands in 1957, and the return to freely convertible currencies in many parts of Western Europe in 1958 were further signs of this success story.

Thanks to the virtually undamaged road and railway network, intact factories, and other readily available physical infrastructure, Switzerland enjoyed an early lead over the neighbouring countries, which also limited the duration of the postwar boom driven by the reconstruction of the domestic economy. Reflecting these conditions, real growth per capita was "only" about 3 per cent between 1950 and 1973.[2] Conversely, these years were characterised by a staggering boom within the Swiss banking sector, whose combined balance sheet expanded from approximately 130 per cent of GDP at the beginning of the 1950s to more than 200 per cent at the beginning of the 1970s (see Fig. 7.1a). Reflecting the limited size of the domestic market, this expansion resulted first and foremost from the burgeoning growth of offshore business. Remarkably, during this "golden age", the worldwide importance of Zurich and Geneva as financial and banking centres lagged perhaps only behind that of New York and London (Cassis, 2010, pp.232ff.). During the 1950s, Zurich turned even briefly into the second-largest market for issuing foreign loans (Cassis, 2010, p.218). Other increasingly important activities included foreign-bond issuing, gold and commodity trading, and foreign-exchange transactions. Given the pivotal role of the commercial banks within Switzerland's financial system,

[2] This growth rate has been calculated from the data of the "Historical Statistics of Switzerland" (www.hsso.ch).

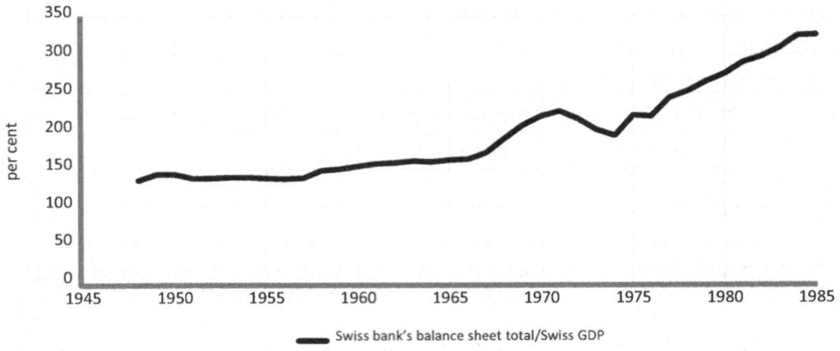

(a) Total balance sheet of Swiss banks in per cent of Swiss GDP

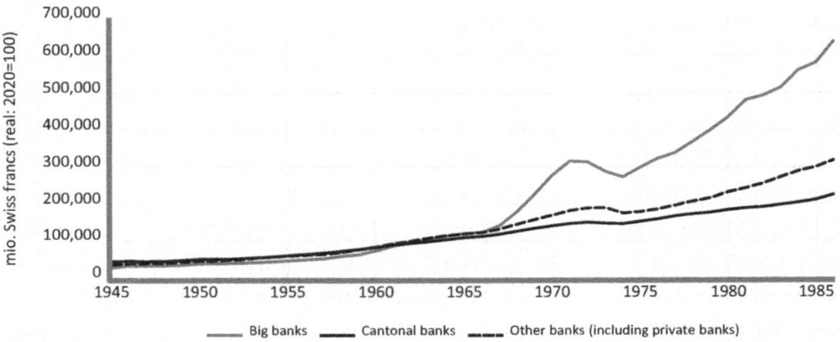

(b) Balance sheet of various types of Swiss banks in real values (1945 to 1985)

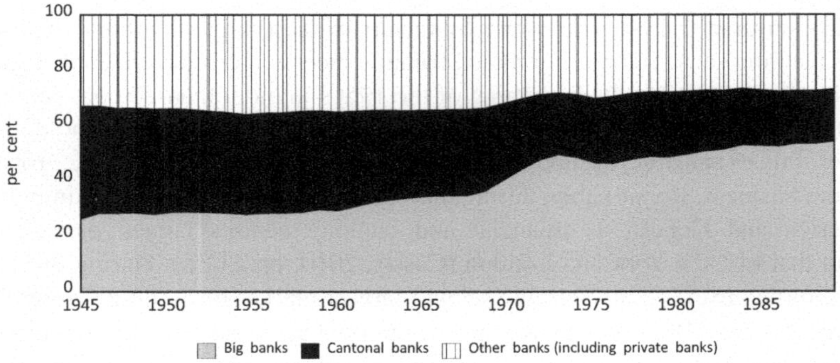

(c) Market share of various types of Swiss banks

Fig. 7.1 Development of Swiss banking during the golden age (own figure. Data sources: Banking data are taken from the "Historical time series and banking statistics" of the Swiss National Bank (SNB). The GDP data used in panel (**a**) are taken from the "Historical Statistics of Switzerland" (www.hsso.ch). The consumer price index to calculate the real values of panel (**b**) has been taken from the SNB statistics)

Table 7.1 Five-year average growth rate of the balance sheet total by type of bank (1946–1980)

Type of bank	Big banks	Private banks	Cantonal banks	Regional banks	Average Swiss inflation
Period	*Growth in percent*				
1946–1950	8	8	4	5	1
1951–1955	6	6	5	6	2
1956–1960	11	11	8	6	1
1961–1965	14	4	9	8	3
1966–1970	22	7	9	7	4
1971–1975	10	−3	9	7	8
1976–1980	11	4	6	4	2

Notes: Data for the growth rates of the various types of banks are taken from Union Bank of Switzerland (1987), *The Swiss Economy, Data, Facts, Analysis 1946–1986*, Zurich, p.99. The inflation rates refer to the change of the consumer price index (CPI) as reported in Mitchell (1992, Table H2) until 1959 and the OECD statistics thereafter

they participated heavily in this internationalisation—or what would later be called "globalisation"—during the second part of the twentieth century.

The remarkable ascent of the Swiss banking sector during the golden age was not evenly distributed across the years or across the various types of financial institutes. Rather, as shown by Fig. 7.1b, the development of the big banks stands out, as their combined balance sheet, measured in real terms, more than doubled after the mid-1960s. This doubling within a decade meant real annual growth rates of almost 20 per cent, with the corresponding nominal figure being even higher due to the upsurge in inflation at the time (see Table 7.1). Underscoring the importance of offshore business, the amount of foreign assets and liabilities held by the big banks increased by factors of six and five, respectively, between 1963 and 1973 (Cassis, 2010, p.234). In a similar vein, the foreign branch network of the big banks also expanded rapidly. Before the 1950s, their international representation did not extend beyond a handful of branches and agencies in London and New York (Jung, 2000, pp.157–159; UBS, 2012, p.24). During the postwar boom, the Swiss Bank Corporation adopted a pioneering role by opening nine foreign branches between 1951 and 1966. Credit Suisse and the Union Bank soon also embarked on ambitious programmes to add to their early footholds in London and New York (Jung, 2000, p.96, pp.159–160; UBS, 2012, p.24). By the early 1970s, the leading Swiss banks were present in virtually all major financial centres of the Western world.[3]

The private banks, which remained the flagships in Geneva, did also well out of the early part of the golden age. It is perhaps not surprising that their long-established connections with foreign clients offered an ideal launch pad for a thriving wealth-management business during the postwar economic boom. As

[3] Simultaneously, the golden age saw also a marked increase of foreign bank branches in Switzerland (Cassis, 2010, pp.234–235).

shown in Table 7.1, real annual growth rates between 5 and 10 per cent were the norm, rather than the exception, during the decades before 1960. However, the decade thereafter was characterised by stagnation, caused by increasingly fierce competition from much larger financial firms at home and abroad. In particular, during the 1960s, Switzerland's big banks began to pursue a more and more universal strategy of complementing their traditional credit-mobilier business with other financial activities, including wealth management for a cosmopolitan clientele (Jung, 2000, pp.159–160; Vogler, 2006, p.48).

Although Switzerland's banks have undoubtedly played a leading role in international wealth management since the second part of the twentieth century, for several reasons, it is actually quite difficult to quantify these activities during that period (Vogler, 2006, p.59; Cassis, 2010, p.234). To begin with, most of the private banks formerly treated the amount of assets under management as a well-kept business secret and, in some cases, even prohibited the compilation of an aggregate figure for internal purposes. Nevertheless, it is estimated that in the 1960s, Switzerland accounted for almost 10 per cent of the foreign assets and liabilities held by commercial banks around the world (Cassis, 2010, p.234, p.275). However, this rough figure neither distinguishes between assets held by private and institutional investors nor accounts for the increasingly important role of off-balance-sheet activities. In general, assets under management can be reinvested abroad in ways that cannot be inferred from balance-sheet data. Owing to the lack of accurate data, the importance of the wealth-management business has sometimes been gauged from indirect measures, such as the volume of the corresponding commission income. Then, again, these figures can be misleading when compared across decades because the standard accounting practices changed substantially over time. Therefore, it was only with the publication of dedicated statistics by the Swiss National Bank since the end of the 1990s, when reliable and comprehensive data on the amount of offshore assets collected and managed by various types of Swiss banks became available. In any case, since the golden age, the discrete world of international wealth management for the rich and the famous has turned into a stereotypical image of Switzerland's financial sector. Against this background, the regular appearance of the "smooth Swiss banker" in popular movies—above all in several episodes of "James Bond" ranging from the "The Spy Who Loved Me", released in 1977, to "Casino Royale", released in 2006—may be a more potent testimony to this development than any statistical number.

Between the 1950s and the 1970s, a new hub for international banking arose in Swiss territory in the southern Canton of Ticino, more precisely in and around the city of Lugano. In particular, during the second part of the twentieth century, Swiss and foreign banks began to open branches in this Italian-speaking part of the country (Büchenbacher, 1977, p.227; Mottet, 1987, p.247). Of course, Lugano has never come close to matching the status of Zurich or Geneva but has specialised mainly in the narrow segment of offering wealth-management and other banking services to Italian customers in currency that was more stable than the lira. Obviously, the cultural and linguistic overlaps provided the basis for this development. However, the risks of the rapid arrival of the Canton of Ticino on the stage of international banking soon hit home, when the so-called Chiasso scandal broke during the second part of the 1970s (see Sect. 8.2).

The Swiss banks oriented towards the domestic economy barely participated in the growth miracle of the golden age (see Fig. 7.1b). Nevertheless, it was only after the 1960s when the cantonal banks were replaced as the most important group when measured by their share of the aggregate balance sheet (see Fig. 7.1c). At the domestic level, they have remained important in the ordinary collection of savings and their transformation into loans for local households and firms. However, with the aforementioned international expansion, the big banks also began to turn their attention to the domestic retail sector by expanding their branch network across the country (Vogler, 2006, p.49). This expansion occurred primarily via the acquisition of smaller regional banks and in some cases through the opening of new branches to enter a certain region (Jung, 2000, p.92–95; UBS, 2012, pp.25–26). By adopting an increasingly universal banking strategy, including the domestic provision of payment services, offering transaction and savings accounts to the broad public, or issuing mortgages, Credit Suisse, the Swiss Bank Corporation, and Union Bank managed to double their share of the domestic retail market from about 20 to 40 per cent between 1945 and 1970. As can be inferred from the real growth rates reported in Table 7.1, the corresponding expansion occurred, to a great degree, at the expense of the cantonal and regional banks.

What factors underlay the spectacular international ascent of Switzerland's banks around the 1960s? Aside from the role of banking secrecy, which will be discussed in detail in Sect. 7.3, the usual attributes of a safe-haven country come to mind. These attributes include the stability of the political system, neutrality in international conflicts (and especially in the Cold War), solid legal protection against expropriation, and low levels of inflation and public debt (Vogler, 2006, pp.30ff.). These pillars of stability cannot, of course, fully explain what happened during the golden age because they were already in place before that period. In this regard, the status of the franc as an exceptional currency in terms of international convertibility is a more suitable candidate for explaining the unique expansion of Switzerland's banks after World War II (Vogler, 2006, pp.42–45). Owing to the relatively low levels of public debt and inflation and the exploitation of a rare trade surplus with the United States, the franc became a rare example of a currency that was more or less freely convertible into gold and US dollars immediately after the conclusion of the Washington Agreement in 1946. This status stood in sharp contrast to that of the currencies of other major European countries, where a similar transition did not occur until the end of the 1950s. Even thereafter, the risk of devaluation loomed large for, e.g., the Italian lira, the French franc, and sterling. Meanwhile, the stability and convertibility of the Swiss franc, bolstered by domestic political hostility towards capital controls that dated back to negative experiences during the interwar period, fostered the cross-border transaction of offshore capital, foreign currency, and gold through Geneva, and especially Zurich. By intermediating the bulk of these transactions, the internationally oriented Swiss banks benefited heavily from the extraordinary status of the franc.

Despite the golden age, the big Swiss banks were still no match for their American or British competitors. For example, in 1960, Credit Suisse and the Swiss Bank Corporation were only about one-tenth the size of the largest financial firm at the time, that is, the Bank of America (Cassis, 2010, p.208). Even after another decade of double-digit growth (see Table 7.1), no entry from Switzerland appeared on the worldwide ranking of the twenty largest commercial banks in 1972 (Vogler, 2006, p.50). In a similar vein, despite the abovementioned expansion of the foreign branch network, Swiss banks still had relatively weak representation abroad. For example, before 1960, they had only opened approximately a dozen foreign branches, as compared with well over 100 by American banks at the time (Cassis, 2010, p.219, p.205, p.226). These figures revealed that Switzerland dominated only certain niches of the banking business. Moreover, the position as one of the largest financial centres after World War II could not be maintained given the relatively small size of the country. From the 1970s onwards, emerging markets, especially Japan with the metropolis of Tokyo, arrived on the scene and quickly caught up with, and eventually surpassed, Zurich and Geneva (Cassis, 2010, pp.238–241).

In addition to the small size of the home market, the development of the Swiss banking sector encountered other obstacles. Above all, the capital inflows associated with the safe-haven status of the franc also gave rise to negative side effects on the domestic economy. More specifically, owing to the mechanisms of the international financial system at the time, e.g., the gold-exchange standard conceived at the Bretton Woods Conference in 1944, these capital inflows encapsulated a potential monetary-policy dilemma for a small open economy. In particular, although Switzerland was not a formal member of the Bretton Woods System, the Swiss National Bank was committed to adhering to the corresponding mechanisms, namely, to stabilising the exchange rate against gold and, in turn, the dollar (Baltensperger & Kugler, 2017, pp.101–105). However, owing to the increasing foreign demand for francs, this "stabilisation" tended to increase the supply of money and credit and, hence, could undermine the stability of the domestic price level. The problem of importing inflation became increasingly acute during the 1960s, when the United States moved to a looser fiscal and monetary policy to finance the Vietnam War and the costly social policies of the so-called Great Society Program. Owing to the centuries-old tradition of defining a currency's value in terms of monetary metal, the time was still not ripe for lowering inflation by severing the link between a stable currency, such as the Swiss franc, and gold—this radical step was, of course, taken in the early 1970s (see Sect. 8.1). Instead, during the 1960s, Switzerland tried to limit the inflow of foreign capital by means of administrative measures.[4] Concretely, based on several gentlemen's agreements with the Swiss National Bank, Switzerland's banks reduced the interest payments on foreign deposits to zero and later even charged a fee on the corresponding inflows (Vogler, 2006, p.43; Baltensperger & Kugler, 2017, p.103). Although these

[4] Conversely, the capital controls in most of the other countries were supposed to stem the outflow of capital.

measures did not solve the fundamental dilemma between retaining a fixed exchange rate and combatting domestic inflation amid a foreign-induced oversupply of money and credit, they created a monetary environment that hampered participation in the emerging "euromarkets" (Cassis, 2010, pp.220ff.). After the return to convertibility of the major European currencies in 1958, these offshore markets underwent a spectacular boom, as some London-based banks quickly realised the potential of accepting deposits, offering loans, and issuing bonds in offshore currencies, above all in so-called eurodollars, rather than sterling. However, unlike the Bank of England, the Swiss National Bank was reluctant to tolerate this type of financial innovation for fear of aggravating the problems associated with foreign capital inflows (Cassis, 2010, p.224).[5]

7.3 The Role of Banking Secrecy

According to a fairly entrenched narrative, Switzerland's role as a leading wealth-management centre rests primarily on an internationally unique protection of financial privacy. In particular, vast amounts of money are allegedly hidden away in numbered accounts to evade taxes or to lubricate other illegal activities. It is perhaps no coincidence that several books popularising this narrative were published during, or shortly after, the international breakthrough of Swiss banks during their golden age.[6] However, more often than not, these books simply take the overwhelming importance of banking secrecy for granted without contemplating the historical circumstances. Moreover, cross-country comparisons are usually not made to check whether, and to what extent, the financial privacy conditions and money-laundering laws in Switzerland actually differ from those elsewhere. Although banking secrecy certainly mattered, the historical evidence suggests that it was probably far less important to the success of Switzerland's banks than is commonly thought.

[5] Similar situations of how to deal with the domestic side effects of large capital inflows did, of course, occasionally reappear within the Swiss financial system during the following decades (see, e.g., Sect. 9.1).

[6] These sometimes quite entertaining books include Fehrenbach's (1966) "Gnomes of Zurich", whose title borrows the words used by British prime minister Harold Wilson to blame the instability of sterling during the 1960s on currency speculators in Zurich. Faith's (1982) "Safety in Numbers" obviously alludes to the role of numbered accounts. One of the sternest critics is Ziegler (1982, pp.48ff.), who accuses Switzerland's banks of nothing less than profiteering from hunger, war, and colonialism by attracting capital from economically underdeveloped countries. These accusations are quite polemical. Capital flight is indeed a problem for the developing world. However, it is unclear how foreign banks can be directly responsible for reluctance to invest in these countries, which typically results from their political instability, the absence of the rule of law, high inflation, or widespread corruption (Vogler, 2006, pp.57–58; 83). Capital flows from low-income countries to banks in high-income countries are merely a symptom of a relatively unattractive economic and political environment. Imposing restrictions to interrupt these transactions would obviously not cure the underlying problems.

Regarding the historical context, it is perhaps worth remembering that banking secrecy was codified in Switzerland only in 1934 in an attempt to address the foreign bank espionage at the time (see Sect. 6.5). However, due to the rapid disintegration of the international financial system during the 1930s and the severe economic disruptions of World War II, the famous Article 47 of the Federal Banking Act became virtually obsolete during these years (Vogler, 2006, p.29). Actually, the global expansion of the Swiss banking sector arose in two waves during the early interwar years and the period from the 1960s onwards (see Sects. 6.2 and 8.1). That these waves occurred before and decades after the introduction of Article 47, obviously, conflicts with efforts to attach overwhelming importance to it.

Furthermore, in contrast to the internationally exceptional stability of Switzerland's currency during the twentieth century, the country's banking-secrecy laws, as well as related practices such as offering numbered accounts, are not as unique as is often thought (see e.g. Emmenegger, 2014, pp.150–151). This should not come as a surprise because financial firms around the world inevitably store and communicate sensitive and confidential information concerning their client's payments, income, and wealth situation. Since the nineteenth century, when banking services were popularised, questions about the protection of the privacy of account holders have not been ignored. In many countries, the resulting rules, guidelines, and traditions have sooner or later been enshrined in formal laws. Consequently, they reflect the underlying history of dealing with these questions in a given place. In this regard, the synoptic comparison between Switzerland and a selected group of European countries in Table 7.2 reveals some remarkable overlaps, as well as differences.[7] For example, Luxembourg can also look back on an outstanding banking-secrecy tradition. The same can be said of Austria, which also boasts a long history of offering numbered accounts. Outside Europe, the laws on banking secrecy in Singapore and Lebanon are partially based on those of Switzerland. Germany took a very similar approach to the protection of financial privacy before World War I. However, this protection was severely curtailed during the Weimar Republic owing to the need to enforce high taxes, in order to pay for the war debt and reparations. After World War II, this policy was generally maintained. The French authorities have had relatively unhindered access to bank-account information since the nineteenth century. In a similar vein, there is no outstanding banking-secrecy tradition in many parts of the Anglo-Saxon world, including the United Kingdom and the United States. Then, again, given this international comparison, the fact that, e.g., Austria, despite a tradition of offering numbered accounts, has not developed into a major financial and banking centre, while Anglo-Saxon countries with relatively weak forms of banking secrecy have dominated the international financial system over the last couple of centuries, suggests that the role of a rigorous legal protection of financial privacy should not be overrated (Vogler, 2006, pp.51ff.).

[7] For a more comprehensive overview of banking-secrecy rules around the world, see Vogler (2006, pp.52–55).

Table 7.2 Banking secrecy: an international comparison (as of 2020)

Country	Brief description
Austria	After World War II, very similar banking secrecy to that of Switzerland. In the wake of the Global Financial Crisis of 2008, banking secrecy is essentially abolished for international owners of an account
France	Most of the banking regulations date back to the 1930s. There is a long established practice that banks have an obligation to treat financial information in a confidential manner. However, since the nineteenth century, they have also wide-ranging obligations to provide information to the fiscal authorities
Germany	Until World War I, uncodified banking-secrecy practices very similar to Switzerland. Banking secrecy was severely curtailed during the 1920s and 1930s. This policy was maintained after World War II
Italy	Although banking secrecy is generally recognised, under Italian law, there is no statutory definition of, or specific regulation on banking secrecy
Luxembourg	Long tradition of banking secrecy. Since 1981, banking secrecy is protected under the criminal law. In the wake of the Global Financial Crisis of 2008, banking secrecy is essentially abolished for international owners of an account
United Kingdom	There is no specific law on banking secrecy in the UK. However, there is a common-law duty to treat information arising from the contractual relationship between a bank and its customers in a confidential manner
Switzerland	Banking secrecy codified at the federal level in 1934. Illegally passing on banking information is treated as an ex officio crime. In the area of taxation, a distinction is made between tax evasion and tax fraud. Although both practices are illegal, banking secrecy is generally only lifted in cases of fraud. In the wake of the Global Financial Crisis of 2008, banking secrecy is essentially abolished for foreign account holders

Notes: International comparisons on banking secrecy, on which this table is based, have been published by Chambost (1982) and more recently by Vogler (2006, pp.53–57) and the OECD

In Switzerland and in other countries, banking secrecy has never held unconditionally. By and large, the outstanding—but not necessarily unique—features of the Swiss version of financial privacy refer to the conditions and procedures, according to which government authorities can obtain information from banks to investigate cases of fiscal fraud or other crimes (Tobler, 2019, pp.27–28). In particular, Article 47 of the Federal Banking Act of 1934 turned the unauthorised release of private financial information into an ex officio offence rather than a mere contractual infringement under civil law. Among other things, this legislation implies that Switzerland's judicial authorities are obliged to prosecute the leakage of bank-account information, even when no formal complaint has been made by, e.g., an affected depositor. Furthermore, there is a fairly unique distinction between the ways in which tax evasion and tax fraud are dealt with (see Roethenmund, 1980, p.57–58). Unlike households and firms in a source-based tax system, those in Switzerland file an annual tax declaration with the canton. In this regard, "tax evasion" refers to cases of unintentionally making a mistake, whereas "tax fraud" refers to acts of deliberate cheating, including forging documents, fabricating false income statements, and manipulating balance sheets. Both evasion and fraud are illegal, despite widespread claims to the contrary.[8] However, only the latter has long been considered sufficiently severe to provide the basis for lifting banking secrecy vis-à-vis the tax authorities (see, e.g., Roethenmund, 1980, pp.59ff.; Delaloye et al., 2012).[9] Before the mid-twentieth century, this distinction hardly mattered at the international level. However, the situation changed with the ascent of Switzerland's banks during their golden age because banking secrecy was lifted only to provide international legal assistance in cases violating both domestic and foreign tax law (see also Roethenmund, 1980, p.57). This principle of so-called double incrimination applies to various areas of international legal assistance to prevent despotic regimes from being able to collect information from, say, the foreign accounts of their political opponents by simply passing the necessary tailor-made domestic laws. By the same token, through this principle, idiosyncrasies, such as the difference between tax evasion and fraud, can also enter foreign countries via the back door. Against this background, the more Switzerland emerged as an important offshore centre for private wealth management, the more banking secrecy became an increasing international irritation. The resulting conflicts intensified after the financial liberalisations of the 1970s and the money-laundering and tax scandals that subsequently came to light. Across these decades, cooperation among various criminal and fiscal authorities across the globalised financial system was strengthened through the conclusion of treaties on international judicial assistance and double taxation. In Switzerland, this process began with a treaty on mutual assistance in criminal matters concluded with the United States in 1973 and culminated with the adoption of the automatic exchange of information (AEOI) with many foreign tax authorities during the aftermath of the Global Financial Crisis (Sects. 8.2 and 9.3).[10]

[8] These claims have even entered the academic literature; see, e.g., Cassis (2010, p.276).

[9] It should be noted that the declaration of bank accounts is incentivised in Switzerland by charging an anonymous withholding tax on their interest-rate income. When an account is reported to the tax authorities, this withholding tax can be deducted from a household's or a firm's tax liabilities. In general, despite banking secrecy, tax evasion and the shadow economy are quite limited in Switzerland compared with other countries (see e.g. Medina & Scheider, 2019).

[10] Banks, by no means, represent the only vehicles of financial crimes (see, e.g., Emmenegger, 2014, pp.150ff.). For example, shell companies and trusts, which are popular in common-law countries, also lend themselves to illegal financial activities and tax evasion. In this regard, a recent international field experiment to set up anonymous companies, whereby the researchers disguised as businessmen indicated their intention to avoid paying taxes, led to the following finding: "Against the conventional policy wisdom, [...] shell companies from tax havens were significantly more likely to comply with the rules than providers in OECD countries like the United States and Britain." (Findley et al., 2017, p.3).

References

Baltensperger, E., & Kugler, P. (2017). *Swiss monetary history since the early 19th century*. Cambridge: Cambridge University Press.

Bauer, H., & Blackman, W. J. (1998). *Swiss banking–An analytical history*. Basingstoke, London: Macmillan Press.

Bordo, M., & James, H. (2007). From 1907 to 1946: Happy childhood or troubled adolescence? In *The Swiss national bank 1907–2007, SNB*. Zurich: NZZ Libro.

Büchenbacher, C. (1977). *Tatsachen über das schweizerische Bankgeheimnis*. Zurich: Nova Press.

Cassis, Y. (2010). *Capital of capital. The rise and fall of international financial centres 1780–2009*. Cambridge: Cambridge University Press.

Chambost, E. (1982). *Die Bankgeheimnisse in den Ländern der Welt*. München: Piper.

Delaloye, F. X., Habib, M. A., & Ziegler, A. (2012). Swiss banking secrecy: The stock market evidence. *Financial Markets and Portfolio Management, 26,* 143–176.

Emmenegger, P. (2014). The politics of financial intransparency: The case of Swiss banking secrecy. *Swiss Political Science Review, 20,* 146–164.

Faith, N. (1982). *Safety in numbers: The mysterious world of Swiss banking*. London: Hamish Hamilton.

Fehrenbach, T. R. (1966). *The Swiss banks. Gnomes of Zurich*. New York: McGraw-Hill.

Frei, D. (1969). Das Washingtoner Abkommen von 1946. Ein Beitrag zur Geschichte der schweizerischen Aussenpolitik zwischen dem Zweiten Weltkrieg und dem kalten Krieg. *Schweizerische Zeitschrift für Geschichte, 19,* 567–619.

Findley, M., Nielson. D., and Sharman, J. (2017). Global shell games: testing money launderers' and terrorist financiers' access to shell companies. Griffith University: Centre for Governance and Public Policy.

Jung, J. (2000). *Von der Schweizerischen Kreditanstalt zur Credit Suisse Group. Eine Bankengeschichte*. Zurich: NZZ Verlag.

Medina, L., & Scheider, F. (2019). Shedding light on the shadow economy: A global database and the interaction with the official one. *CESifo Working Paper No. 7981*.

Mitchell, B. R. (1992). *International historical statistics. Europe 1750–1988*. New York: Stockton Press.

Mottet, L. H. (1987). Die Genfer Bankiers. In L. H. Mottet (Ed.), *Geschichte der Schweizer Banken*. Zurich: Verlag Neue Zürcher Zeitung.

Obstfeld, M., & Taylor, A. (2004). *Global capital markets integration, crisis, and growth*. Cambridge: Cambridge University Press.

Perrenoud, M., Lopez, R., Adank, F., Baumann, J., Cortat, A., & Perers, S. (2002). *La place financerère et les banques suisses à l'époque du national-socialisme. Publication de la Commission Indépandante d'Experts Suisse-Seconde Guerre Mondiale*. Zurich: Chronos.

Roethenmund, R. (1980). *The Swiss banking handbook. A complete manual for practical investors*. New York: Books in Focus.

SNB, (2007). The Swiss National Bank 1907–2007. Zurich: NZZ Libro.

Tobler, S. (2019). *Der Kampf um das Schweizer Bankgeheimnis. Eine 100-jährige Geschichte von Kritik und Verteidigung*. Zurich: NZZ Libro.

UBS (2012). *150 years of banking tradition*. Zurich.

Vogler, R. U. (2006). *Swiss banking secrecy: Origins, significance, myth*. Contributions to Financial History (Vol. 7). Association for Financial History.

Ziegler, J. (1982). *Eine Schweiz - über jeden Verdacht erhaben*. Darmstadt: Luchterhand.

Chapter 8
Swiss Banking During Financial Globalisation (1970s–2008)

8.1 Causes and Consequences of Financial Globalisation

During the last quarter of the twentieth century, the world returned to levels of international economic integration not seen since the collapse of the classical gold standard in 1914 (Obstfeld & Taylor, 2004, pp.121ff.). More specifically, in the decades after the 1970s, an extraordinary upsurge occurred in cross-border activities ranging from the export and import of goods to the exchange of information and the voluntary migration of people. In a similar vein, the trading of vast amounts of money and capital around the world by banks with subsidiaries in all major financial centres again became a potent symbol of the globalised economy. The foundations of this development had been laid by restoring the international convertibility of major currencies during the 1950s and the subsequent success of the euromarkets during the 1960s (see Sect. 7.2). The disintegration of the Bretton Woods System during the 1970s, and its replacement with a "non-system" based on more or less freely floating exchange rates, indicated that the tide had definitely turned against imposing rigid trade barriers and capital controls. Their dismantling, indeed, triggered a dramatic expansion of short-term capital movements, through which differences in interest rates between countries are exploited, or financial risks can be diversified across a broad international asset portfolio. The path-breaking developments in using computer technology to exchange and process vast amounts of information, the popularisation of financial instruments, such as derivatives in foreign-exchange trading, and the collapse of the centrally planned economies all gave additional impetus to globalisation during the 1980s and 1990s (Cassis, 2010, pp.242ff.). Last but not least, until the turn of the millennium, the financial sector, and especially the large banks, benefitted greatly from the popularity of free-market policies, which led to the abolishment of official interest-rate ceilings, revoked most prohibitions on combining commercial with investment banking, removed many taxes on financial transactions, and lowered the administrative barriers to entry into a range of trading and brokerage activities. Of course, these policies were not

N. Herger, *Switzerland and its Banks*, Frontiers in Economic History,
https://doi.org/10.1007/978-3-031-35904-0_8

implemented everywhere to the same extent or at the same time. Furthermore, they did not reflect a return to a completely deregulated financial system—especially when compared with the laisser-faire conditions during the classical gold standard. Rather, deregulation at the national level was often met by a countermovement at the international level. For example, within the banking sector, a more and more elaborate system of minimum equity-capital requirements was developed under the auspices of the Bank for International Settlements (BIS). Referring to the head-office location of this supranational organisation in Switzerland, where the corresponding negotiations took place, these international capital regulations have become known as the "Basel rules".

Until the 1970s, Switzerland was at the forefront of the movement towards a deregulated international financial system. Above all, the convertibility of the franc was quickly restored after the end of World War II, which is about ten years earlier than the major European currencies (see Sect. 7.1). Moreover, the foreign outreach of Switzerland's banks during their golden age can be interpreted as a harbinger of financial globalisation. Finally, by letting the franc float against the dollar as one of the first currencies to do so in January 1973, Switzerland adopted a pioneering role in abandoning the constraints of the Bretton Woods System. A key motive for making this remarkable decision at the time was a widespread desire to tighten monetary policy and, thus, to combat the domestic inflation of up to 10 per cent during the 1970s, instead of trying to stabilise the exchange rate (see Schiltknecht, 1994; Baltensperger & Kugler, 2017, pp.101–107).[1]

However, Switzerland did not manage to retain this pioneering role in the deregulation of money and banking, when economic globalisation genuinely took off after the 1970s. In opposition to a trend of ambitious financial deregulation programmes in the United Kingdom and the United States, between the end of the 1970s and the beginning of the 1980s, the Swiss franc became the subject of new administrative measures that were intended to halt large inflows of foreign capital (Cassis, 2010, pp.244ff.). They had arisen mainly because the Swiss National Bank had quickly seized its newly achieved monetary-policy autonomy to push inflation down from a level of almost 10 per cent during the early 1970s to well below 5 per cent towards the end of that decade (Baltensperger & Kugler, 2017, pp.106ff.). As many countries continued to suffer from double-digit increases in the average price level around 1980, this outstanding degree of monetary stability reinforced the franc's status as a safe-haven currency. However, to tame the resulting capital inflows and combat the associated appreciation, which manifested in a strengthening

[1] In addition to a broadly shared preference for price stability, it probably mattered that Switzerland's neutrality represented an obstacle to joining some of the most important international organisations until the end of the Cold War. In particular, Switzerland was not a formal member of the Bretton Woods institutions until the 1990s (Baltensperger & Kugler, 2017, p.104). Moreover, during the 1970s, Swiss economists were well acquainted with the emerging ideas of monetarism, including the benefits of exchange rates determined through the private demand and supply of currency (Friedman, 1953). The term "monetarism" was actually coined by the Swiss economist Karl Brunner (1916–1989) (see Moser & Savioz, 2022).

of the franc against the German mark by 15 per cent and against the US dollar by almost 30 per cent in 1978 alone, Switzerland resorted to imposing constraints and introducing fees on bank deposits as well as on the purchases of bonds and shares by nonresidents during that year (Roethenmund, 1980, pp.100ff.). Most of these emergency measures to, in the official wording, "safeguard the franc and the national economy", were not lifted until the mid-1980s. In addition to these measures and restrictions on cross-border transactions, until the 1990s, it was fairly common for Switzerland's banks to conclude cartel-like agreements on the domestic market or to employ more or less overt forms of collusion to restrict competition and prevent market entries into, e.g., brokerage activities (Jung, 2000, pp.39–40; Cassis, 2010, p.247). Moreover, in contrast to most of the foreign countries, financial intermediaries are subject to stamp duties on issuing new bonds until today, which has hampered the development of the corresponding markets. Finally, Switzerland has not joined the European Union and is, therefore, not bound by its competition laws regarding the provision of state aid to banks and other (financial) firms. As a result, the traditional links between the cantonal banks and their local governments have, by and large, been preserved. The same can be said of the publicly owned Swiss postal bank (called "Post Finance"), which holds a key position in arranging domestic payments and handling the deposits of small savers.

Given this environment, Switzerland began to lag behind in the globalisation of the banking sector. Indeed, according to a commonly used measure for this development depicted in Fig. 8.1, the foreign assets and liabilities held by Swiss banks stagnated at levels of approximately 60 and 40 billion US dollars, respectively, throughout the 1980s. It was only during the following decade when these assets and liabilities increased substantially to 340 and 270 billion at the beginning of the 1990s and to 770 and 680 billion at the beginning of the new millennium,

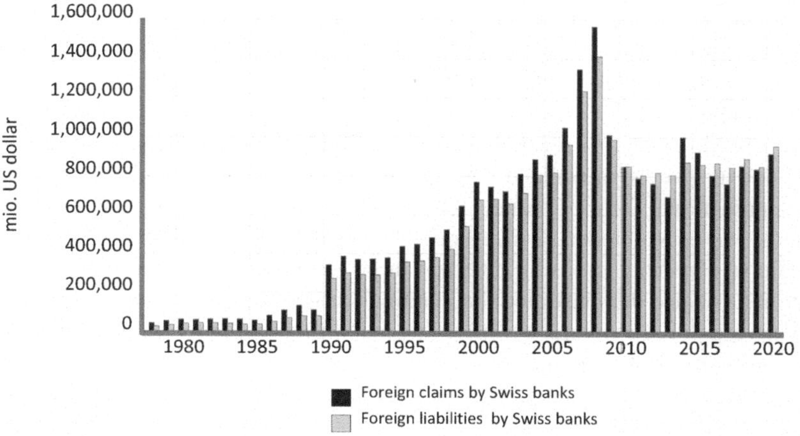

Fig. 8.1 Globalisation in Swiss banking (own figure. Data source: Locational banking statistics of the Bank for International Settlements (BIS))

respectively. The climax of this upsurge was reached shortly before the outbreak of the Global Financial Crisis in 2008 when the corresponding amounts stood at 1.6 and 1.4 trillion, respectively. Even when accounting for the effect of inflation, this more than tenfold increase within roughly 15 years reflects a massive cross-border expansion of Switzerland's banking sector. Of course, this expansion followed a worldwide trend that gave rise to increasingly large, and globally interconnected, financial firms. Above all the investment banks, which raise vast amounts of money for business and governments, act as brokers and dealers on the money and capital markets, and offer financial services for undertaking cross-border mergers and acquisitions, became broadly recognised landmarks of this aspect of globalisation.

In relative terms, the wave of globalisation during the last quarter of the twentieth century represented a setback for Switzerland's banking sector, whose outstanding role had definitely come to an end. To interpret this development, the fact that the conditions during the golden age were exceptional should not be overlooked. Under normal circumstances, the banking centres of the United States, Germany, France, and Britain can obviously draw on sizable home markets to outclass the rivals in smaller countries. For the same reason, the emergence of Japan, and later the return of China as an important economy, was inevitably intertwined with the arrival of new international financial centres in, e.g., Tokyo, Singapore, Shanghai, and Hong Kong. However, several home-grown factors also added to the relative decline of Switzerland. In addition to the reluctance to deregulate the financial industry as vigorously as, e.g., the United Kingdom, it probably mattered that the Swiss franc was no longer an exceptional currency in terms of convertibility and stability. In particular, low inflation rates became more and more common during the so-called period of the Great Moderation, which began in the 1990s and lasted for more than a decade. In a similar vein, the benefits of political neutrality became far less obvious after the demise of the bipolar world order with the collapse of the Soviet Union in 1991. Finally, for historical and political reasons (see Sect. 2.3), Switzerland was reluctant to fully participate in European integration, let alone to adopt the euro as a common currency. Especially, during the 1990s, the resulting lack of a joint economic and monetary framework with neighbouring countries was accompanied by serious concerns that the domestic economy could stagnate or even be doomed to irreversible decline. There were also fears that the franc could not survive as an isolated currency unit on a European continent dominated by a supranational form of money. Eventually, it became clear that these fears and concerns were overblown. Switzerland continued to prosper during globalisation. The Global Financial Crisis of 2008 and more recently the international upsurge in inflation have also demonstrated that national currencies can offer the advantage of allowing a tailored response to instability within the banking sector or within the wider economy (Baltensperger & Kugler, 2017, pp.122–123).

Regardless of these relative setbacks, Switzerland's banks continued to punch above the weight of the country. In particular, Zurich and Geneva still belonged to the leading international banking centres during financial globalisation and managed to retain their leading position in the niche of offshore wealth management by accounting for around one-third of this market (Cassis, 2010, pp. 274–276). Within this niche, Geneva has remained an important player, despite the absence of a homegrown multinational financial firm. Conversely, the big banks accounted for the bulk of the development of the financial sector in Zurich. As shown back in Fig. 1.1c of Chap. 1, their balance sheet underwent a period of exponential growth from the 1980s onwards. Consequently, they turned into the dominant financial firms within the Swiss banking sector. This expansion resulted, among other things, from a series of domestic and international mergers and acquisitions. As an important result of this restructuring and consolidation, which mainly took place during the 1980s and 1990s, Credit Suisse and UBS grew into large, multinational financial firms.

The remaining parts of this chapter discuss the reorientation, restructuring, and consolidation of the Swiss banking sector during the last decades of the twentieth century in more detail. However, before turning to these issues, the next section is devoted to the paradigm change in governance, which became all but inevitable after a series of major scandals shook Switzerland's banking sector during the early period of financial globalisation.

8.2 Paradigm Change in Governance

Allegations that Swiss banks are mainly vehicles for money laundering and tax evasion did not disappear during the final decades of the twentieth century. If anything, the familiar criticism by foreign governments dating back to at least the 1920s was reinforced by that of international and nongovernmental organisations (NGOs), which became increasingly powerful agencies in a globalised world. Although many banking scandals announced with much fanfare by these organisations later turned out to be exaggerated or even completely unfounded,[2] the "golden years" of Switzerland's banking sector had clearly created an environment of remarkably lax attitudes towards governance. Reflecting these attitudes, a series of genuine scandals, most of which were associated with tax evasion and money laundering, came to light during and after the 1970s. Table 8.1 presents a far from exhaustive list of some of the most notorious examples linking Swiss banks with the financial misconduct of celebrities, criminal organisations, and infamous despots.[3]

[2] A famous example of an unfounded scandal involved Evita Perron (1919–1952), the glamorous wife of the Argentinean dictator Juan Perron (1895–1974). The claim that she had a Swiss bank account to hide money has never been supported by evidence (Vogler, 2006, p.75.). On a much larger scale, the stories of billions' worth of dormant accounts from World War II stand in sharp contrast to the amounts that have actually been uncovered by several wide-ranging inquiries (see Sects. 6.6 and 8.4).

[3] For a much more extensive overview of actual and alleged Swiss-banking scandals since 1945, see Vogler (2006, pp.74–90). Furthermore, the fiscal fraud involving the Basler Handelsbank during the 1930s and the discussions regarding the dormant accounts dating back to World War II are summarised in Sects. 6.3 and 6.6, respectively.

Table 8.1 Some banking scandals during the 1970s and 1980s

Year	Scandal	Brief description	Sources
1977	Chiasso scandal	The Credit Suisse branch in Chiasso suffers from severe losses from unauthorised investments in financial firms in Liechtenstein. These unauthorised investments went on for more than ten years without being detected	Büchenbacher (1977, ch.8) and Jung (2000, pp.245–287)
1979	Shah of Persia affair	Before being overthrown, it is alleged that the Shah of Persia had moved large amounts of money out of the country with the help of banks in New York, Paris, and Zurich. The Islamic regime in Teheran demanded foreign governments to block the corresponding assets. Switzerland did not comply with this demand	Roethenmund (1980, pp.60–61)
1986	Duvalier affair	Around eight billion Swiss francs held by Haitian President Jean Claude Duvalier were frozen (together with around 120 billion US$ in France)	Vogler (2006, p.87)
1986	Marcos affair	Around 700 million Swiss francs held by Philippine dictator Ferdinand Marcos on Swiss bank accounts were frozen	Vogler (2006, p.87)
1988	Lebanon connection	A Lebanese criminal organisation had laundered money from drug dealing through Swiss banks	Jung (2000, pp.297ff.)
1989	Medellin drug cartel	Around ten billion Swiss francs of assets held by a Columbian drug cartel on Swiss bank accounts were blocked. Money was also seized in Austria, Luxembourg, the United Kingdom, and the United States	Vogler (2006, p.90)

The public outrage following these scandals has often been anything but harmless for the banking business, which relies, after all, on a fair amount of economic and political trust. Eventually, Switzerland's banks began to recognise the potential threat of this "reputation risk". Whether they liked it or not, the gravity of the situation at the end of the 1970s warranted a paradigm change in governance and especially in attitudes towards combatting financial crimes.

A path-breaking event for the paradigm change in governance was the so-called Chiasso scandal, which hit the headlines in 1977 (Jung, 2000, pp.245–287). The origin of this scandal was dubious off-balance-sheet investments by the Credit Suisse branch in Chiasso, a small town in southern Switzerland next to the Italian border. This town had benefitted from a boom in cross-border banking since the 1960s owing to capital flight from Italy, which suffered from entrenched fiscal problems and widespread tax evasion (see Büchenbacher, 1977, pp.227ff.). As indicated by the discussion above, this type of boom also lent itself to excessive risk taking, careless attitudes towards financial crimes, and negligent behaviour in corporate governance (see Sect. 7.2). In particular, within this environment, the Chiasso branch of Credit Suisse had offered its Italian clientele deposit accounts with attractive interest rates. Part of the funds collected through these accounts was, in turn, channelled through a dedicated trust company in Liechtenstein, which served as a vehicle for unauthorised, and often risky and untaxed reinvestments. Despite several internal and external warnings about the Chiasso branch over more than ten years, the top management in Zurich failed to recognise the impending financial and legal risks associated with these off-balance-sheet transactions. When the full extent of the corresponding problems came to light in April 1977, the general public was stunned not only by this ignorance but also by the fact that the scandal involved Credit Suisse, which had cultivated the reputation of conservative bank known for having survived the Great Depression and World War II without incurring unsustainable losses or requiring outside help. That Credit Suisse was for months unable to quantify the losses resulting from the bad debt in Chiasso added to the consternation and inevitably gave rise to pervasive speculations in domestic and foreign media. Towards the end of 1977, it finally became clear that slightly more than one billion Swiss francs had to be written off—at the time, this was a truly staggering amount. Although Credit Suisse could draw on a sufficiently large equity buffer and own reserves to absorb this loss, the general director (i.e., the CEO) was forced to resign. Furthermore, the Chiasso bankers directly involved in the scandal were arrested and later convicted of disloyal management, fraud, the forgery of documents, and other financial crimes.

With every further scandal that emerged during the 1970s and 1980s, suspicions about Swiss banks and their unwillingness to diligently check the identity and background of their international customers increased. The revelations of 1977 finally led to the conclusion that tighter rules, better internal controls, and more public oversight are warranted to remedy apparent governance problems and especially to prevent cases of outright mismanagement and misconduct. In terms of concrete measures, the members of the Swiss Bankers Association reacted by concluding a gentlemen's agreement to increase transparency in financial transactions and to strengthen the fight against tax evasion (Roethenmund, 1980, pp.59ff.; Jung, 2000, pp.290–293; Vogler, 2006, pp.63ff.).[4] By means of the resulting self-regulation, which is enshrined in the clumsily named "Agreement on the Swiss banks' code of conduct with regard to the exercise of due diligence",[5] path-breaking principles against fraud and money laundering have been introduced. In particular, these principles include a duty to identify bank customers, the so-called know-your-customer rule, to stop the practice of accepting money through lawyers or shell companies, behind which the final owners can hide. Furthermore, it was also

[4] Furthermore, the Chiasso scandal entailed a political discussion, with numerous enquiries and questions raised in parliament. To reinforce this debate, the social democrats partly launched a popular initiative calling for a loosening of banking secrecy, the introduction of public deposit insurance, an increase in transparency, and the severing of links between banks and industrial companies (Jung, 2000, pp.293–295). This initiative was rejected by more than 70 per cent of the population in 1984.

[5] In German: "Vereinbarung über die Standesregeln zur Sorgfaltspflicht der Banken". In French: "Convention relative à l'obligation de diligence des banques".

agreed to end any form of active assistance of illegal capital transfers or tax evasion. Of note, these principles were more than cheap talk, as the Swiss Bankers Association can actually fine a member for violating them. Moreover, they became an established business standard during the following decades and provided the blueprint for the legislation against money laundering introduced in Switzerland during the 1990s (see below).

The scandals that emerged during the 1980s (see Table 8.1) exposed other supervisory shortcomings and legal loopholes. For example, after substantial diplomatic pressure was exerted by the US administration, a clause was added to the Swiss penal code in 1988 to outlaw cases of insider trading (Jung, 2000, pp.295–297). Owing to the principle of "double incrimination", this clause was necessary to provide US authorities with bank-account information when, say, a Swiss bank trades securities in New York on behalf of a customer, who is involved in an alleged case of insider trading.

Towards the end of the 1980s, the fight against international money laundering moved to the top of the agenda. In this regard, an outstanding case was the so-called Lebanon connection, which uncovered payments through Swiss banks by members of Lebanese criminal organisations involved in illegal drug dealing, among other forms of organised crime. It was again the big banks that found themselves at the centre of these allegations. Moreover, in a quite unusual event for Switzerland, this scandal led to the resignation of the federal councillor and minister for justice, Elisabeth Kopp (*1936), after it was revealed that she had tipped off her husband about an imminent money-laundering investigation of a foreign-exchange trading company with him as a board member.

As a reaction to these, and many other, infamous revelations about the Swiss banking sector, the codes of conduct and laws against money laundering and other financial crimes were tightened during the 1990s. In particular, since 1998, banks have been obliged to actively report suspected cases of money laundering to a dedicated agency within Switzerland's federal police (the so-called Meldestelle für Geldwäscherei or Bureau de communication en matière de blanchiment d'argent). Taken together, the codes of conduct and laws introduced since the 1970s reflect a paradigm change in dealing with alleged cases of fraud and financial crimes. Compared with the period before the 1970s, it is today probably more widely recognised by Switzerland's banking community that the reputation risk and embarrassment following financial scandals sooner or later outweigh the corresponding benefits.

8.3 Real-Estate Crisis and Banking Merger Wave

For Switzerland's banking sector, the 1990s were difficult years characterised by profound restructuring and consolidation. In particular, the number of banks decreased by almost 30 per cent from just below 500 in 1990 to approximately 350 in 1999 (see Fig.. 1.1a of Chap. 1). In a similar vein, numerous branches were closed across the country and, for the first time in decades, the total number of people employed within the sector declined from just above 120,000 at the beginning of the 1990s to slightly more than 100,000 at the end of the decade (Jung, 2000, p.40). This restructuring and downsizing first and foremost affected the smaller regional and savings banks, whose market share declined considerably (see Fig. 1.1c of Chap. 1). Conversely, the big players managed to strengthen their position, thanks mainly to the burgeoning growth of their foreign business driven by the globalising financial system. Nevertheless, significant consolidation also took place within this segment as the number of big banks decreased from five to two during the 1990s.

This restructuring resulted from several unaddressed structural problems within Switzerland's banking sector. As mentioned above, financial deregulation during the last part of the twentieth century changed the international, and later also the domestic, environment by, e.g., fostering competition within the financial industry (see Sect. 8.1). Moreover, the remarkable progress in information technology opened new ways to make payments and to gather, store, and process the data required to provide loans or offer other financial services. To benefit from these novel technologies, considerable investments in the necessary computer hardware, software, and telecommunication infrastructure were needed. Additionally, the importance of personally approaching bank customers and collecting information about the local economy through the traditional branch network declined. The combination of the investments in expensive information technologies and the reorganisation of the branch network often caused overwhelming problems for smaller banks with strong roots in a particular region.

Switzerland's banking sector had long tried to resist structural change by resorting to anti-competitive measures, such as collusive agreements that essentially divided the domestic market into spheres of influence (Jung, 2000, p.40; Birchler, 2007, p.394). Due to the lack of an effective antitrust policy, in Switzerland, these types of agreements were fairly commonplace in many domestically oriented industries until the 1990s. Antitrust legislation generally outlawing these types of cartels and other forms of collusion came into force only in 1996. During the 1980s, it was also possible to temporarily ignore the entrenched problems resulting from domestic overbanking because of a generally benign economic environment. However, the situation changed when economic growth collapsed at the beginning of 1990, and remained extraordinarily low by international standards over the following years (see Sect. 8.4). The boom-and-bust cycle around 1990 was magnified by speculative overheating and a subsequent downturn within Switzerland's real-estate market. In particular, while property prices doubled during the 1980s, which also witnessed a construction boom partially fuelled by loose monetary-policy conditions with low interest rates, the real-estate market crashed in 1991 (Birchler, 2007, p.394; Rich, 2007, pp.308ff.). Subsequently, housing prices fell by roughly 20 per cent. In addition, the first part of the 1990s was characterised by an upsurge in inflation, which peaked at a level of almost 6 per cent in 1991 (Rich, 2007, pp.313ff.; Baltensperger & Kugler, 2017, pp.116–117). To restore price stability, the Swiss National Bank increased the level of interest rates. Unsurprisingly, this monetary-policy tightening temporarily aggravated the real-estate crisis and was associated with a protracted economic downturn until the mid-1990s. These developments reflect a widely documented pattern, according to which economies tend to recover relatively slowly from a systemic real-estate crisis (see e.g. Abiad et al., 2011).

In combination, the stubborn recession and declining real-estate prices had dire consequences for the Swiss banking sector, including a reduction in loan demand and a sharp increase in mortgage defaults. In particular, between 1991 and 1996, commercial banks had, on average, to write off approximately 10 per cent of their loan portfolios (Birchler, 2007, p. 394). Small regional banks suffered disproportionately from the real-estate crisis, as they were often heavily exposed to a collapse in their local housing market with scant possibilities for risk diversification. As a result, during the 1990s, the number of regional banks was halved from roughly 200–100 (see Fig. 1.1a of Chap. 1).[6] Of note, this reduction was accompanied not by a wave of bankruptcies, but rather by a series of mergers and acquisitions through which smaller and weaker banks were taken over by larger and financially more potent competitors (Birchler, 2007, pp.395ff.). There were virtually no cases of outright failure. A notable exception was a run in 1991 on the "Spar- und Leihkasse Thun", a small savings and loan institute in the Canton of Bern. The following liquidation resulted in a total shortfall of about 200 million Swiss francs, and left thousands of depositors with losses of up to 40 per cent on the underlying savings.

The recession and real-estate crisis did not leave the cantonal banks unscathed. In particular the Cantonal Bank of Bern, which is one of the largest as well as the oldest financial institute of this type, took a severe hit during the first part of the 1990s by incurring a massive loss of more than three billion Swiss francs. This loss resulted mainly from accumulated bad debt on the mortgage portfolio. Owing to public ownership, approximately 1.5 billion francs of the corresponding loss had to be borne by the (cantonal) taxpayer (Birchler, 2007, pp.397–398). Due to this financial debacle, the Canton of Bern suffered from high public debt levels, and local tax increases over the following decades. As a political response to these unpleasant fiscal consequences, the Bernese cantonal bank was converted from a public institution into a joint-stock company in 1998. Similar, albeit less severe, "debacles" occurred in the Cantons of Appenzell, Geneva, Vaud, and Solothurn (Jung, 2000, pp.40–41). The corresponding restructuring measures, cases of privatisation, and mergers led to a reduction in the number of cantonal banks from 29 in 1990 to 24 in 2000 (see Fig. 1.1a of Chap. 1).

Despite incurring, on average, losses of almost 10 per cent on the loan portfolios, Switzerland's big banks weathered the real-estate crisis of the 1990s relatively well. Overall, they played a stabilising role during this decade, and managed to strengthen their domestic and international position thereafter (Birchler, 2007, p.396). More specifically, although the big players did not fare particularly well in the domestic mortgage market, their large and diversified balance sheets, as well as ample amounts of undisclosed reserves that had been set aside during the 1980s,

[6] As these banks were typically small, the corresponding effect on the banking sector's aggregate balance sheet was negligible. In this regard, the international development of the big banks determined the picture (see Fig. 1.1c of Chap. 1).

provided the basis for absorbing these losses, while simultaneously pursuing a quite aggressive growth strategy (Birchler, 2007, 396). In addition to the acquisition of many struggling regional banks, more far-reaching consolidation took place within the big-banking segment itself. Credit Suisse took the lead in 1991 by acquiring the Bank Leu, meaning that one of the oldest financial firms in Europe disappeared after 236 years in existence (Jung, 2000, pp.131–135). Two years later, the next coup involved the "Volksbank", which had never fully recovered from its near bankruptcy during the Great Depression, and had been critically weakened by the effects of tumbling Swiss housing prices at the beginning of the 1990s (Jung, 2000, pp.131–135; pp.137–142). With these, and other, acquisitions, Credit Suisse endeavoured to turn itself into a large and diversified company fit for competition in a rapidly changing domestic and international environment. However, by far the most spectacular event of this consolidation process occurred with the mega-merger of the Swiss Bank Corporation and the Union Bank, announced in 1997 and completed in 1998. Combining two leading financial firms of the country into UBS for the first time created a Swiss bank that could match the size of the largest competitors in the world (Cassis, 2010, p.269). Despite the many organisational challenges, as well as sceptics denouncing this project—rightly or wrongly—as managerial hubris, the merger was seen by its initiators as a necessary step for competing successfully within a globalised economy (UBS, 2012, pp.31–33). At the emotional level, some of the scepticism also reflected an ancient rivalry between the financial centres of Zurich and Basel. In particular, Zurich became the head-office location of UBS, while the Bank Corporation, with its strong roots in Basel, disappeared as an independent firm. Hence, this city lost its most potent representative of a long, and proud history as an international financial centre (see Sects. 3.3 and 5.4).

Within the financial industry, the era of globalisation also saw attempts to converge banking with the insurance business. A Swiss case in point of this convergence was the acquisition of the "Winterthur" insurance company by Credit Suisse in 1997, which was however reversed ten years later (Jung, 2000, pp.227ff.). A strategy to transform the Zurich Insurance Company into a broad financial services provider was similarly short-lived. By way of contrast, the expansion of Switzerland's big banks from their traditional credit-mobilier and wealth-management activities into the growing segment of global investment banking has had a more lasting legacy. As the issuing and trading of shares, bonds, and derivatives as well as the provision of all kinds of financial services associated with these activities are traditionally concentrated in the top-tier financial centres, the corresponding growth took place mainly in New York and London rather than in Zurich. To participate in this growth, the big Swiss banks had already begun to venture into these activities by forming alliances with various American investment banks in the 1960s and 1970s. A case in point was the alliance between Credit Suisse and the First Boston Corporation. In the 1990s, some of these collaborations were replaced by full integration. Credit Suisse took this step in 1990 with the acquisition of a controlling stake in the First Boston Corporation (Jung, 2000, pp.182ff.). In a similar vein, the Bank Corporation acquired the London-based S.G. Warburg in 1995. Hence, an in-house investment bank was available when UBS was formed two years later (UBS, 2012, pp.27–28).

8.4 More Setbacks During the 1990s: Swiss Economic Disease, European Integration, and US Lawsuits

The restructuring and consolidation of the Swiss banking sector was intertwined with additional economic challenges and international political troubles. With respect to the economic environment during the 1990s, Switzerland suffered from the aforementioned stagflation and the following slow recovery (Kleinewefers Lehner, 2007, pp.232–235). The associated combination of relatively high levels of unemployment, inflation, and low levels of growth over an entire decade even gave rise to speculations about the existence of a "Swiss economic disease", which was thought to lower the development potential of rich democracies with open markets (Kehoe & Prescott, 2002, pp.2–3; Abrahamsen et al., 2005). In addition, unprecedentedly high government deficits, which arose mainly at the federal level, pushed the corresponding public debt-to-GDP ratio from approximately 10 per cent in 1990 to 25 per cent in 2005 (see Fig. 8.2). Although this indebtedness was low by international standards, the trend was nevertheless worrying. Switzerland only came to grips with its fiscal problems after introducing a so-called debt brake in 2003, which aimed to stabilise the total amount of outstanding debts at the federal level at 120 billion Swiss francs.[7] As shown in Fig. 8.2, this fiscal-policy rule was remarkably successful in turning entrenched deficits into surpluses, and hence reversing the public-debt trend after 2005 (Beljean & Geier, 2013).

Regarding the international political environment, concerns arose mainly about the role of a small neutral country on a continent no longer divided by the decades-old antagonism of the Cold War. Contrary to the movement towards closer economic and political integration in Europe, the participation of Switzerland in the single market of the European Union (EU) was rejected by a referendum in 1992. This path-breaking verdict of the population, which came after a remarkably fierce domestic debate, created much consternation among the political leadership as well as the intellectual and economic elites, which had come together in a broad coalition to advocate deeper European integration as the only way to safeguard Switzerland's prosperity (see Sect. 2.3). For them, the referendum of 1992 represented a massive setback, and greatly reinforced worries about the imminent political and economic decline of the country. Unsurprisingly, this mood also beset the banking community, especially the internationally connected big banks. The entry of several new member countries into the European Union during the 1990s, including neighbouring Austria, only aggravated the situation, as Switzerland visibly became an island on

[7] For the details on the mechanism of this public debt brake (or "Schuldenbremse"), see Beljean and Geier (2013, p.118).

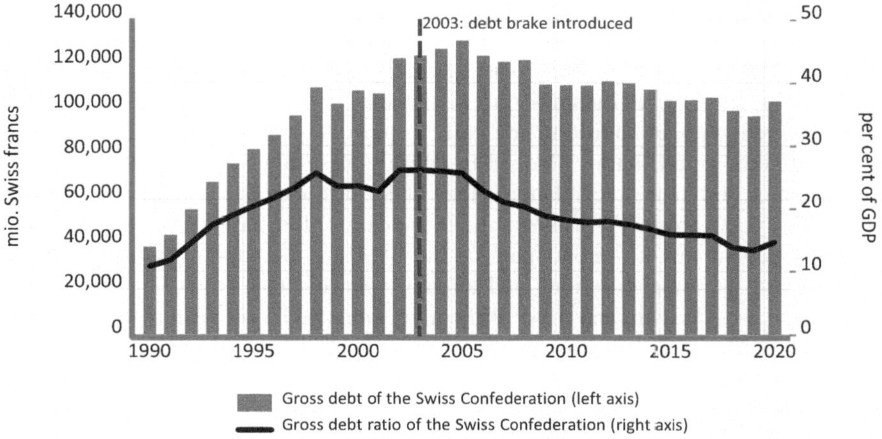

Fig. 8.2 Effect of the public debt brake (1990–2020) (own figure based on Beljean & Geier, 2013, p.116)

the political map of Europe. In a similar vein, after the introduction of the euro as the common European form of money in 1999, the Swiss franc also became a national "currency island".

During the first part of the new millennium, Switzerland managed to maintain its status as a prosperous country backed by an internationally successful economy, including a leading banking sector. Apparently, it is possible for a small European economy to thrive without entering the single market.[8] Of course, Switzerland has had a free-trade agreement with the European Union since 1972. Moreover, since the referendum of 1992, a series of bilateral agreements has been concluded to, at least temporarily, settle issues, such as the free movement of labour or a participation in the Schengen passport-free area.[9] Conversely, these bilateral agreements have hitherto not covered the mutual acceptance of financial and banking regulations (Brunetti, 2019, pp. 10–11). Currently, it remains unclear whether such a financial services agreement, which would be of direct relevance for the Swiss banking sector, will ever be concluded with the European Union.

A perhaps rather surprising element of the international political troubles for Switzerland and its banks during the 1990s was the reopening of the old debate

[8] Nonetheless, according to some commentators, the rejection of deeper legal and economic integration with the European Union in 1992 was an important culprit in the slow recovery of the Swiss economy during the 1990s (Bodmer, 2004). However, in all likelihood, the structural problems ran deeper than the issue of whether or not to participate in the single market. It is at least noteworthy that the stagflation began with the real-estate crisis in 1991, that is, well before the vote, which took place at the end of the year 1992.

[9] Recall that Switzerland became a full member of the IMF and the Worldbank in 1992, and the United Nations in 2002 (see Sect. 2.3).

about the dormant accounts of holocaust victims. At the origin of this renewed debate stood a class-action lawsuit filed by international Jewish organisations in 1996 in a district court in New York. Legally, this lawsuit resulted, after three years of litigation, in an outside-court settlement, through which UBS and Credit Suisse agreed, without admitting any guilt, to pay compensation of 1.25 billion US dollars. Jewish organisations pledged to employ these funds to support victims of the holocaust and their descendants, if they had lost money in a Swiss bank account during the years around World War II. In hindsight, the ferocity of the dormant-accounts debate in the second part of the 1990s is perhaps astonishing. After all, the corresponding questions had already been discussed decades earlier, the broad facts were known, and most of the allegations had long been made (see also Sect. 6.6).[10] Moreover, most of the people involved in this debate had personally suffered neither from World War II, nor from the horrific events of the holocaust. Nevertheless, emotions ran high, with some critics claiming that Switzerland and its banks had managed to come unscathed through World War II only because of close financial, economic, and political collaboration with Nazi Germany (see e.g. Eizenstat Report published in 1997). It was retorted that it would be a historical distortion to put Switzerland, which had after all maintained its independence under difficult circumstances and resisted the temptation of totalitarianism when this was widely seen as a promising form of government, on par with a rogue dictatorship (see e.g. Blocher, 1997). However that may be, domestically, the conduct of Switzerland's banking sector during World War II probably pushed emotions to astonishingly high levels during the 1990s, because this debate resonated strongly with the controversy over finding a new role for the country after the end of the Cold War. In particular, for political groups wanting to preserve the traditional policy of neutrality, independence from foreign political influence, and direct democracy, the events during World War II provided a perfect case to illustrate that the country could survive as an "island" within Europe under virtually any circumstances. Conversely, the proponents of closer European integration had every incentive to debunk the international isolation of Switzerland between 1939 and 1945 as a historical myth.

[10] Switzerland's parliament reacted to the debate of the 1990s by commissioning an in-depth historical inquiry into the role of the country during the period of national socialism, including studies dedicated to banking aspects, such dormant accounts (Bonhage et al., 2001), the role of the big banks (Perrenoud et al., 2002), and a case study on the conduct of a Swiss mortgage bank at the time (Bonhage, 2002). Furthermore, in 1996, the Swiss Bankers Association and international Jewish organisations set up a so-called Independent Committee of Eminent Persons (ICEP, 1999) to undertake a comprehensive search for dormant accounts dating back to the 1930s. This commission essentially completed the search for dormant accounts that had begun, in earnest, in 1962 with the "Meldebeschluss" (see Sect. 7.2). By and large, these investigations and reports confirmed, although in much greater detail, the facts that had already been established. See Sect. 6.6 for a corresponding discussion.

8.5 Overview of Swiss Banking During the Twentieth Century

As in the first wave of globalisation around 1900 (see Sect. 5.5), the upsurge in cross-border trade and payments taking place a century later was a blessing for internationally oriented banks located in top-tier financial centres (Cassis, 2010, pp.243–244). Of course, the subtleties of economic history imply that modern events are never exact replicas of the past. For example, the first wave of globalisation occurred during the classical gold standard, which was an international monetary system organised around fixed parities between the major currencies, whereas floating exchange rates have become the norm since the 1970s. More relevant in the present context, Swiss banks found themselves at the periphery of the global economy in 1900. In particular, before the outbreak of World War I, Switzerland not even appeared on the list of the twenty largest banks around the world, whereas two entries featured on the corresponding top-ten list in 2001 (Cassis, 2010, pp.92, 269). At around that year, representatives from Switzerland held just below ten per cent of worldwide foreign bank assets and liabilities and, hence, ranked fourth in this regard (Cassis, 2010, p.275). As banking centres, Zurich and Geneva owed their worldwide importance mainly to their specialisation in wealth management. In particular, data that have become available since 1999 suggest that, at the time, roughly one-third of private offshore wealth was managed in Switzerland, positioning it ahead of Britain with roughly one-fifth, and the United States with one-eight (Cassis, 2010, p.275). Last but not least, by being involved in six per cent of all foreign-exchange transactions in 2001, the Swiss franc was the fifth most important currency, behind the dollar, the euro, the yen, and sterling (BIS, 2001). To put these numbers in perspective, note that Switzerland is roughly the twentieth largest economy in the world—the exact position depends on the measurement and currency conversion of GDP—and ranks much further down in terms of population size.

Although Switzerland's ascent into an internationally important banking centre was, obviously, brought about by a century of strong growth within this sector, the sharp disintegration and subsequent recovery of the global economy and financial system over the twentieth century also mattered. The trough of the corresponding deglobalisation was reached somewhen during the Great Depression and the massive economic and political turmoil of both world wars. By offering a safe haven with relatively liberal financial conditions, a stable political system, and a comparatively freely convertible currency, Swiss banks capitalised, metaphorically and literally, on this fragmentation and instability. Unsurprisingly, as worldwide conditions gradually normalised during the second part of the twentieth century, Switzerland began to lose, in relative terms, its exceptional role in international banking. Reflecting this return to a more natural economic order, Zurich and Geneva have been unable to outperform top-tier centres in such activities, as the development of derivatives trading, during the recent age of financial globalisation.

Over the twentieth century, the big banks managed to greatly strengthen their role and, through both internal growth and a series of domestic and international

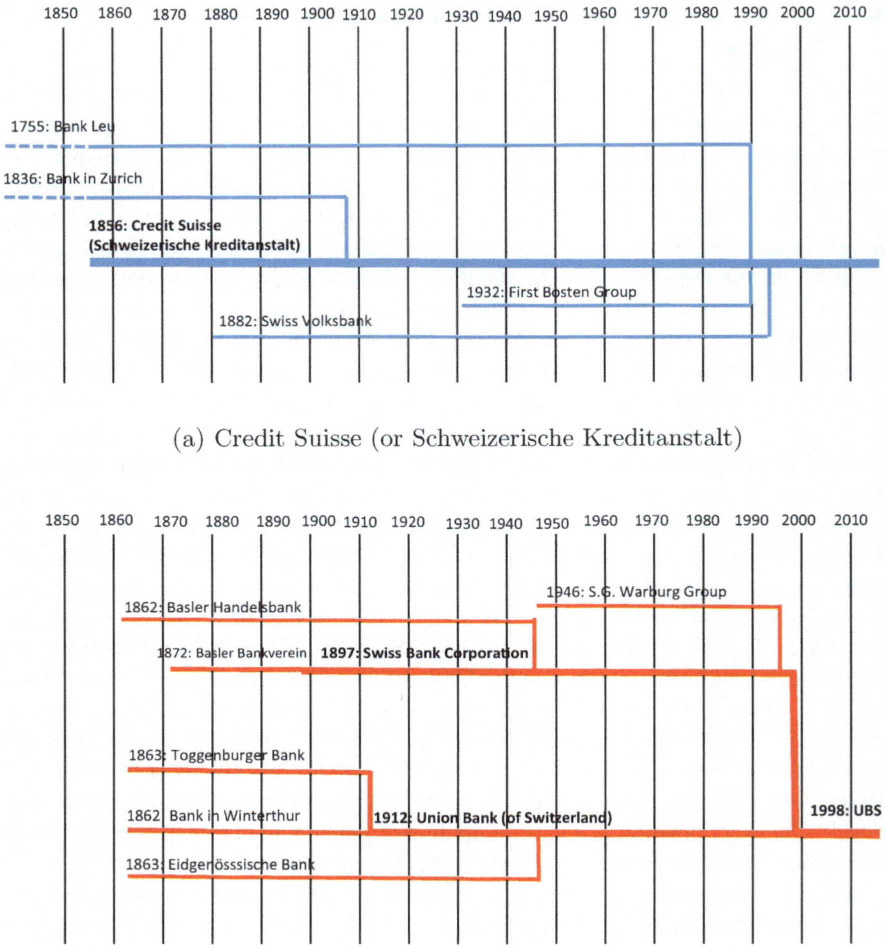

(a) Credit Suisse (or Schweizerische Kreditanstalt)

(b) UBS

Fig. 8.3 Main mergers and acquisitions of Switzerland's big banks during the nineteenth and twentieth centuries (own figure based on Jung (2000, p.413), in panel (**a**) and UBS (2012, pp.6–7) in panel (**b**))

mergers and acquisitions, became the main Swiss financial protagonists. To adopt this role, these banks transformed themselves from important domestic players in industrial finance into multinational financial firms with an extensive network of subsidiaries in all major economies around the globe. Figure 8.3 provides a synoptic overview of the underlying concentration process by depicting key events that eliminated some of Switzerland's big banks, or involved the takeover of well-known foreign investment banks during the nineteenth and twentieth centuries. Around the change of millennium, the outcome of this process was essentially a duopoly of multinational banks consisting of UBS and Credit Suisse, which were, respectively, the sixth and ninth largest banks in the world in 2001. That these multinational banks were headquartered in Zurich reflected the further consolidation of this city's position as the leading Swiss financial centre, ahead of Geneva, Basel, and Lugano.

Of course, the international banking sector is not confined to the big players. Above all, wealth management has never been the exclusive domain of the multinational firms in Zurich, but also rests on another strong pillar in the form of private banks, which can look back on a long tradition to serve a cosmopolitan clientele. Geneva (e.g., Lombard Odier, and the Pictet and Mirabaud Groups) is still an important base for these types of activity, but representatives from Basel (e.g., Bank Sarasin) and Zurich (e.g., Julius Bär, and Vontobel) have also kept some of these financial traditions alive (Cassis, 2010, pp. 261).

Another twentieth-century phenomenon reflecting the internationalisation of the financial sector was the number of foreign bank branches and subsidiaries that were set up in Zurich, Geneva, and Lugano. Around 1900, almost no foreign bank was present in Switzerland. Conversely, in 2000, the number of foreign banks in Switzerland had reached approximately 150. In a sense, this development merely represented a counter-reaction to the international expansion of Switzerland's banks. More specifically, while they reached out to the world by opening subsidiaries and branches in, e.g., London, New York, and Tokyo to access overseas markets and participate in activities, such as investment banking, foreign banks entered Switzerland to carve out their share of the offshore wealth-management business.

Finally, the domestic savings and loan business should not be overlooked. Owing to the relatively modest size of the domestic economy, the development of the cantonal as well as the regional and savings banks mainly associated with these activities was, of course, less remarkable. Although the cantonal banks have managed to maintain a key position within Swiss retail banking, the overhaul in information technology to offer modern financial services required investments that went beyond the capabilities of many smaller financial institutes. Hence, a considerable number of regional and savings banks were acquired by larger rivals during the final quarter of the twentieth century. This development explains why the total number of Swiss banks peaked at more than 500 during the 1960s, but fell back to roughly 350 by the end of the century (see Fig. 1.1a of Chap. 1). Of note, this reduction does not necessarily reflect stagnation, or even decline. The further development of the domestic banking sector has continued, rather, within larger financial institutes, and especially within the retail branches of the big banks, the cantonal banks, and, last but not least, the postal (called "Post Finance") as well as the Raiffeisen bank.

Taken together, the current Swiss banking sector encompasses large multinational firms, medium-sized and internationally oriented private banks specialising in specific activities (e.g., wealth management), and financial firms focusing on the domestic market. This mixture not only appears in banking and finance, but is a fairly common feature of the modern Swiss economy. For example, in manufacturing, the global food producer and distributor Nestlé, or the pharmaceutical company Novartis are examples of the multinational sector. Internationally oriented, and specialised manufacturing firms can be found in the watchmaking industry. Sometimes, this mixture of companies can be a source of tension. For example, during Switzerland's growth crisis of the 1990s, the domestically oriented sector, including the small regional banks, was widely seen as a source of inefficiency and hence, an obstacle to economic growth. Conversely, national champions, including the multinational banks, quite rightly prided themselves on being the main producers of Switzerland's high living standard. The new millennium showed how quickly fortunes can change, as global banking stars in Switzerland and elsewhere suddenly found themselves at the origin of a major episode of financial instability. The next chapter turns to these events.

References

Abiad, A., Dell'Ariccia, G., & Li, G. B. (2011). Creditless recoveries. *IMF Working Paper 11/58.*

Abrahamsen, Y., Aeppli, R., Atukeren, E., Graff, M., Müller, C., & Schips, B. (2005). The Swiss disease: Facts and artefacts: A reply to Kehoe and Prescott. *Review of Economic Dynamics, 8,* 749–758.

Baltensperger, E., & Kugler, P. (2017). *Swiss monetary history since the early 19th century.* Cambridge: Cambridge University Press.

Beljean, T., & Geier, A. (2013). The Swiss debt brake - has it been a success? *Swiss Journal of Economics and Statistics, 149,* 115–135.

Birchler, U. (2007). Developments in the banking sector. In . *The Swiss National Bank 1907–2007, SNB* (pp. 392–403). Zurich: NZZ Libro.

BIS (2001). *Triennial central bank survey of foreign exchange and over-the-counter (OTC) derivatives markets.* Basel: BIS.

Blocher, C. (1997). *Switzerland and the Second World War: A Clarification.* Mimeo.

Bodmer, F. (2004). *Ausmass und Gründe der Wirtschaftskrise der 90er Jahre.* Basel: WWZ-Forschungsbericht 06/04.

Bonhage, B. (2002). *Schweizerische Bodenkreditanstalt. Aussergewöhnliche Zeiten bringen aussergewöhnliche Geschäfte.* Zurich: Chronos Verlag.

Bonhage, B., Lussy, H., & Perrenoud, M. (2001). *Nachrichtenlose Vermögen bei Schweizer Banken.* Zurich: Chronos Verlag.

Brunetti, A. (2019). *Finanzplatz Schweiz Wohin? Analyse Nr. 22.* St.Gallen: Wirtschaftspolitisches Zentrum (WPZ).

Büchenbacher, C. (1977). *Tatsachen über das schweizerische Bankgeheimnis.* Zurich: Nova Press.

Cassis, Y. (2010). *Capital of capital. The rise and fall of international financial centres 1780–2009.* Cambridge: Cambridge University Press.

Friedman, M. (1953). The case for flexible exchange rates. In *Essays in positive economics* (pp. 157–203). Chicago: University of Chicago Press.

ICEP (1999). *Report on Dormant Accounts of Nazi Prosecution in Swiss Banks.* Geneva.

Jung, J. (2000). *Von der Schweizerischen Kreditanstalt zur Credit Suisse Group. Eine Bankengeschichte.* Zurich: NZZ Verlag.

Kehoe, T. J., & Prescott, E. C. (2002). Great depressions of the 20th century. *Review of Economic Dynamics, 5,* 1–18.

Kleinewefers Lehner, A. (2007). Economic trends. In *The Swiss National Bank 1907–2007, SNB* (pp. 230–236). Zurich: NZZ Libro.

Moser, T., & Savioz, M. (2022). *Karl Brunner and Monetarism.* New York: Random House.

Obstfeld, M., & Taylor, A. (2004). *Global capital markets integration, crisis, and growth*. Cambridge: Cambridge University Press.

Perrenoud, M., Lopez, R., Adank, F., Baumann, J., Cortat, A., & Peters, S. (2002). *La place financerère et les banques suisses à l'époque du national-socialisme. Publication de la Commission Indépandante d'Experts Suisse-Seconde Guerre Mondiale*. Zurich: Chronos.

Rich, G. (2007). Swiss monetary targeting 1974–1996: The role of internal policy analysis. *Swiss Journal of Economics and Statistics, 143,* 283–329.

Roethenmund, R. (1980). *The Swiss banking handbook. A complete manual for practical investors*. New York: Books in Focus.

Schiltknecht, K. (1994). Geldmengenpolitik und Wechselkurs: Der schweizerische Weg. In F. Alterbini (Ed.), *Schweizerische Geldpolitik im Dilemma: Geldmenge oder Wechselkurs* (pp. 57–68). Chur: Rüegger.

UBS (2012). *150 years of banking tradition*. Zurich.

Vogler, R. U. (2006). *Swiss banking secrecy: Origins, significance, myth*. Contributions to Financial History (Vol 7). Association for Financial History.

Chapter 9
Global Financial Crisis, Too-Big-to-Fail Problem, and the End of Banking Secrecy (Since 2008)

9.1 Switzerland and the Global Financial Crisis

The Global Financial Crisis of 2008, and the following deep economic recession around the world, had a profound effect on the banking business in Switzerland (and elsewhere). Without going into the details of the numerous and interrelated economic, financial, and political causes, the crisis essentially originated in a real-estate boom-and-bust cycle in the United States.[1] In particular, although US housing prices increased markedly during the early part of the new millennium, they underwent an unprecedented nationwide decline after 2007 (see, e.g., Blinder, 2013, pp.31ff.). Especially, within the so-called subprime segment, which basically encompasses low-income households, this decline triggered an upsurge in mortgage defaults (see, e.g., Rajan, 2010, pp.31ff.). These correlated defaults threatened, in turn, to wipe out the equity buffers of banks and nonbank financial firms heavily exposed to the corresponding loans. As such, these developments reflected a fairly normal anatomy of a financial crisis rooted in a credit boom, which is associated with an unsustainable economic expansion that sooner or later ends up in an economic and financial bust associated with a wave of bankruptcies. However, the crisis around 2008 was aggravated by several idiosyncratic factors. First, long-standing government programs to foster home ownership had inflated the subprime segment of the US mortgage market. For better or worse, these public programs to make housing more affordable had also lowered the lending standards in terms of the equity and income required to obtain a mortgage. The unsurprising outcome was an accumulation of risky loans. Second, in the years prior to the crisis, an unprecedented "securitisation" of these, and other, types of financial risk occurred in terms of pooling them into assets, such as "mortgage-backed securities". These

[1] Comprehensive accounts of the Global Financial Crisis can, e.g., be found in Rajan (2010) and Blinder (2013).

N. Herger, *Switzerland and its Banks*, Frontiers in Economic History,
https://doi.org/10.1007/978-3-031-35904-0_9

assets became very popular in the banking sector because trading them in secondary markets was widely seen as an innovative way to reduce default and liquidity risks in, e.g., mortgage lending. However, when financial instability struck, these expectations proved to be overoptimistic. In particular, rather than absorbing the financial shocks of 2008, the widespread securitisation had actually created an opaque environment with respect to the true amounts and final bearers of the losses coming to light in the real-estate market. Against this background, pervasive levels of uncertainty arose as to which financial firms held large portfolios of mortgage-backed securities or other problematic assets. Unfortunately, entrenched suspicions about imminent losses also threatened the survival of some of the leading investment banks in New York, such as Bear Stearns or Merrill Lynch. Owing to their close interconnections with key parts of the financial system, especially with the money markets as well as central components of the wholesale payments system, the potential failure of these banks posed a systemic risk. When they found themselves in deep trouble by the middle of 2008, the US government had to resort to bailouts and hastily arranged takeovers by competitors to contain the crisis (see, e.g., Blinder, 2013, pp.100ff., pp.166–167).

The US investment bank Lehman Brothers met a different fate in the sense that no bailout or takeover was arranged. The resulting failure, which hit the headlines in mid-September 2008, acted as a major catalyst for a worldwide escalation of financial and economic instability (see Blinder, 2013, pp.129ff.). More precisely, this failure triggered a chain reaction not seen since the Great Depression by turning a crisis into a panic, a case of local into global instability, and an ordinary economic downturn into an extraordinary recession. At an early stage, this escalation manifested in a collapse of the interbank market, in which commercial banks used to grant each other large amounts of short-term loans. The evaporation of this important source of liquidity destabilised, above all, some of the largest multinational banks and forced them into fire sales of assets. These developments resulted in a stock market crash as well as a bank credit crunch and, in turn, hampered investments. Through these kinds of knock-on effects, the systemic financial crisis spread into the real economy. The first drop in global trade in several decades was a clear sign of the magnitude of the downturn. In countries, such as Britain, Greece, Iceland, Ireland, and Spain, homegrown real-estate bubbles or overexpansions in the banking or public sector aggravated the panic and further deepened the downturn. These countries demonstrate that the US real-estate bust was a major, but by no means the only fault line of the crisis. To mention some of the other weaknesses and lacunas in the financial system before the fateful events of 2008, banks around the world had apparently not set aside sufficiently large capital buffers to absorb losses, central banks had been reluctant to end the real-estate boom at an early stage, too many households and governments had accumulated unsustainable levels of debt, and the "experts" working for rating agencies, as banking supervisors, or in academia had clearly overlooked some of the relevant risks associated with securitised assets.

Especially during the post-Lehman panic, there were genuine worries about a return of the treacherous economic and political environment that had destabilised the world during the Great Depression of the 1930s. However, the monetary-policy responses to the events in September 2008 differed from those after the New York stock market crash of October 1929. Above all, at an early stage of the crisis, central banks intervened in a decisive and coordinated manner in their capacity as lenders of the last resort (or ultimate liquidity providers). For example, jointly with the Federal Reserve System and the European Central Bank (ECB), the Swiss National Bank injected large amounts of money and slashed its target band for the official Swiss franc interest rate from a range between 2.25 and 3.25 per cent in September 2008 to 0 and 1 per cent only three months later (Baltensperger & Kugler, 2017, p.127). In parallel with these monetary-policy responses, governments around the world began to put together fiscal stimulus packages to boost aggregate demand and, hence, counteract some of the real economic losses of the Global Financial Crisis. Furthermore, regulatory reforms followed almost immediately. Above all, the Bank for International Settlements coordinated the efforts to tighten the international capital adequacy rules. Referring again to the place where these negotiations took place, this third package of internationally agreed-upon minimum standards appeared under the label of the "Basel III rules", which were published at the end of 2010.

For the Swiss economy and financial system, the Global Financial Crisis after 2008 shared some similarities with the situation of the 1930s (see Sect. 6.3). Notably, both events impacted on the country as a large external shock, and the collapse in foreign demand represented an outstanding problem that affected, first and foremost, the export-oriented industry, especially the machinery industry. However, owing to the international monetary system with more or less freely floating exchange rates, these economic problems had more rapid repercussions after 2008 than in the 1930s. In particular, during the Global Financial Crisis, Switzerland's currency almost immediately paid tribute to its safe-haven status. To express this status in terms of numbers, the franc appreciated from a rate of approximately 1.50 per euro (and 1.10 per US dollar) in 2008 to approximately 1.20 (0.90) in 2011. This steep appreciation greatly reduced the international competitiveness of large parts of Switzerland's manufacturing sector as well as the tourism industry. As for the financial sector, the Lehman panic primarily involved the big players' investment banking branches located in New York and London. Conversely, the wealth-management business traditionally carried out from Zurich and Geneva remained fairly stable. In a similar vein, there was only minor instability within the group of domestically oriented banks, implying that the Swiss economy did not suffer from an outstanding credit crunch or from problems with a domestic property crash. Against this background, there was also a fairly broadly shared view that comprehensive fiscal stimulus measures would be futile, or even counterproductive, given that they would end up inflating a quite stable domestic demand.

9.2 Too-Big-to-Fail Banks

For Switzerland, a key difference between the situation during the Great Depression and the Global Financial Crisis was that the banking sector had grown massively and had become much more internationally interconnected. In particular, as illustrated by Fig. 9.1, the individual market share of the biggest Swiss banks did not go beyond 10 per cent in 1930, and none of their balance sheets exceeded 20 per cent of Swiss GDP. In combination, they accounted for less than one-third of the Swiss banking sector and held assets and liabilities worth only about half of the size of Switzerland's economy. By contrast, in 2007, the balance sheet of UBS alone was more than twice as large as Switzerland's GDP and accounted for almost 50 per cent of the balance sheet of all Swiss banks combined.[2] These numbers reflect a dramatic expansion and internationalisation that exposed the big banks heavily to the epicentre of the turmoil in New York in 2008. Hence, the financial instability during that year affected Switzerland almost immediately.

Recall from the discussion above that the Global Financial Crisis revealed some dangerously low levels of loss-absorbing capital, on which the worldwide financial system around the turn of the millennium rested. Switzerland's banks were by no means an exception to this development. As depicted in Fig. 9.2, the crude ratio between (equity) capital and the balance sheet had rather dropped to historically

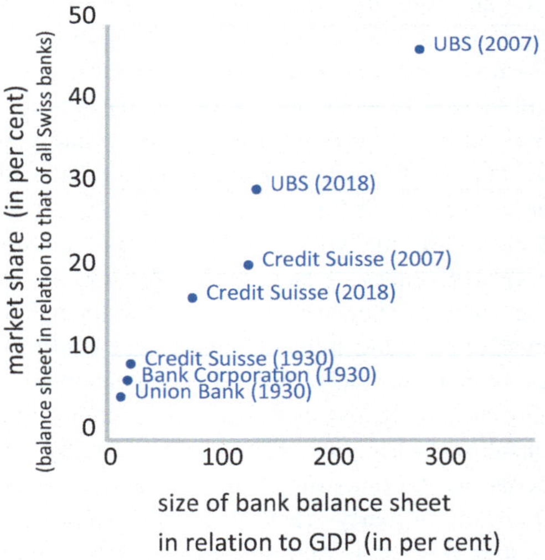

Fig. 9.1 Size of the big banks in 1930, 2007, and 2018 (own figure. Data sources: GDP: Historical statistics of Switzerland (www.hsso.ch) and SNB data portal. Bank balance sheets: Ritzmann (1973, p.265), Raff (1962, p.112), Jöhr (1956, p.93), Bauer (1972, pp.480–481), and annual reports of Credit Suisse and UBS. The balance-sheet values refer to the parent company and not to the group or holding level)

[2] Figure 9.1 is compiled on the basis of the balance-sheet totals referring to the parent company rather than to the group or the holding level. This distinction matters mainly for the situation at UBS and Credit Suisse in 2007 and 2018. Accounting for the various majority stakes in other banks and financial firms would have led to even higher market shares and sizes of the balance sheet in relation to GDP.

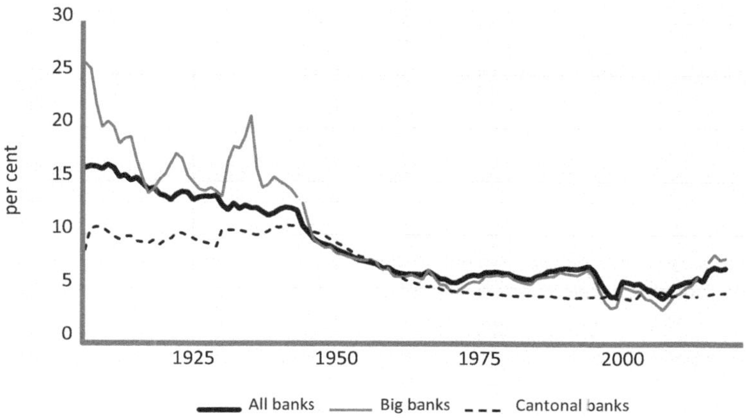

Fig. 9.2 Capital ratio (unweighted) of Swiss banks (1906–2018) (own figure. Data sources: 1906–2008: SNB, historical time series and banking statistics. Since 2008: SNB, annual banking statistics. The balance-sheet values refer to the parent company and not to the group or the holding level. Here, (bank) capital encompasses the following balance-sheet items: Statuary share capital, statuary capital reserve, voluntary retained earnings reserve, and profit/loss carried forward)

low levels of less than five per cent at the dawn of the new millennium.[3] Most of all, the big banks had become highly leveraged during financial globalisation (see Junge & Kugler, 2013, pp.321ff.).[4] Economically, these low capital ratios implied that relatively small losses were enough to give rise to bankruptcy. There is a telling comparison with the situation before World War II, when the big banks' capital ratio stood at 15 per cent and more, and even that of the cantonal banks was approximately 10 per cent—despite their explicit state guarantee. However, since the golden age (1945–1970s), a gradual decline had occurred. Around 2000, the big banks had even begun to operate with relatively smaller amounts of loss-absorbing capital than the cantonal banks. This development reflected that during the multinational expansion of the 1990s as well as the economic boom before the Global Financial Crisis, the balance sheets of UBS and Credit Suisse considerably outgrew the underlying capital.[5]

[3] These figures are again calculated at the level of the parent company. For the sake of simplicity and long-term data availability, Fig. 9.2 ignores the different risks of the underlying assets to calculate the capital ratio. In other words, Fig. 9.2 reports an unweighted ratio to reflect the amount of capital held within the banking sector.

[4] The reciprocal value of the capital ratio of Fig. 9.2 would reflect the leverage ratio, e.g., how large a balance sheet has been compiled on the basis of a given amount of capital.

[5] The leveraged expansion of the banking sector has been associated with neither an increase of Switzerland's real GDP growth nor a decline in the interest-rate spread between mortgages and savings as a measure of the financial sector's efficiency (Baltensperger & Kugler, 2017, pp.202ff.). Taken together, there is no evidence that the Swiss economy as a whole benefitted from the expansion of the big banks during financial globalisation.

At the outset of the Global Financial Crisis, the abovementioned development of the big banks left Switzerland in a highly delicate situation. In particular, owing to their leveraged growth as well as their size and interconnectedness with the domestic and international economy, they were clear examples of financial institutes that are "too big to fail". Above all, after a particularly rapid expansion of the investment banking branch since the dawn of the new millennium, UBS had become a financial giant with a substantial exposure to the types of assets, such as mortgage-backed securities, that were at the centre of the financial instability of 2008. During that year, bankruptcy no longer seemed impossible. Taken together, a too-big-to-fail problem had arisen that posed a severe risk for Switzerland and its financial sector. The remaining part of this chapter discusses these events as well as the political and regulatory reactions that followed.

9.3 Rescue of UBS and Too-Big-to-Fail Legislation

The following paragraphs focus on the delicate problems at UBS during and after 2008, including the extraordinary rescue measures taken by the Swiss National Bank and government and the regulatory reform to address the too-big-to-fail problem. These extraordinary events, as well as their causes and consequences, are merely one example of dozens of other public interventions and government bailouts to stabilise financially weakened banks in Europe and in North America during the Global Financial Crisis.

When the merger between the Bank Corporation and Union Bank was announced in 1997, the planned creation of UBS was greeted with much scepticism (see Sect. 8.3). However, the commercial success that followed quickly silenced these voices. Above all, the rapid expansion in investment banking, which became a potent division within UBS, represented an unmistakable sign of the global role that Switzerland's largest bank wanted to play. During the heyday of globalisation, this division, whose financial activities were concentrated within the top-tier financial centres of London and New York, indeed outperformed the wealth-management business traditionally associated with a Swiss bank.

Fortunes changed during the Global Financial Crisis, which revealed that the profits in investment banking had not only been high but also encapsulated aggravated levels of risk. In particular, at UBS, years of apparently lucrative trades had created large portfolios of mortgage-backed securities and other problematic assets on the balance sheet. Owing to the role played by these assets during the imminent financial and economic downturn, it is perhaps not surprising that after years of generating several billions in annual profits, the UBS investment banking division posted a large loss of almost 16 billion Swiss francs in 2007. During the entire run-up to the failure of Lehman Brothers in 2008, UBS had to write-off approximately 40 billion Swiss francs and, hence, featured among the largest victims of the early part of the crisis (Cassis, 2010, p.281). By comparison, the write-offs and losses at Credit Suisse during the same period amounted to "only" 15 billion Swiss francs.

As the worldwide economic circumstances turned from crisis to panic in autumn 2008, the stability of UBS, and hence the entire Swiss banking sector, suddenly hung in the balance. Recall from the discussion above that the failure of Lehman Brothers triggered the collapse of key components of the financial system, including the interbank lending market. Furthermore, due to the freezing of these components, as well as the distortions resulting from fire-sales, there was pervasive uncertainty regarding the adequate valuation of a whole range of financial instruments and assets. With respect to the broader situation, the economic outlook worsened by the day. On top of these perilous developments, Switzerland found itself in the uncomfortable position of having two globally interconnected banks that were clearly too big to fail—cynics even claimed that they were too big to be rescued (see Fig. 9.1). In all likelihood, a collapse of UBS would have had catastrophic consequences at the domestic and international levels.

Against this background, an extraordinary package of public rescue measures was hastily put together in October 2008 to stabilise UBS. Concretely, the federal government decided to inject six billion Swiss francs of fresh capital in the form of mandatory convertible bonds ("Pflichtwandelanleihen" or "emprunt à conversion obligatoire").[6] Furthermore, the Swiss National Bank contributed to the public rescue by setting up a so-called Stabilisation Fund, by means of which illiquid assets could be withdrawn from the UBS' balance sheet against the payment of liquid central bank reserves (Baltensperger & Kugler, 2017, p.127). The problematic assets transferred to this fund were, in turn, backed by a loan from Switzerland's central bank as well as by a 10 per cent equity stake from UBS. In essence, the Stabilisation Fund represented a bad banking scheme under the full control of the Swiss National Bank but operated jointly with UBS. Until spring 2009, securities, derivatives, and loans worth almost 40 billion US dollars (at the time roughly 35 billion Swiss francs)—the bulk of which were associated with the US real-estate market—were moved into this fund. Taken together, these public rescue measures almost immediately silenced speculation about the possible failure of a big Swiss bank. During the following years, the challenge of how to reduce the financial risks for the taxpayer resulting from the stabilisation of UBS moved to the forefront. To reduce this risk, the Swiss government sold its equity stake as soon as the situation within the international financial system had calmed down in 2009. This sale yielded a profit of more than one billion Swiss francs. Moreover, winding up the Stabilisation Fund took several years, during which the corresponding assets were gradually sold off to repay the loan from the Swiss National Bank. This process was completed in 2013 and yielded a total profit of about five billion Swiss francs (see SNB, 2013, p.37).

---

[6] During the same month, Credit Suisse managed to raise ten billion Swiss francs of fresh capital from private investors.

Given the profits from the Stabilisation Fund, it is tempting to ask whether UBS would not have survived the turmoil of 2008 without outside support by simply holding on to, e.g., the mortgage-backed securities portfolio. After all, in contrast to a stand-alone investment bank, such as Lehman Brothers, the relatively stable wealth-management business and home market could have carried Switzerland's biggest financial firm through the turbulent months after 2008. Furthermore, in contrast to other banks, UBS had already written off large amounts of its problematic asset portfolio between 2007 and early 2008. However, it should not be overlooked that the value of the assets administered by the Stabilisation Fund initially declined in early 2009. Furthermore, UBS began to show tentative signs of recovering by announcing a return to profitability only later during that year. Most importantly, it would have been irresponsible to speculate with the bankruptcy risk of a big bank. Shortly after the Lehman panic, the domino effects caused by such an event almost certainly would have wreaked havoc across the domestic and international financial system. Owing to the outstanding size and interconnectedness of UBS, Switzerland was much more exposed to the potential failure of its largest bank than most other countries in Europe or North America, including the United States and the United Kingdom (Birchler, 2007, pp.400). Plainly and simply, this acute too-big-to-fail problem necessitated extraordinary interventions in autumn 2008.

Despite the consensus that a stabilisation of UBS was urgently needed, government support for a multinational bank proved to be highly unpopular with the broader public. That investment bankers based in New York, rather than wealth managers in Zurich, were seen as the main culprit in the instability only added to the consternation within Switzerland. Given this political environment and similar to conditions during the 1930s, the extraordinary government interventions to stabilise UBS paved the way for tighter rules and regulations within the financial sector. Reflecting the key problem that emerged during 2008, the main goal of introducing new legislation in Switzerland was to do something about the too-big-to-fail problem, e.g., the dilemma when there is no viable option but to rescue a bank, whose collapse would have catastrophic consequences. As for the concrete steps, the Swiss government appointed an expert commission with the mandate to propose possible measures to tame the big banks. Based on the resulting recommendations, a so-called too-big-to-fail legislation was passed by Switzerland's parliament in 2011 and entered into force in 2012. The key parts of this legislation included a strengthening of the capital adequacy and liquidity requirements, as well as the introduction of contingency plans (so-called living wills) to keep systemically relevant financial activities, such as the payments system, in operation in case an acute crisis reemerged. The tightened capital-adequacy requirements referred, by and large, to the international minimum standard agreed-upon through the Basel III process. However, for systemically important banks, the Swiss requirement goes beyond the international minimum standard (see, e.g., Junge & Kugler, 2013, pp.317–320). In particular, their capital-adequacy ratios include a larger conservation buffer and an additional convertible-bonds layer. The corresponding rules were gradually phased in until 2020.

After 2008, the big banks were indeed tamed to some degree. In particular, the investment banking division of UBS was considerably downsized. As shown in Fig. 9.1, by 2018, this development had resulted in a large reduction of the balance-sheet size of UBS. By contrast, the corresponding reduction was much more modest at Credit Suisse. Moreover, taken together, these numbers still added up to a joint market share of the big banks of almost 50 per cent and a combined balance sheet approximately twice the size of Switzerland's GDP.

9.4 The End of International Banking Secrecy

The bank bailouts and the fiscal stimuli to alleviate the economic consequences of the Global Financial Crisis were, of course, not costless policies, but rather involved a reallocation of massive amounts of debt from private firms and households to the government. In several countries, this reallocation led to an almost seamless transition from a banking to a public-debt crisis. For the following reasons, members of the euro area, especially Greece, Italy, Portugal, and Spain, were particularly prone to making this transition or even moving perilously close to a default during the economic downturn after 2008. First, they had become accustomed to operate a loose fiscal policy by paying little attention to the euro membership obligations of limiting the annual government budget deficit to 3 per cent of GDP and the overall public debt level to 60 per cent of GDP. Second, the euro-area members had deprived themselves of a national currency with an independent monetary policy, and hence, no longer had the option to devalue the currency to regain much-needed international competitiveness or to counteract a balance-of-payments crisis. After 2010, it became quite obvious that some form of transfer from fiscally stable to weaker members would be needed to avoid outright sovereign defaults (especially, in Greece). However, reflecting entrenched disagreements regarding the principles of an appropriate fiscal and monetary policy within the euro area, the corresponding negotiations—and with them the public-debt crisis—dragged on for years. Particularly fierce controversies arose over whether to impose fiscal rules in a rigid or flexible manner, to trust in austerity programmes and structural reforms or in a fiscal stimulus to revive the economy, and to preserve national sovereignty or further deepen European integration through, e.g., the creation of a banking union (Brunnermeier et al., 2016, pp.85ff.). Although Switzerland was not completely decoupled from these debates, its fiscal and economic situation was nevertheless much more benign than that of most other European countries. In particular, the Swiss debt burden was more manageable thanks to the success of the "debt brake" (see Sect. 8.4), the rescue of UBS had resulted in a profit rather than a loss (see Sect. 9.2), and, last but not least, national sovereignty in monetary policy had been preserved.

Within the financial and banking system, the European Debt Crisis manifested primarily in a capital flight from vulnerable to safer members, especially Germany. Owing to the lack of risk-sharing mechanisms, such as a common fiscal policy or a banking union, speculation over an imminent sovereign default in Greece, arguably, also gave rise to financial contagion effects on other countries of the euro area (Brunnermeier et al., 2016, pp.210ff.). Then, again, as a non-EU country, Switzerland was not directly affected by these developments, but nevertheless felt the effect of the flight to safety through a burgeoning demand for Swiss francs, whose exchange rate moved from roughly 1.50 per euro in 2009 to almost parity in 2011. This steep appreciation by one-third within two years added yet another chapter to the franc's safe-haven history. However, in contrast to the earlier episodes during the 1930s (see Sect. 6.3) and the 1970s (see Sect. 7.1), Switzerland did not resort to administrative controls, or similar instruments, to stem the capital inflows caused by the European Debt Crisis. Instead, the Swiss National Bank intervened heavily in the foreign-exchange market in the form of purchases of large amounts of euros. In a more radical step to limit appreciation, Switzerland's central bank introduced an exchange-rate floor of 1.20 francs per euro in September 2011 (Baltensperger & Kugler, 2017, p.128). This floor was removed only in 2015, after the situation within the euro area had calmed down.

In contrast to the export industry, which suffered heavily from the extraordinary appreciation of the domestic currency, the safe-haven effect was, in itself, no direct cause for concern for the Swiss banking sector. Nevertheless, severe indirect problems arose because capital inflows in times of an international public-debt crisis are often politically intertwined with foreign allegations regarding Switzerland's role as a so-called tax haven.[7] After the Global Financial Crisis, the international taxation of offshore wealth indeed moved to forefront of the political agenda, and cracking down on tax evasion, even by means that are incompatible with the law, again became a popular policy.

To deal with structural government deficits by stepping up the fight against tax evasion, the European Union had already begun to put pressure on nonmember countries across the continent, and especially on Switzerland, during the 1990s. In particular, they were encouraged to accept a common European framework with withholding taxes levied on bank accounts and a comprehensive exchange of fiscal information among national governments. Because the latter was clearly incompatible with domestic banking-secrecy law, after lengthy negotiations concluded in 2003, Switzerland agreed only to collect an anonymous withholding tax on accounts held by EU residents. This policy caused little concern, as a similar

[7] It is perhaps worth noting that the term "tax haven" has no commonly accepted definition (see e.g. Dharmapala, 2008, pp.66). Hence, the corresponding discussions remain necessarily vague and subjective (Hines & Rice, 1994, p.76; Dharmapala, 2008, pp.662). This observation also holds true for the blacklists that have been published by the OECD to identify tax havens since 1999 (see, e.g., Emmenegger, 2015, pp.156ff.). After 2009, Switzerland briefly appeared on such a list. However, politics probably plays a role in the OECD's campaign against tax havens, insofar as only small countries and island states have ever ended up on its blacklist. Despite a comparable lack of financial transparency or international legal assistance to combat fiscal fraud, large countries, especially the United States, have hitherto never been labelled tax havens by the OECD (Emmenegger, 2014, p.159).

system had long been in place at the domestic level (see Sect. 7.3). However, after this withholding-tax system had been extended to cover EU account holders, the revenue collected and transferred to their national tax authorities without providing individual information fell short of expectations; the corresponding amounts added up to "only" about half a billion Swiss francs per year (Delaloye et al., 2012, pp.147–151). Arguably, these disappointingly low transfers reflected the readily available possibilities to bypass the withholding tax by, e.g., reallocating offshore assets to stocks or bonds, subscribing to life insurance policies with payment streams similar to fixed income assets, or turning to non-EU-based trust companies (Delaloye et al., 2012, p.168; Johannesen, 2014).

The Global Financial Crisis exacerbated the latent conflicts regarding the taxation of offshore wealth. For example, based on information gathered via methods reminiscent of the espionage employed in the 1930s (see Sect. 6.5), renewed allegations about tax evasion through banks in Switzerland (and Liechtenstein) emerged in Germany in early 2008. Despite these foreign allegations, Switzerland's government and banking community long believed that the key elements of financial privacy could be preserved by offering selective concessions, such as expanding the aforementioned anonymous withholding-tax system to countries outside the European Union. However, a dramatic escalation of the conflict occurred, when an investigation was launched in the United States against UBS based on information received from a former employee, who had agreed to cooperate after pleading guilty to charges of conspiracy to defraud the US tax authorities (Emmenegger, 2015, pp.483–485). In 2009, this investigation resulted in a request to hand over the Swiss account details of thousands of US citizens suspected of tax evasion. The US Department of Justice also indicted the head of UBS wealth management on charges of helping numerous clients evade their federal income taxes—several years later, he was acquitted of these charges. However, that may be, in 2009, the biggest Swiss bank faced the dilemma of being confronted with aggressive US legal pressure to hand over blanket account information, which violated both Swiss banking-secrecy law and the procedures stipulated within the relevant double-tax treaty. Given the precarious situation at the time (see Sect. 9.3), the Swiss authorities feared that these charges could further destabilise UBS. If a US court had decided to block access to the dollar financial market, bankruptcy would no longer have been inconceivable. To prevent this from happening, Switzerland's government resorted to emergency decrees giving UBS blanket permission to reveal the identities of thousands of US clients to their national tax authority (Emmenegger & Eggenberger, 2018, p.813).

Although Switzerland and its banks had withstood foreign attacks on banking secrecy for many decades, the increasing dependence on the US dollar market during financial globalisation had clearly led to a new environment, within which the established principles had to be hastily abandoned in the wake of the Global Financial Crisis (Emmenegger, 2015). Obviously, multinational banks, such as UBS and Credit Suisse, were particularly vulnerable to any kind of unilateral legal action that could result in the loss of their access to the world's preeminent financial and money market. However, when the US authorities turned their attention to other Swiss banks, it became clear that they were not immune to this type of legal risk, regardless of whether they are small or have no branch in the United States or anywhere else in the world. In this regard, the indictment of the Wegelin Bank in a district court in New York in 2012 represented a pioneering case that quickly led to the downfall of this ancient private bank (Emmenegger, 2015, pp.485–487). It would be going too far to review the many allegations and counterallegations, legal disputes, and settlements between numerous banks, their clients, and the US tax authorities that followed.[8] In any event, the aggressive litigation by US authorities set the tone for the policies pursued by other countries, as well as international organisations, such as the OECD, to reform the international tax system (Palan & Wigan, 2014). In particular, under the combined pressure exerted by the United States, France, Germany, and other countries and international organisations, the distinction between tax evasion and fraud in assisting foreign investigations was revoked in 2009. Furthermore, following an international trend, Switzerland abandoned its opposition to an automatic exchange of information in 2012. Since then, tax treaties on the so-called OECD compatible standard have been concluded with many countries around the world, including those with major financial centres (Schauwecker, 2018, p.13). With respect to these countries, the release of information for tax purposes no longer requires the prior consent of the offshore account holder or the presentation of specific evidence that a fiscal crime could have been committed. Taken together, these reforms put an end to Swiss banking secrecy in matters of taxation for foreign account holders.

In summary, a period of pervasive financial instability, when Switzerland became the target of intense foreign criticism for serving as a tax haven, led to the codification of banking secrecy during the Great Depression of the 1930s (see Sect. 6.5). Ironically, quite similar economic events unfolding seven decades later resulted in a more or less complete dismantling of this type of financial privacy protection at the international level. By contrast, at the domestic level, the traditional form of Swiss banking secrecy, including the system with anonymous withholding taxes and the legal distinction between tax evasion and tax fraud, has not been overturned. In a similar vein, there is as yet no automatic exchange of information between the banks and the cantonal or national tax authorities. There are several reasons for this disparate development at the domestic and international levels. First, because of the fiscal discipline enshrined in the "debt brake", Switzerland's federal government achieved a fiscal surplus during the years after 2008 rather than having to deal with the precarious increase in public debt that occurred elsewhere (see Sect. 8.4). Hence, there was no urgent quest for additional tax revenue during and after the Global Financial Crisis. Second, the instruments of direct democracy, through which Switzerland's citizens can determine their tax burden through regular votes on public budgets at all levels of government, have

[8] Landmann (2013) interprets these legal disputes as an undeclared "tax war" between Switzerland and the United States. However, virtually all alleged cases of tax evasion were resolved through outside court settlements. Because ordinary litigation and formal judgements were avoided, it remains difficult to gauge whether the US accusations against Swiss banks had any legal merit (Emmenegger & Eggenberger, 2018, p.816).

probably cultivated a political environment, within which the relationship between the population and the tax authority is based on a fair amount of trust rather than rigid administrative control. This special environment could also explain why tax morale within Switzerland is comparatively high, and the size of the shadow economy is small by international standards, despite the strict form of banking secrecy (see e.g. Feld & Schneider, 2010).

9.5 Return of the Too-Big-to-Fail Problem: Downfall of Credit Suisse

For Switzerland's banking sector, the downfall of Credit Suisse in March 2023 was yet another large shock. Compared with UBS, which had come perilously close to failure during the most dramatic period of the Global Financial Crisis, Credit Suisse weathered the turbulent years around 2008 comparatively well, especially without receiving a government bailout (see Sect. 9.3). However, during the following years, the opportunity to further strengthen the reputation of a solid bank was wasted. Quite the opposite happened when Credit Suisse became embroiled in a series of tax-evasion, money-laundering, data-leakage, and other scandals. Moreover, the risks on its balance sheet were not reduced as aggressively as those of UBS (see Fig. 9.1). The obvious differences of the balance-sheet development of Switzerland's main multinational banks at the time reflected, by and large, that Credit Suisse did not substantially downsize its investment banking branch. This branch was, in turn, responsible for several catastrophically bad investments that led to heavy losses in 2021 and 2022. These losses, together with the earlier scandals that resulted in costly lawsuits in Britain, France, and the United States, created a stream of bad headlines, which began to fatally undermine the trust in Credit Suisse.

Amid increasing deposit outflows and a collapsing share price, the situation aggravated during 2022. To stabilise the situation, Credit Suisse had to raise four billion Swiss francs of fresh capital towards the end of that year. However, this injection did not restore the necessary trust, without which even the best capitalised bank cannot survive. In particular, at the beginning of 2023, it became known that the precarious deposit outflows had not stopped but rather accelerated, which signaled a continued loss of confidence. In March 2023, the financial uncertainty following the collapse of two banks in the United States (Silicon Valley Bank and Signature Bank) as well as the announcement that shareholders were not willing to participate in yet another round of capital injections triggered a panicky increase of deposit outflows and raised doubts whether interbank lending to Credit Suisse would continue. To avoid bankruptcy, the Swiss government and the Swiss National Bank saw no other option, but to arrange an emergency takeover of Credit Suisse by UBS. The result of this hastily arranged takeover is a Swiss mega bank with a balance sheet that is much larger than Switzerland's GDP. Hence, the too-big-to-fail problem of Swiss banking remains, obviously, acute.

The emergency takeover of Credit Suisse was a sobering experience for the too-big-to-fail legislation, which failed its first test to prevent these types of government interventions from happening again (see Sect. 9.3). Above all, it became clear that the regulatory instrument of preparing contingency plans (or "living wills") is no panacea for unwinding a systemically important bank in an ordinary manner during a period with aggravated levels of uncertainty. Conversely, the tightened capital requirements probably helped to limit the domestic and international contagion of Credit Suisse's downfall and, at least initially, provided the necessary buffer to absorb the corresponding losses through private means rather than a public bailout.

At the time of writing (April 2023), the takeover of Credit Suisse by UBS has not been completed and many questions as regards the way forward remain open. Sorting out the corresponding details will probably take several years. When adopting a historical perspective, it is clear that the downfall of the oldest big bank in Switzerland represented merely the latest example of a series of shocks and major setbacks since the heyday of financial globalisation. In combination, these multiple shocks were associated with an apparent decline in the Swiss banking sector during the second decade of the new millennium.

9.6 Decline

Since the second decade of the new millennium, the Swiss banking sector has witnessed an extraordinary series of economic, financial, and regulatory shocks (Straumann, 2018; Brunetti, 2019). By and large, these shocks originated in various international developments, including financial deglobalisation in the wake of the bankruptcy of Lehman Brothers, the European Debt Crisis, the ensuing tightening of banking regulations, the economic and social restrictions from the COVID-19 pandemic, and recently the financial sanctions imposed on Russia due to the war with Ukraine as well as the upsurge in inflation within the developed world. In addition, Switzerland's banks had to cope with several home-made shocks, such as the instability associated with the UBS bailout and more recently the downfall of Credit Suisse, the outstanding too-big-to-fail problem, and, last but not least, the cross-border tax controversies that resulted in the dismantling of banking secrecy for offshore accounts. Taken together, this challenging environment has been associated with a period of stagnation or even decline. In particular, the relative importance of the Swiss banking sector in terms of the value added to GDP declined from almost 9 per cent before 2008 to 5 per cent around 2020. During the same period, the total workforce employed in this sector within Switzerland also shrank from approximately 110,000–90,000. Meanwhile, at the international level, rival banking centres, especially Hongkong and Singapore, have managed to strengthen their position at the expense of Zurich and Geneva (Brunetti, 2019, p.4).

Of course, parts of this decline represented a countermovement to the overexpansion before the Global Financial Crisis. Expressed in absolute values, the decline was also more modest, as the Swiss economy expanded, in real terms, by more

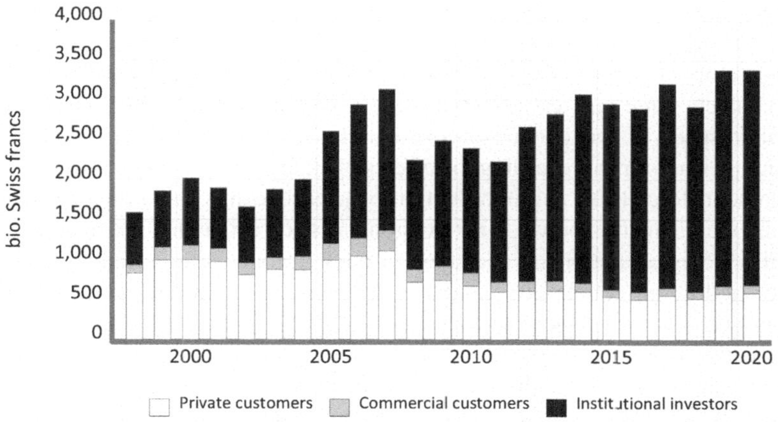

Fig. 9.3 Amount of foreign assets collected and managed by Swiss banks (own figure. Data source: Swiss National Bank. The data refer to non-resident holders of Swiss bank and custody accounts at the end of the year)

than 15 per cent between 2008 and 2020. Moreover, the strengthening of financial centres in Asia simply reflected the reality of the growing economic importance of the countries on this continent. Taken together, Swiss banks remain an important force, at both the domestic and international levels. Remarkably, the country still hosts large multinational financial firms[9] and has hitherto managed to defend its leading position within the segment of offshore wealth management. As shown in Fig. 9.3, although the amount of foreign assets under management initially declined during the turmoil of the Global Financial Crisis and the European Debt Crisis, the years thereafter saw a rebound. In international private banking, Zurich and Geneva have also retained their top position by accounting for roughly one-quarter of this market in 2018 (Boston Consulting Group, 2018). By comparison, Hongkong, which ranked second, was only half this size. In a similar vein, in 2015, Switzerland accounted for one-quarter of the entire offshore wealth-management business for private, commercial, and institutional customers combined. Although this share is impressive, it nevertheless represented a substantial decline when compared with the situation ten years earlier, when Switzerland accounted for approximately half of this market (Straumann, 2018, p.114).

The total foreign assets under management disguise considerable shifts within this segment across the abovementioned period. As shown by the breakdown in Fig. 9.3, after 2008, a decline occurred in private customers and to a smaller extent in the—quantitatively far less important—commercial customers. Conversely, foreign assets managed on behalf of institutional investors have grown considerably since

9 In the non-banking parts of the financial sector, Switzerland is, e.g., also an important centre for reinsurance due to the presence of Swiss Re (see James et al., 2013, Ch.20).

the beginning of the new millennium. This growth was not interrupted between 2010 and 2020. Institutional investors, which encompass mainly foreign hedge funds, holding companies, insurance companies, and pension funds, currently account for approximately three-quarters of the offshore wealth managed by Swiss banks.

With respect to the abovementioned multiple shocks, the historically most relevant questions arose regarding the effects of changes within the international tax environment. Recall that the introduction of a European withholding-tax scheme, revoking the distinction between tax evasion and tax fraud at the international level, and introducing an automatic exchange of bank-account information with a large number of foreign countries essentially removed the traditional pillars of Swiss banking secrecy for offshore clients (see Sect. 9.3). According to a widely held narrative, this secrecy was crucial for the worldwide success of Switzerland's banks. However, the empirical developments associated with these changes cast doubt on this view. In particular, a stock-market study by Delaloye et al. (2012) on the effect of the tax negotiations between Switzerland and the EU before 2003, and the legal disputes between UBS and the US tax authorities around the year 2009 suggests that these events barely affected the valuation of the big banks. Conversely, for private banks, the value of banking secrecy was, probably, much higher. However, it was arguably the events closely associated with the undermining of financial privacy, such as the unhindered exchange of information between national tax authorities, rather than the measures tailored to the fight against tax evasion, such as the withholding-tax scheme, that reduced the stock-market value of the private banks.[10] As for the impact of double-tax treaties with an automatic exchange of information, in Switzerland and elsewhere, they arguably had only a modest effect on the allocation of bank deposits (Johannesen & Zucman, 2014). Taken together, these developments suggest that banking secrecy mattered but was by no means the only, let alone the outstanding, factor in Switzerland's success as a banking centre. Of course, the economically highly unstable conditions during and after the Global Financial Crisis could have obscured, to some degree, the impact of the changing international tax environment that followed. Certainly, a conspicuous reduction in the volume of offshore assets under management by Swiss banks could be observed after 2008 (see Fig. 9.3). However, the extent to which this reduction reflects withdrawals of undeclared assets, or rather reallocations, losses, and defaults within an extraordinarily turbulent environment, remains unclear. It is even more difficult, or plainly impossible, to establish whether these reallocations were made by bank account holders wanting to avoid paying taxes or reflected genuine privacy concerns as well as fears that some countries could abuse their power to tax or that

[10] Another remarkable change within the private-banking segment occurred with respect to the legal organisation. Before the Global Financial Crisis, there were still banks in Geneva and other Swiss cities organised in the form of private partnerships with unlimited liability. This legal organisation was reminiscent of the family banks that used to dominate the European banking scene in the eighteenth century (see Sect. 3.1). However, in the new regulatory and tax environment in the wake of the Global Financial Crisis, the last private banks upholding these traditions have moved to some form of limited liability company.

some governments might have careless attitudes towards the protection of private financial information.

References

Baltensperger, E., & Kugler, P. (2017). *Swiss monetary history since the early 19th century*. Cambridge: Cambridge University Press.

Bauer, H. (1972). *Schweizerischer Bankverein 1872–1972*. Basel: Schweizerischer Bankverein.

Birchler, U. (2007). Developments in the banking sector. In *The Swiss National Bank 1907–2007, SNB* (pp. 392–403). Zurich: NZZ Libro.

Blinder, A. S. (2013). *After the music stopped: The financial crisis, the response, and the work ahead*. New York: The Penguin Group.

Boston Consulting Group (2018). *Global wealth 2018: Seizing the analytics advantage*. Boston.

Brunnermeier, M., James, H., & Landau, J. P. (2016). *The Euro and the battle of ideas*. Princeton: Princeton University Press.

Brunetti, A. (2019). *Finanzplatz Schweiz Wohin? Analyse Nr. 22*. St.Gallen: Wirtschaftspolitisches Zentrum (WPZ).

Cassis, Y. (2010). *Capital of capital. The rise and fall of international financial centres 1780–2009*. Cambridge: Cambridge University Press.

Delaloye, F. X., Habib, M. A., & Ziegler, A. (2012). Swiss banking secrecy: The stock market evidence. *Financial Markets and Portfolio Management, 26,* 143–176.

Dharmapala, D. (2008). What problems and opportunities are created by tax havens? *Oxford Review of Economic Policy, 24,* 661–679.

Emmenegger, P. (2014). The politics of financial intransparency: The case of Swiss banking secrecy. *Swiss Political Science Review, 20,* 146–164.

Emmenegger, P. (2015). The long arm of justice: U.S structural power and international banking. *Business and Politics, 17,* 473–493.

Emmenegger, P., & Eggenberger, K. (2018). State sovereignty, economic interdependence and US extraterritoriality: The demise of Swiss banking secrecy and the re-embedding of international finance. *Journal of International Relations and Development, 21,* 798–823.

Feld, L., & Schneider, F. (2010). Survey on the shadow economy and undeclared earnings in OECD countries. *German Economic Review, 11,* 109–149.

Hines, J., & Rice, M. E. (1994). Fiscal paradise: Foreign tax havens and American business. *The Quarterly Journal of Economics, 109,* 149–182.

James, H., Borscheid, P., Gugerli, D., & Straumann, T. (2013). *The value of risk: Swiss Re and the history of reinsurance*. Oxford: Oxford University Press.

Johannesen, N. (2014). Tax evasion and Swiss bank deposits. *Journal of Public Economics, 111,* 46–62.

Johannesen, N., & Zucman, G. (2014). The end of bank secrecy? An evaluation of the G20 tax haven crackdown. *American Economic Journal: Economic Policy, 6,* 65–91.

Jöhr, A. (1956). *Schweizerische Kreditanstalt 1856–1956*. Zurich: Conzett and Huber.

Junge, G., & Kugler, P. (2013). Quantifying the impact of higher capital requirements on the Swiss economy. *Swiss Journal of Economics and Statistics, 149,* 313–356.

Landmann, V. (2013). *Die verschwiegene Geiselnahme. Der Steuerkrieg der USA gegen die Schweiz*. Zurich: Offizin Verlag.

Palan, R., & Wigan, D. (2014). Herding cats and taming tax havens: The US strategy of "not in my backyard". *Global Politics, 5,* 334–343.

Raff, H. (1962). *Schweizerische Bankgesellschaft 1862–1912–1962*. Zurich: Orell Füssli.

Rajan, R. (2010). *Fault lines*. Princeton: Princeton University Press.

Ritzmann, F. (1973). *Die Schweizer Banken. Geschichte - Theorie - Statistik*. Bern: Verlag Paul Haupt.

Schauwecker, M. A. B. (2018). Das Bankgeheimnis im Steuerbereich. *Jusletter*.

SNB (2013). *UBS purchases StabFund from the SNB Profit of USD 3.762 billion for the SNB*. Zurich: SNB Press Release.

Straumann, T. (2018). Zurich and Geneva - The End of the Golden Age. In Y. Cassis & D. Wojcik (Eds.), *International financial centres after the Global Financial Crisis and Brexit*. Oxford: Oxford University Press.

Chapter 10
Why Are There So Many Banks in Switzerland? A Tentative Answer

Let us return to the opening question of this book: why are there so many banks in Switzerland? By reflecting on the previous chapters covering several centuries of Swiss banking history, the following paragraphs endeavour to provide a tentative answer to this question.

Owing to the landlocked location, linguistic and religious fragmentation, large areas of inhospitable terrain, and relatively small size, Switzerland does not necessarily lend itself to being a location for a major banking centre with many internationally oriented financial firms. To develop into such a centre, these natural disadvantages had to be overcome by providing an environment that was attractive in other regards. More precisely, the key factor in Switzerland's success in banking has, probably, been the relatively high degree of economic and political stability or, in other words, the safe-haven status of the country. As illustrated by twentieth century history, with two worldwide wars and a catastrophic economic depression or more recently by the shocks associated with the Global Financial Crisis, aggravated levels of uncertainty undermine the development of the banking sector. This is anything but surprising, as this sector is supposed to facilitate the management and safekeeping of wealth and to help pre-funding investments. The payoffs of these types of financial activity depend, of course, on many future developments and, therefore, are impaired by unnecessarily high levels of uncertainty. Against this background and in very broad terms, Switzerland has been able to offer an economic, legal, political, and social environment that has been less unstable than that of other countries during recent centuries. Factors that have contributed to this stability include a mature democratic system, long-standing neutrality in international affairs, a broadly shared understanding that political conflicts or labour disputes should be solved by consensus, a monetary framework with a stable national currency, and last but not least the luck of not being involved in international wars or suffering from severe internal conflicts since the nineteenth century. The Swiss banking sector has also thrived within this environment due to elements, such as a high savings rate, low public indebtedness, tax competition among the cantons, a cosmopolitan

N. Herger, *Switzerland and its Banks*, Frontiers in Economic History,
https://doi.org/10.1007/978-3-031-35904-0_10

environment in cities, such as Geneva and Zurich, and, until recently, strict banking secrecy.

Although Switzerland can look back on a centuries-old history with respect to federalism and democratic rule, which both date back to the Old Confederation before 1848, and neutrality, which has been recognised by the major European powers since the conclusion of the Peace Treaty of Westphalia in 1648, other factors of success for the banking sector have appeared more recently. For example, banking secrecy was not codified until the Great Depression of the 1930s and became an internationally important feature only for several decades during the second part of the twentieth century. Since the dawn of the millennium, key elements of this secrecy, especially the distinction between tax evasion and tax fraud as well as the high hurdles to exchanging bank-account information with foreign authorities, have been dismantled. In a similar vein, the Swiss franc, which was introduced in 1850, was initially seen as a rather weak currency subordinated to the dominant, and more stable, French franc. Above all, Swiss banks themselves have only recently become an icon on the international financial stage. Despite their ancient roots in wealth management in Geneva during the eighteenth century and early industrialisation during the nineteenth century, the genuine ascent of Switzerland's banks began only during the twentieth century. In particular, the country's safe-haven status gradually emerged after the outbreak of World War I in 1914, and the truly golden age of Swiss banking lasted merely a couple of decades after the end of World War II.

This answer highlighting the relative stability of the political and economic environment and the associated safe-haven status for the success of Switzerland's banks concludes this book but is of course not conclusive for their history. Regarding the general outlook, especially in the world of finance, the only things known about the future are that it is unknown and that shocks, crises, and scandals have a nasty habit of reappearing in an often unexpected manner. In all likelihood, episodes of instability will remain major catalysts for the transformation of the banking business. Moreover, the many uncertainties that remain are not only restricted to short-term events but also include gradual, but over time often more pervasive, economic, political, and technological developments. Against this background, it should not be taken for granted that Swiss banks will handle future uncertainty as successfully as they have done in the past. In terms of the immediate outlook, several obvious challenges lie ahead.

An outstanding example of a technological challenge is the ongoing digitalisation and the resulting financial innovations. Online banking, payments via mobile phones, crowdfunding via the Internet, and the invention of cryptocurrencies and blockchain technology have already transformed the ways in which payments are made, savings are mobilised, and credit is allocated in a digital economy. As these activities are at the heart of the banking business, its disruption through financial technology could lead to a profound transformation. For banks in Switzerland and elsewhere, this journey has probably just begun. Whether it will be a story of success, or decline, remains to be seen.

The ongoing changes in banking secrecy and the global tax environment could also be path-breaking for Switzerland's banks, as they have regularly been embroiled in cases of money laundering and tax evasion in recent decades. These cases have given rise to a large number of bewildering stories and, therefore, feature prominently in this book. However, it would be a distortion to portray the history of Swiss banking mainly as a series of money-laundering and tax-evasion scandals. Although everyday business rarely hits the headlines, Swiss banks have, of course, for decades and centuries provided an increasingly broad public at home and abroad with financial instruments to collect savings, make payments, manage wealth, and provide credit in a perfectly legal manner. Countless ordinary transactions have been made and other financial services have been offered to make this happen. At the domestic level, these types of services are today taken for granted. However, not long ago, the broad public had at most access to a simple savings account, and the payment system suffered from severe inefficiencies, such as during the free-banking period of the nineteenth century. In a similar vein, it should not be overlooked that numerous foreign clients suffering from high inflation, the risk of expropriation from their government, banking instability, or financial underdevelopment in their respective home countries have greatly benefitted from the stability in Switzerland by making use of its banking sector. Against this background, the future success of Switzerland's banks will, probably, depend on whether they manage to avoid scandalous transactions and at the same time remain sufficiently stable to excel in the provision of innocent financial services to numerous ordinary clients at home and abroad. It may sound strange, but the indicators of success will be whether Swiss banks will be too boring to make the headlines and whether Switzerland continues to be too stable to attract much international attention.

Appendix A
Timeline

1700 At around this time, the first private banks in Geneva are founded.
1755 Foundation of the Bank Leu in Zurich.
1789 After the French Revolution, the French government defaults on its debts. This default bankrupts most of Geneva's private banks.
1800 At around this time, industrialisation begins in Switzerland and numerous small savings banks are established across the country.
1826 First banknote issued by a Swiss bank.
1834 First cantonal bank founded in Bern.
1836 Bank in Zurich founded as the first stock-traded bank in Switzerland.
1848 Adoption of the Federal Constitution of Switzerland.
1850 Creation of the Swiss franc as national currency.
1856 Foundation of the "Schweizerische Kreditanstalt" ("Credit Suisse").
1881 Federal Banknote Act ends the period of unfettered banknote competition. This act forces note-issuing banks to convert all banknotes at par value and imposes common minimum-reserve requirements.
1897 Establishment of the Swiss Bank Corporation in Basel. During the following year, this bank opens a foreign branch in London.
1907 Foundation of the Swiss National Bank (SNB) as central note-issuing bank. This marks the end of the free-banking era, as banknote issuing becomes a government monopoly.
1912 Creation of the Union Bank of Switzerland in Zurich via a merger between the Bank in Winterthur and the Toggenburger Bank.
1914 The outbreak of World War I in August triggers a liquidity crisis within Switzerland. Several smaller banks have to be restructured or fail.
1931 Bank for International Settlements founded in Basel to handle (or settle) the German war reparations.
1931 Standstill Agreement in connection with Germany's foreign debt. Large parts of the loans provided by Swiss banks (and other foreign lenders) remain frozen in Germany.

N. Herger, *Switzerland and its Banks*, Frontiers in Economic History,
https://doi.org/10.1007/978-3-031-35904-0

1933 Public bailout of the "Swiss Volksbank".
1934 Failure of the "Banque d'Escompte Suisse" in Geneva.
1935 Entering into force of the Federal Act on Banks and Savings Banks. Codification of banking secrecy in Article 47 of this act.
1936 Devaluation of the Swiss franc against gold by 30 per cent.
1945 Consolidation among the big banks as the "Basler Handelsbank" and the "Eidgenössische Bank" are acquired by, respectively, the Bank Corporation and Union Bank.
1946 Washington Agreement: Switzerland agrees to pay 250 million Swiss francs to the Allies in compensation for the gold acquisition during World War II.
1962 "Meldebeschluss" forces Swiss banks to report to the government all dormant account dating back to World War II.
1977 Chiasso scandal hits Credit Suisse. The scandal is quickly followed by the introduction of a code of conduct with regard to the exercise of due diligence by the Swiss Bankers Association.
1991 Outbreak of a real-estate crisis in Switzerland. Subsequently, numerous regional banks are acquired by bigger rivals. One small regional bank, the "Spar und Leihkasse Thun", suffers from a bank run.
1993 As a result of the real-estate crisis, the Cantonal Bank of Bern has to be restructured and supported by the local government.
1998 Merger between the Bank Corporation and Union Bank to form UBS.
2005 Entering into force of a withholding-tax agreement with the EU. Henceforth, Switzerland collects a withholding tax on accounts held by EU citizens and disburses the corresponding revenue to their national government.
2008 Global Financial Crisis: Public rescue of UBS through a capital injection by the Swiss Confederation and the establishment of a dedicated Stabilisation Fund with the Swiss National Bank.
2011 Too-big-to-fail legislation is passed by Swiss parliament. This legislation imposes tighter equity capital rules and forces systemically important banks to prepare contingency plans (the so-called living wills) in case of a failure.
2012 Introduction of an automatic exchange of information (AEI) between the tax authorities of Switzerland and France. The AEI has since then been introduced with a large number of countries and essentially marks the end of international banking secrecy.
2023 Emergency takeover of Credit Suisse by UBS.

Appendix B
Major Swiss Banks in Different Languages

English	German	French	Italian
Credit Suisse	Schweizerische Kreditanstalt	Credit Suisse	–
Discount Bank of Switzerland	–	**Banque d'Escompte Suisse**	–
Federal Bank (of Switzerland)	**Eidgenössische Bank**	Banque Federale (Suisse)	–
Merchant Bank of Basel	**Basler Handelsbank**	Banque Commerciale de Bâle	–
Swiss Bank Corporation (since 1998 part of **UBS**)	Schweizerischer Bankverein	Société de Banque Suisse	Società di Banca Svizzera
Swiss National Bank (SNB)	Schweizerische Nationalbank	Banque Nationale Suisse	Banca Nazionale Svizzera
Swiss Volksbank (People's bank of Switzerland)	Schweizerische Volksbank	Banque Populaire Suisse	Banca Populare Svizzera
Union Bank of Switzerland (since 1998 part of UBS)	Schweizerische Bankgesellschaft	Union de Banques Suisses	Unione di Banche Svizzere

Notes: Name in bold letters is used in the main part of the book

N. Herger, *Switzerland and its Banks*, Frontiers in Economic History,
https://doi.org/10.1007/978-3-031-35904-0

Appendix C
Data

See Tables C.1 and C.2.

Table C.1 Number, and balance-sheet total of Swiss banks (1800–1943)

Type	Big banks		Cantonal banks		Land banks		Savings banks		Other banks		Total	
year	nr.	*bs.*	*nr.*	bs.	*nr.*	bs.	*nr.*	bs.	*nr.*	bs.	*nr.*	bs.
1800							3	0.7	1	6.8	4	7.5
1801							3	0.7	1	6.8	4	7.5
1802							3	0.6	1	6.8	4	7.4
1803							3	0.6	1	6.5	4	7.1
1804							3	0.6	1	6.3	4	6.9
1805							4	0.6	1	6	5	6.6
1806							4	0.6	1	6	5	6.6
1807							4	0.6	1	5.9	5	6.5
1808							5	0.6	1	5.8	6	6.4
1809							6	0.6	1	5.8	7	6.4
1810							5	0.6	1	5.7	6	6.3
1811							6	0.7	1	5.6	7	6.3
1812							9	0.8	1	5.6	10	6.4
1813							9	0.9	1	5.5	10	6.4
1814							9	1	1	5.5	10	6.5
1815							9	1.1	1	5.4	10	6.5
1816							14	1.4	1	5.4	15	6.8
1817							16	1.5	1	5.4	17	6.9
1818							20	1.9	1	5.4	21	7.3
1819							25	2.3	1	5.4	26	7.7
1820							31	3	1	5.3	32	8.3
1821							34	3.5	1	5.3	35	8.8
1822							37	4.2	1	5.3	38	9.5

(continued)

N. Herger, *Switzerland and its Banks*, Frontiers in Economic History,
https://doi.org/10.1007/978-3-031-35904-0

Table C.2 (continued)

Type	Big banks		Cantonal banks		Land banks		Savings banks		Other banks		Total	
year	nr.	*bs.*	*nr.*	bs.	*nr.*	bs.	*nr.*	bs.	*nr.*	bs.	*nr.*	bs.
1823							41	4.9	1	5.4	42	10.3
1824							48	6.1	1	5.5	49	11.6
1825							48	7.1	2	5.6	50	12.7
1826							53	8.1	2	6.3	55	14.4
1827							58	9.2	2	6.5	60	15.7
1828							64	10.2	2	6.6	66	16.8
1829							70	11.4	2	6.7	72	18.1
1830							72	12.1	2	6.7	74	18.8
1831							73	13	2	6.6	75	19.6
1832							74	13.9	2	6.6	76	20.5
1833							84	14.8	2	7	86	21.8
1834			1				98	16.1	2	6.8	101	22.9
1835			1	1.8			106	17.5	2	7.1	109	26.4
1836			1	2.3			112	18.8	2	7.3	115	28.4
1837			1	3.3			125	20.1	4	7.7	130	31.1
1838			1	5.8			132	21	4	13.2	137	40
1839			1	5.6			132	22.2	4	15.7	137	43.5
1840			1	5.8			134	23.6	4	16.3	139	45.7
1841			1	6.2			135	25.7	4	16.9	140	48.8
1842			1	6.5			139	27.7	4	17	144	51.2
1843			1	6.6			146	29.3	4	17.4	151	53.3
1844			1	7.6			147	31.6	5	17.7	153	56.9
1845			1	7.3			149	33.7	5	18.9	155	59.9
1846			3	8.2			147	36.4	6	24.7	156	69.3
1847			4	17.3			147	36.9	8	25.9	159	80.1
1848			5	20.6	1		147	37.9	9	31.9	162	90.4
1849			5	21.1	2	0.1	148	40.9	11	31.1	166	93.2
1850			5	26	3	0.7	150	45.4	13	32.3	171	104.4
1851			5	30	5	2	158	50	14	34	182	116
1852			5	34	6	5	169	55	15	38	195	132
1853	1	1	5	36	6	7	171	60	16	44	199	148
1854	1	5	5	37	9	16	178	63	17	41	210	162
1855	1	15	5	40	11	23	183	65	18	54	218	197
1856	2	20	5	45	13	30	185	71	19	61	224	227
1857	2	56	6	53	14	42	191	76	21	88	234	315
1858	2	56	7	62	16	47	197	82	22	93	244	340
1859	2	63	7	67	18	50	197	89	23	98	247	367
1860	2	69	7	73	20	55	199	96	24	100	252	393
1861	2	72	7	80	21	62	201	99	29	109	260	422
1862	4	74	7	91	21	71	204	104	36	119	272	459
1863	5	113	7	97	27	83	200	110	49	135	288	538

(continued)

Table C.1 (continued)

Type	Big banks		Cantonal banks		Land banks		Savings banks		Other banks		Total	
year	nr.	*bs.*	*nr.*	bs.	*nr.*	bs.	*nr.*	bs.	*nr.*	bs.	*nr.*	bs.
1864	5	125	8	104	29	104	203	114	58	154	303	601
1865	5	130	8	115	35	121	201	118	64	175	313	659
1866	5	128	8	123	37	140	197	123	73	188	320	702
1867	5	114	8	126	39	160	200	129	82	203	334	732
1868	5	113	10	143	41	173	205	143	96	212	357	784
1869	5	119	10	154	46	187	210	158	102	223	373	841
1870	5	127	11	170	47	193	208	168	103	227	374	885
1871	5	146	12	207	49	212	209	178	105	245	380	988
1872	5	175	12	233	51	221	210	188	110	271	388	1088
1873	5	201	12	263	53	250	212	194	120	324	402	1232
1874	5	196	12	304	58	279	207	201	131	368	413	1348
1875	5	198	12	332	58	302	210	212	135	401	420	1445
1876	5	201	12	370	59	326	213	225	141	438	430	1560
1877	5	201	13	420	60	352	212	235	143	416	433	1624
1878	5	187	13	464	61	374	213	244	144	426	436	1695
1879	5	200	14	503	63	397	219	253	145	445	446	1798
1880	5	223	14	536	64	418	217	265	148	466	448	1908
1881	5	218	14	532	65	438	215	281	148	477	447	1946
1882	5	221	14	554	66	456	212	294	147	499	444	2024
1883	5	230	17	607	67	469	214	307	147	501	450	2114
1884	5	220	17	622	68	477	214	317	149	513	453	2149
1885	5	220	17	630	69	482	210	335	148	515	449	2182
1886	5	226	18	701	68	455	207	346	146	483	444	2211
1887	5	238	19	710	68	469	204	358	148	524	444	2299
1888	5	236	18	720	70	496	202	359	147	530	442	2341
1889	5	301	18	746	73	508	202	371	150	543	448	2469
1890	5	348	20	789	73	538	197	380	151	587	446	2642
1891	5	319	20	856	73	546	192	382	146	598	436	2701
1892	5	314	22	919	72	562	192	388	141	568	432	2751
1893	5	315	22	1026	72	592	187	396	141	587	427	2916
1894	5	329	22	1024	71	625	186	405	140	605	424	2988
1895	5	339	22	1073	72	673	183	417	138	623	420	3125
1896	6	495	23	1143	73	715	180	432	140	659	422	3444
1897	6	582	23	1300	74	755	180	453	141	688	424	3778
1898	6	615	23	1345	74	812	180	473	141	731	424	3976
1899	6	640	24	1438	77	860	180	489	142	759	429	4186
1900	6	674	25	1537	76	893	182	503	143	801	432	4408
1901	6	707	25	1677	75	926	182	524	145	838	433	4672
1902	6	761	25	1757	74	941	183	553	144	862	432	4874
1903	6	854	25	1786	75	980	183	572	147	931	436	5123
1904	6	922	25	1861	75	1025	186	599	152	1005	444	5412

(continued)

Table C.1 (continued)

Type	Big banks		Cantonal banks		Land banks		Savings banks		Other banks		Total	
year	nr.	*bs.*	*nr.*	bs.	*nr.*	bs.	*nr.*	bs.	*nr.*	bs.	*nr.*	bs.
1905	6	1090	25	2010	78	1079	183	630	158	1083	450	5892
1906	6	1306	25	2168	80	1180	183	611	158	1161	452	6426
1907	6	1376	25	2334	80	1253	183	631	155	1090	449	6684
1908	7	1610	25	2430	80	1150	179	657	163	1137	454	6984
1909	7	1849	25	2516	79	1229	179	658	162	1185	452	7437
1910	7	1976	25	2649	80	1331	178	700	159	1231	449	7887
1911	7	2141	25	2873	75	1408	176	727	158	1301	441	8450
1912	7	2428	25	3135	73	1374	168	732	149	1198	422	8867
1913	7	2487	26	3463	67	1311	165	763	146	1206	411	9230
1914	7	2485	27	3597	65	1282	164	766	139	988	402	9118
1915	8	2807	28	3789	65	1292	160	770	138	1022	399	9680
1916	8	3214	28	3979	65	1307	160	792	137	1109	398	10,401
1917	8	3689	28	4246	65	1353	159	817	136	1204	396	11,309
1918	8	4151	28	4462	65	1389	157	890	135	1363	393	12,255
1919	8	4610	28	4729	66	1410	156	1022	131	1383	389	13,154
1920	8	4814	28	4961	65	1361	150	961	127	1354	378	13,451
1921	8	4360	28	5144	65	1331	146	966	122	1317	369	13,118
1922	8	4141	28	5235	66	1272	144	1000	122	1249	368	12,897
1923	8	4255	28	5301	68	1263	140	1032	118	1254	362	13,105
1924	8	4686	28	5612	68	1268	136	1057	119	1293	359	13,916
1925	8	4924	28	5836	67	1242	133	1087	119	1305	355	14,394
1926	8	5615	28	6091	68	1453	133	960	119	1383	356	15,502
1927	8	6336	28	6470	69	1522	133	1007	121	1521	359	16,856
1928	8	7162	28	6684	70	1648	132	1040	121	1630	359	18,164
1929	8	8195	28	7094	72	1766	132	1096	122	1776	362	19,927
1930	8	8578	28	7600	72	1916	132	1178	122	1935	362	21,207
1931	8	7171	28	7709	74	2047	131	1256	121	1870	362	20,053
1932	8	6430	28	7834	75	2114	131	1311	118	1819	360	19,508
1933	7	5547	28	7915	76	2135	131	1344	115	1749	357	18,690
1934	7	4998	28	8061	77	2144	131	1355	114	1618	357	18,176
1935	7	4157	28	7968	77	2226	130	1465	115	1408	357	17,224
1936	7	4600	28	8159	77	2201	126	1355	115	1340	353	17,655
1937	7	4662	28	8410	77	2275	126	1392	110	1337	348	18,076
1938	7	4487	28	8284	76	2285	124	1444	108	1192	343	17,692
1939	7	4280	28	7993	78	2260	124	1443	107	1142	344	17,118
1940	7	4392	28	8003	78	2250	119	1410	103	1112	335	17,167
1941	7	4493	28	8141	80	2278	117	1430	102	1158	334	17,500
1942	7	4732	28	8241	80	2323	117	1478	99	1209	331	17,983
1943	7	4989	28	8397	91	2358	118	1536	98	1269	342	18,549

Notes: nr. refers to the number, and bs. to the aggregate balance sheet (in mio. Swiss francs) of the type of bank. The data are taken from Ritzmann (1973, pp.263–266). Between 1800 and 1944, statistics on private banks and stock-market banks are not available

Table C.2 Number and balance-sheet total of Swiss banks (since 1944)

Type	Big banks		Cantonal		Reg./savings		Private		Raiffeisen		Branches		Other		Total	
year	nr.	bs.	nr.	bs.	nr.	bs.	nr.	bs.	nr.	bs.	nr.	bs.	nr.	bs.	nr.	bs.
1944	7	5199	27	8562	291	5484	76	407	2	670	8	74	52	232	463	20,628
1945	5	5543	27	8747	293	5661	76	439	2	723	8	116	56	254	467	21,483
1946	5	6429	27	8988	292	5987	81	537	2	782	8	131	56	297	471	23,151
1947	5	6834	27	9316	295	6357	81	656	2	845	7	145	56	417	473	24,570
1948	5	7155	27	9676	292	6556	79	683	2	885	7	201	57	472	469	25,628
1949	5	7344	27	10,189	292	6922	76	667	2	936	7	198	62	535	471	26,791
1950	5	7977	27	10,536	290	7244	73	657	2	984	7	183	65	644	469	28,225
1951	5	8410	27	11,011	289	7672	74	693	2	1042	7	222	70	766	474	29,816
1952	5	8847	27	11,521	288	8179	74	712	2	1116	7	224	77	912	480	31,511
1953	5	9272	27	12,119	289	8776	72	744	2	1202	7	223	78	1007	480	33,343
1954	5	9686	27	12,728	290	9408	71	840	2	1301	7	236	80	1157	482	35,356
1955	5	10,494	28	13,700	289	9831	70	860	2	1404	7	266	84	1268	485	37,823
1956	5	11,255	28	14,631	288	10,372	66	904	2	1513	7	295	89	1456	485	40,426
1957	5	12,198	28	15,818	285	10,801	65	953	2	1597	8	364	99	1671	492	43,402
1958	5	13,904	28	17,081	285	11,528	62	1125	2	1700	9	472	110	2106	501	47,916
1959	5	14,771	28	18,261	285	12,386	60	1184	2	1831	8	559	115	2555	503	51,547
1960	5	17,545	28	19,864	284	13,382	61	1443	2	1992	8	805	122	3218	510	58,249
1961	5	21,180	28	22,022	283	14,676	62	1724	2	2195	8	807	133	4203	521	66,807
1962	5	24,275	28	23,967	282	15,967	57	1659	2	2439	8	848	137	5427	519	74,582
1963	5	27,694	28	26,071	278	17,468	53	1652	2	2682	9	1112	143	6734	518	83,413
1964	5	31,002	28	28,355	278	18,794	51	1751	2	2925	9	1236	151	7797	524	91,860
1965	5	33,867	28	30,862	278	19,952	50	1775	2	3173	9	1574	159	8933	531	100,136
1966	5	36,700	28	33,379	274	21,125	49	1770	2	3418	9	1997	165	10,211	532	108,600
1967	5	43,513	28	36,428	270	22,627	47	2017	2	3721	10	2618	167	12,439	529	123,363
1968	5	57,127	28	39,934	261	23,289	47	2529	2	4051	11	3071	169	16,143	523	146,144

1969	5	74,249	28	43,555	260	25,086	47	2490	2	4417	11	4106	180	19,505	533	173,408
1970	5	94,357	28	47,558	254	27,280	38	2487	2	4866	12	4901	184	22,812	523	204,261
1971	5	114,353	28	52,790	248	29,260	38	2990	2	5446	13	6405	193	28,096	527	239,340
1972	5	121,256	28	57,856	244	32,345	37	2691	2	6203	14	6164	196	31,663	526	258,178
1973	5	121,152	28	61,687	237	32,573	36	2566	2	7047	15	6134	198	37,543	521	268,702
1974	5	125,811	28	67,106	234	34,800	32	2450	2	7810	15	5718	192	35,460	508	279,155
1975	5	146,997	28	74,612	232	37,459	31	2125	2	8607	14	5878	188	39,605	500	315,283
1976	5	161,382	28	79,369	225	38,138	28	2043	2	9416	14	6249	185	43,267	487	339,864
1977	5	171,511	28	84,443	225	40,252	27	2077	2	10,271	14	6378	183	46,794	484	361,726
1978	5	188,752	28	88,382	223	42,287	27	2346	2	11,192	14	6848	181	50,230	480	390,037
1979	5	212,240	29	93,812	220	42,911	26	2343	2	12,207	15	7682	178	57,217	475	428,412
1980	5	239,394	29	101,201	220	45,759	26	2635	2	13,216	16	9215	176	66,730	474	478,150
1981	5	282,225	29	110,995	219	49,218	25	2857	2	14,493	16	10,817	178	76,345	474	546,950
1982	5	305,749	29	119,015	218	52,181	25	3501	2	15,621	17	12,398	181	87,503	477	595,968
1983	5	328,657	29	126,705	217	55,914	25	3708	2	17,148	17	11,901	178	97,614	473	64,1647
1984	5	368,229	29	134,337	217	59,954	24	3509	2	18,863	15	14,195	186	107,723	478	706,810
1985	5	394,627	29	144,007	216	64,388	24	4226	2	20,747	16	15,985	189	114,371	481	758,351
1986	5	436,825	29	154,570	215	69,621	24	4621	2	23,048	16	18,178	197	121,018	488	827,881
1987	5	460,752	29	167,481	214	76,082	23	5494	2	25,387	17	19,894	202	126,782	492	881,872
1988	5	483,497	29	179,701	213	82,414	22	5025	2	28,109	17	24,071	205	142,091	493	944,908
1989	5	509,713	29	195,173	210	88,607	22	5624	2	31,225	17	27,432	209	153,628	494	1,011,402
1990	4	523,526	29	213,879	204	93,595	22	5581	2	34,042	16	18,479	218	167,737	495	1,056,839
1991	4	543,187	28	228,282	189	92,741	19	5334	2	36,876	16	15,201	222	172,235	480	1,093,856
1992	4	567,281	28	238,830	174	89,941	19	5858	2	39,438	14	11,356	227	176,723	468	1,129,427
1993	4	611,841	28	253,080	155	83,460	18	7456	2	42,579	13	11,385	230	186,845	450	1,196,646
1994	4	621,989	27	259,281	135	71,650	17	6847	1	45,747	13	13,915	226	184,116	423	1,203,545

(continued)

Table C.2 (continued)

Type	Big banks		Cantonal		Reg./savings		Private		Raiffeisen		Branches		Other		Total	
year	nr.	bs.	nr.	bs.	nr.	bs.	nr.	bs.	nr.	bs.	nr.	bs.	nr.	bs.	nr.	bs.
1995	4	730,587	25	261,527	127	72,264	17	7126	1	49,868	14	15,566	225	186,490	413	1,323,428
1996	4	869,370	24	265,858	119	71,271	17	9298	1	53,343	16	18,576	199	207,617	380	1,495,333
1997	4	1,121,233	24	268,994	117	70,750	16	11,494	1	57,296	18	23,906	193	228,542	373	1782,215
1998	3	1,373,548	24	274,323	108	71,719	16	12,961	1	61,532	21	27,320	185	236,521	358	2,057,924
1999	3	1,504,757	24	296,195	106	74,065	17	15,448	1	65,556	21	21,534	184	266,293	356	2,243,848
2000	3	1,340,310	24	303,385	103	75,808	17	18,424	1	77,142	23	18,843	191	290,968	362	2,124,880
2001	3	1,415,981	24	304,779	94	77,682	17	17,374	1	82,409	25	17,010	193	312,180	357	2,227,415
2002	3	1,444,462	24	312,804	88	78,820	15	16,222	1	92,684	25	16,436	189	290,447	345	225,1875
2003	3	1,408,660	24	310,664	83	80,619	15	17,427	1	10,2140	26	16,013	181	301,519	333	2,237,042
2004	3	1,643,506	24	314,331	83	81,492	14	16,807	1	106,098	25	14,925	180	313,610	330	2,490,769
2005	2	1,910,445	24	326,997	79	83,878	14	17,207	1	108,187	28	17,427	182	382,315	330	2,846,456
2006	2	2,198,373	24	343,080	78	85,942	14	18,561	1	113,998	29	23,657	176	410,586	324	319,4197
2007	2	2,341,136	24	356,580	76	85,311	14	29,513	1	123,076	30	34,444	176	487,838	323	3,457,898
2008	2	1,885,316	24	389,316	75	89,922	14	40,677	1	131,575	31	23,717	180	519,097	327	3,079,620
2009	2	1,444,799	24	403,548	70	92,276	14	39,211	1	139,520	33	23,891	181	524,978	325	2,668,223
2010	2	1,482,146	24	421,548	69	96,070	13	45,798	1	147,239	32	24,912	179	496,813	320	2,714,526
2011	2	1,466,696	24	449,385	66	101,117	13	54,399	1	155,889	32	56,813	174	508,666	312	2,792,965
2012	2	1,364,750	24	482,278	66	104,307	13	61,768	1	164,670	28	94,121	163	506,389	297	2,778,283
2013	2	1,322,279	24	495,555	64	106,426	11	65,636	1	173,619	27	78,652	154	606,990	283	2,849,157
2014	2	1,460,240	24	522,628	63	108,954	7	7407	1	185,703	27	59,248	151	697,541	275	3,041,721
2015	3	1,424,231	24	537,441	62	113,076	7	6699	1	202,412	26	72,667	143	669,591	266	302,6117
2016	4	1,454,808	24	553,231	62	116,141	6	5942	1	215,262	26	75,919	138	680,073	261	3,101,376

2017	4	1566,435	24	575,343	62	118,131	6	6198	1	225,253	23	93,320	133	664,763	253	324,9443
2018	4	1,520,781	24	600,318	60	120,283	5	6323	1	225,333	23	90,944	131	661,020	248	3,225,002
2019	4	1,540,711	24	626,727	60	126,317	5	5753	1	248,345	24	98,154	129	671,609	247	3,317,616
2020	4	1,566,626	24	697,083	59	111,439	5	6833	1	259,653	26	114,261	126	711,341	245	3,467,236

Notes: nr. refers to the number, and bs. to the aggregate balance sheet (in mio. Swiss francs) of the type of bank. The data are taken from the Swiss National Bank (SNB), historical time series, and banking statistics. Regional and savings banks are summarised into one group. Other banks include stock-market banks and foreign owned banks

Reference

Ritzmann, F. (1973). *Die Schweizer Banken. Geschichte - Theorie - Statistik*. Bern: Verlag Paul Haupt.

Appendix D
Glossary

Arbitrage refers to the simultaneous purchase and sale of identical goods or assets in different markets. As long as the corresponding prices differ, and transaction costs are sufficiently low, arbitrage transactions yield virtually risk-free profits. The exploitation of these profits tends to eliminate the underlying price differences.

The **Bank for International Settlements (BIS)** was originally designed to facilitate the transfer of German war reparations from World War I to the Allies. The BIS was opened in 1931 in Basel. Today, the BIS supports central banks to maintain monetary and financial stability through international cooperation and by acting as bank for central banks.

Banking secrecy refers to legal and professional obligations to keep financial information obtained through the relationship between a bank and its customers confidential. Banking secrecy holds never unconditionally and can, e.g., be lifted in connection with criminal investigations or to combat tax evasion.

Basel is a Swiss city. Its banking history resonates until today through the presence of the Bank for International Settlements (BIS), whose head office is located in Basel. Therefore, the international standards regarding capital and liquidity adequacy agreed through negotiations at the BIS are also referred to as "Basel rules".

Bern is the capital city of Switzerland.

In terms of total assets, earnings, and staff numbers, the **big banks** (Grossbanken; grandes banques) are the largest bank category in Switzerland. Nowadays, they are typically universal banks offering a broad range of financial services both within Switzerland and abroad.

A **bill of exchange** is a financial security, with which cashless payments in international trade and finance used to be made. In particular, a bill of exchange was a written order by an issuer, called the drawer, instructing a counterparty, called the drawee, to pay a certain amount of money at a specific place. Bills of exchange could be sold before their due date to a third party, called the acceptor, who adopted

N. Herger, *Switzerland and its Banks*, Frontiers in Economic History,
https://doi.org/10.1007/978-3-031-35904-0

responsibility to make the final payment. For this financial service, the acceptor charged an interest rate called "discount rate".

The **Bretton Woods System** was an international currency system during the decades after World War II. Within this currency system, the US dollar was convertible at 35$ per ounce into gold. Other currencies of countries within the Western hemisphere were convertible according to fixed exchange rates into US dollars. Formally, Switzerland was not a member of the Bretton Woods System. Informally, the Swiss National Bank followed the rules of this system.

Cantonal banks (Kantonalbanken, banques cantonales) are the publicly supported banks of the cantons. During the nineteenth century, many of these banks had, among other things, the right to issue own forms of paper money (note-issuing banks). Cantonal banks are today ordinary commercial banks focusing on the savings and mortgage business. Most cantonal banks have a (explicit or implicit) state guarantee (e.g., by the canton).

The jurisdictions of the Swiss confederation are called **cantons**. They have a status comparable to that of the states of the United States of America.

Capital controls are administrative measures and constraints to regulate the cross-border exchange of money and capital.

The **central bank** is a financial institute—nowadays usually under public law—responsible for setting monetary policy. Central banks wield influence over the economy, because they have been granted the monopoly over the issuance of currency. Among other things, this monopoly gives them the power to steer interest rates and, hence, determine how much money and credit circulates within the economy. By employing a range of monetary-policy instruments, modern central banks pursue macroeconomic goals, such as keeping the price level stable (preserving purchasing power) or smoothing the business cycle. Among many other tasks, central banks play a leading role within the financial system in terms of acting as lenders of last resort to the banking sector in times of financial crisis. The central bank of Switzerland is called the Swiss National Bank (SNB).

Commercial banks are financial intermediaries that accept deposits, but can also be refinanced through other sources, such as debt and equity, and at the same time provide loans to firms and households.

The **democratic movement** summarises the broad opposition in Switzerland against the liberal establishment, which dominated the political and economic system during the second part of the nineteenth century. The movement was democratic in terms of advocating the introduction of direct-democratic rights (referendum and initiative) on all levels of government to break the power of the political and economic establishment.

Direct democracy refers to a system of government, within which laws and budgets are directly approved by the voters through dedicated assemblies or at the ballot box rather than indirectly through an elected parliament. Switzerland actual combines direct and indirect forms of democratic rule and therefore is also referred to as a "semi-direct democracy".

A **dormant account** has had no financial activity for a long period of time, except for the posting of interest. According to current Swiss legislation, bank assets are treated as dormant when the contact with the account holder has been interrupted for more than 10 years.

With respect to money and banking, **double criminality** stipulates a principle, according to which international legal assistance, including the lifting of banking secrecy, is only provided, when an alleged financial crime is outlawed in both the domestic and foreign country involved in the corresponding investigation.

Eurocurrency encompasses bank deposits and other assets that are not denominated in the currency of the local financial centre. For example, dollar-denominated assets held outside the United States (say, in London or Tokyo) are called eurodollars.

Federalism is a political system, within which the local jurisdictions retain a large degree of political power (especially in the areas of organising the local government, holding elections, raising taxes, policing, and jurisprudence). In Switzerland, citizens belong to three levels of government, namely the municipality, canton, and confederation.

A **fire sale** refers to the hasty sale of assets at extremely discounted prices in response to an emergency, such as a financial crisis.

A **free-banking system** is characterised by the absence of regulations, and other forms of government interference, in the market for paper money. In other words, banks can issue their own form of banknotes in a more or less competitive manner.

Geneva is a relatively ancient banking centre in Switzerland. Aside from the financial industry, Geneva is also the headquarter location of major international organisations, including parts of the United Nations, as well as an important watchmaking centre.

The **Great Moderation** is a period between the 1990s and 2007 characterised by low levels of inflation and moderate business-cycle fluctuations in many countries around the world.

Gresham's law refers to arbitrage transactions within a bimetallic currency system, within which the official form of money (e.g., coins) is convertible into two precious metals (e.g., silver and gold) at fixed mint-pars. If the market price of these monetary metals deviates substantially from the official mint-par, the officially overvalued form of currency will flood into circulation, while the more valuable metal in the market will no longer circulate as coins. In that sense, "bad money drives out good money".

The popular **initiative** is a political instrument to propose a new clause in, or a partial amendment of, the constitution. When citizens manage to collect a certain number of signatures for their proposed constitutional change, it has to be put on the ballot. A majority of the voters and the cantons is required for approval.

Investment banks raise money for business and governments and act as brokers and dealers in financial markets. Investment banking used to be limited to the subscription of shares and bonds and the trading of financial assets in secondary markets. Today, investment banking is thought to include participation in mergers and acquisitions and consulting, among other activities.

A **mandatory convertible bond** is a bond issued by a bank or a company. Upon the demand of the bearer, this bond must be converted into shares on or before a specific date.

Similar to investment banks, **merchant banks** typically specialised in mercantile operations, including large international transactions of assets, capital, commodities, and money.

Money laundering refers to illegal processes of making large amounts of money earned through criminal activities, such as drug trafficking and terrorist funding, appear to have come from a legitimate source. The money is considered dirty, and the process "launders" it to make it look clean.

Neutrality is an international status, through which a country announces that it is neither directly, nor indirectly, involved in a military conflict between foreign countries. By pursuing a policy of the so-called permanent neutrality, Switzerland goes further by announcing that it will not be involved in any future military conflicts between foreign powers. This status has officially been recognised by the international community since at least the Peace Treaty of Westphalia of 1648. The rights and obligations of neutral countries are stipulated in the Hague Conventions of 1912.

Note-issuing bank refers to a financial institute with the right to issue paper money in the form of banknotes. In a free-banking system, several banks compete over issuing banknotes. Currently, in virtually all countries, banknotes are issued through a government monopoly with a central note-issuing bank, which is generally identical with the central bank.

The **Old Confederation** (Alte Eidgenossenschaft) refers to the loose alliance between the ancient cantons in Switzerland before the foundation of the modern Swiss Confederation in 1848. The Old Confederation had no fully fledged federal institutions. It was essentially organised around an informal diet meeting (called "Tagsatzung") comprising the delegates of the cantons.

Private banks (Privatbanken, banques privées) are typically organised as private partnerships with a more or less unlimited liability regarding the partner's own wealth. Most of the oldest banks in Switzerland were private banks owned by wealthy financiers or aristocrats. However, today, this legal structure has become rare in banking.

The **referendum** is a political instrument to challenge a piece of legislation that has been approved by parliament. Typically, when a certain quorum of the citizens signs a referendum within a given period (at the national level in Switzerland currently 50'000 signatures within three months), the piece of legislation has to be put on the ballot. A majority of the voters is required for approval.

A **rente** was an annual payment of fixed-income securities during the ancien régime. Rentes could be paid in perpetuity, over a lifetime (rente viagère), or over some other period. Rentes viagères were popular financial instruments to fund French sovereign debt during the eighteenth century.

In the area of banking and finance, **safe havens** are countries and currencies to which investors flock in times of crisis. Hence, safe-haven currencies tend to appreciate during international episodes of political and economic instability.

Savings banks (Sparkassen, caisses d'épargne) are financial institutes dedicated to mobilising savings from low-income households. Especially during the nineteenth century, the savings-banks movement promoted these financial institutes to address poverty. During the second part of the nineteenth century, a large number of savings banks disappeared.

Securitisation is the financial activity of transforming the liquidity and risks of an asset by bundling it into a pool (or group) of more or less similar assets, which together form a new security that can be traded in a financial market. A prominent example for this financial activity is the bundling of individual mortgages and their underlying default risks into a mortgage-backed security.

With the **Standstill Agreement** of 1931, creditor countries, including Switzerland, agreed to grant Germany a deferral for fulfilling its financial obligations on foreign loans and deposits.

The **Swiss Bankers Association** (SBA) is the association representing banks in Switzerland.

The **Swiss National Bank** (SNB) is the central bank (or monetary authority) of Switzerland.

Tax evasion refers to a situation, when a person or firm fails to pay a tax liability due to negligent behaviour. In Switzerland, this type of negligence infringes the law but is prosecuted under the civil law.

Tax fraud refers to a situation, when a person or firm deliberately avoids paying a tax liability (by forging documents, manipulating balance sheets, etc.). In Switzerland, this type of activity is illegal and officially prosecuted under the criminal law.

A **tax haven** is a relatively loosely defined term for jurisdictions offering foreign firms and individuals an environment with minimal, or even no, tax liabilities, or other attributes designed to appeal to foreign tax evasion.

Too-big-to-fail refers to the problem that an economic unit—typically a bank—has become so large, or systemically relevant, that a bankruptcy would have massive negative effects on virtually all parts of the economy.

Wealth management refers to the delegation by an asset owner (individual or institutional) of the corresponding managerial decisions to a financial firm, typically a bank. Based on a relationship of trust, it is expected that the asset manager complies with the given instructions as well as the applicable rules and regulations. In the case of wealthy private individuals, this type of activity is also referred to as "private banking".

Zurich is the largest city of Switzerland and its economic and financial centre.

Index

A
Automatic exchange of information, 148, 150, 154

B
Bank espionage, 95
Bank for International Settlements, 22, **82**, 120, 141
Banking Act, 92, 94
Banking scandals, 123
Banking secrecy, 93–97, 113–116
  end of, 150
Bank in Winterthur, 67
Bank in Zurich, 63
Bank Leu, 38, **62**, 81, 129
Bank Sarasin, 135
Banque Générale Suisse, 69
Basel, 11, 14, 22, 68, 78, 129
  Council of Basel, 36
Basel rules, 120, 141, 146
Basler Handelsbank, 69, 79, 81, 89, 95, 105
Bern, 11, 14, 37, 57
Bernoulli, Daniel, 14, 37
Bernoulli, Jacob, 35, 37
Big banks, 18, 65, 78, 81, 86, 99, 109, 111, 128, 133, 142, 147, 154
Bill of exchange, 29
Bretton Woods System, 25, 112
Brunner, Karl, 120

C
Calvin, Jean, 9, 32
Cantonal banks, 41, **55**, 58, 81, 91, 99, 111, 128, 135
  Cantonal Bank of Bern, 50, 128
  Cantonal Bank of Zurich, 56
Capital controls, 86, 112, 120
Catholicism, 15
Charles the Bold, 13
Chiasso scandal, 111, **124**
Civil War of 1847, 15, 17
Coal central, 79
Code of conduct with regard to the exercise of due diligence, 125
Cold War, 106, 130, 132
Collusion, 121, 127
Comptoir d'Escompte de Genève, 81, 91, 92
Congress of Vienna, 15
Covid-19 pandemic, 26
Credit Suisse, 63, **67**, 81, 89, 99, 109, 124, 132
  downfall of, 151

D
Debt brake, **130**, 147, 150
Democratic movement 19–20, 66
De Pury, David, 41
Devaluation (of 1936), 87
Direct democracy, 10, 19
Dormant accounts, **99**, 132
Double incrimination, 116, 126
Dunant, Henry, 22

E
Eidgenössische Bank, 81, 89, 105
Escher, Alfred, 19, 43, **66**
Euler, Leonhard, 14, 37
Euro, 25, 26
Euromarkets, 113, 119

N. Herger, *Switzerland and its Banks*, Frontiers in Economic History,
https://doi.org/10.1007/978-3-031-35904-0

European Debt Crisis, 147
European Union, 25, 122, 148, 154

F
Fazy, James, 70
Federal Banking Act, 96
Federal Banknote Act, 53
Federal bonds (Bundesanleihen), 99
Federal Constitution of 1848, 17–19
Federal Council, 18
First Boston Corporation, 129
France, 14
Franco-Prussian War, 19, 52, 67
Free-banking system, 48–53
Free floating, 120
French Revolution, 14, 34, 35, 63

G
General Strike, 21
Geneva, 9, 11, 14, 22, **32**, 122
Gentlemen's agreements, 112
German Reichsbank, 98
Germany, 17
Global Financial Crisis, 26, 139–144
Globalisation, 20, 26, 119–122
Gnomes of Zurich, 113
Gold block, 84
Golden age, 107–111
Gold transactions, 99
Gotthard, 64
Gotthelf, Jeremias, 40
Great Britain, 16
Great Depression, 22, 83–91, 95
Great Moderation, 122

H
Haldimand, Antoine Francois, 41
Haller, Albrecht von, 14
Huguenots, 16, 32

I
Industrialisation, 17, 62
Inflation, 120, 127
Initiative, 19, 23, 25, 96, 125
Insider trading, 126
Interest island, 76
International Monetary Fund, 25

J
Julius Bär, 135

L
Latin Monetary Union, 51
Lausanne Agreement, 82
Law, John, 30
Lebanon Connection, 126
Lehman Brothers, 140
Lenin, 21
Lombard Odier, 135
Lugano, 110

M
Machinery industry, 83
Mallet, Guillaume, 41
Mandatory convertible bonds, 145
Meldebeschluss, **101**, 132
Mercenaries, 13–16, 31, 37, 43
Merchant bank, 30
Mirabaud Group, 135
Mississippi bubble, 34
Mobilisation bonds, 79
Monetarism, 120
Money laundering, 126

N
Napoleon, 15, 16
Necker, Jacques, 35, 41
Neutrality, 10, 13, **20**, 25, 31, 98, 111, 122, 130
Note-issuing bank, 30
Numbered account, 100

O
Office Suisse de Compensation, 97
Old Confederation, 10–17, 29, 62

P
Peace Treaty of Versailles, 82
Peace Treaty of Westphalia, 13
Pictet Group, 135
Post Finance, 41, 121, 135
Private banks, 109, 135, 154
Protestantism, 15, 16, 40
  Protestant diaspora, 33

R
Raiffeisen, 135
Railways, 17, 18, 61, **64**
Real-estate crisis, 127

Réduit nationale, 24
Referendum, 19, 25, 57, 130
Reformation, 9, 32
Regional banks, 127, 135
Rentes viagères, 34
Rossini, Gioachino, 11
Rousseau, Jean-Jacques, 14

S
Safe-haven country, 22, 76–77, 112, 141, 148
Savings banks, 39–41, 127
Schiller, Friedrich, 11
Securitised assets, 144
Shadow economy, 151
Silver drainage, 53
Slave trade, 42
Stabilisation Fund, 145
Standstill Agreement, 87
Suisse Re, 67
Swiss Bank Corporation, 69, 72, 78, 81, 89, 99
Swiss Banker's Association, 125
Swiss economic disease, 130
Swiss Financial Society, 79
Swiss franc, 10, 18, 23, 26, 51, 53, 84, 111, 121, 148
Swiss Guard, 9, 16
Swiss National Bank, 18, 20, 26, 56–58, 78, 79, 97, 98, 113, 141, 145
Swiss Re, 26, 153
Swiss Volksbank, 81, 91, 92, 129

T
Tax evasion, 115, 149, 150, 154
Tax fraud, 115, 150, 154
Tax haven, 148
Textile industry, 83
Thirty demoiselles, 35
Thirty Years War, 13
Ticino, 15, 110
Tontines, 34
Too big to fail, 144–146
  legislation, 146, 152

U
Union Bank of Switzerland (UBS), 67, 69, 81, 89, 109, **129**, 132, 149
  rescue of 2008, 144
United Nations, 25

W
Warburg, S.B., 130
Washington Agreement, **106**, 111
Watchmaking industry, 16, 83
Wealth management, 76, 81, 110, 122, 141, 153
Weber, Max, 40
Wegelin Bank, 150
Willhelm Tell, 11
Winterthur Insurance, 129
Withholding tax, 116, 148, 150
Worldbank, 25
World War I, 20–22, 78–79
World War II, 23–24, 97–101

Z
Zurich, 11, 18, 38, 57, **62**, 81, 122
Zurich Insurance Company, 129
Zwingli, Huldrych, 9, 38, 62

The manufacturer's authorised representative in the EU is Springer Nature Customer Service Centre GmbH, Europaplatz 3, 69115 Heidelberg, Germany. If you have any concerns regarding our products, please contact ProductSafety@springernature.com

Printed and bound by CPI Group (UK) Ltd, Croydon, CR0 4YY
01/10/2026
02225852-0010